4-12-65 (64-13991)

THE STRANGE TACTICS OF EXTREMISM

Books by H. A. Overstreet

ABOUT OURSELVES
INFLUENCING HUMAN BEHAVIOR
THE GREAT ENTERPRISE
THE MATURE MIND

Books by The Overstreets

THE MIND ALIVE
THE MIND GOES FORTH
WHAT WE MUST KNOW ABOUT COMMUNISM
THE WAR CALLED PEACE
THE IRON CURTAIN
THE STRANGE TACTICS OF EXTREMISM

Books by Bonaro W. Overstreet

UNDERSTANDING FEAR (HARPER)
HANDS LAID UPON THE WIND

THE
STRANGE TACTICS
OF EXTREMISM

HARRY AND **BONARO OVERSTREET**

W · W · NORTON & COMPANY · INC ·
NEW YORK

TO
E. G.

CONTENTS

7

PART TWO

AND OTHERS

PART THREE

THE RADICAL RIGHTIST MOVEMENT

FOREWORD

This book is one kind of invitation to learning. It is about the ways in which extremism operates among us to accomplish its peculiar purposes. Because we have in our three books on Communism dealt at length with the tactics of Marxism-Leninism, our major stress here is upon those of the Radical Right. But the similarities and the competition between the two extremes—each of them wanting to reshape our common ways of looking at things, in order to gain power enough to reshape our society—make up a significant part of our theme.

There is one fortunate thing about the writings and the methods of the far Left and the far Right. While they can catch us off guard and do tremendous harm so long as we do not familiarize ourselves with their character, they are far more stereotyped and repetitive than are those of the general run of Americans. Hence, they can be taken apart, as it were, and studied, to see what makes them function. When they have been studied, they can be recognized with a fair degree of accuracy in our further encounters with them. And when they are recognized for what they are, they lose most of their power to confuse our minds and to set us against one another.

We are deeply grateful to many persons—far more of them than we can name—who have made available to us materials without which we could not have written this book. Even materials to which we make no specific reference in the text have, in many cases, so contributed to our understanding that they have become part of our approach to the subject.

Many of our readers will surely wonder why we have omitted all discussion of this particular leader or that particular group. In most cases, the answer lies in the multiplicity of far-right groups and in the limitations of space. We have had to pick and choose; and we have been guided in our picking and choosing by our wish to make our coverage of the field representative rather than exhaustive.

Also, our basic purpose has required that we give enough space to each leader and group discussed to make possible a more than surface exploration of outlooks and methods. We have had to leave out, therefore, even a passing mention of a veritable host of organizations and spokesmen for the far Right that might be expected to have a place in a book of this type. We hope, however, that at least some of our readers will supplement with further studies of their own what we have been able to make one book include.

Harry Overstreet
Bonaro Overstreet

Falls Church, Virginia

THE STRANGE TACTICS OF EXTREMISM

PRELIMINARY TO THE WHOLE

THE extravagances of extremism—their forms of expression, their impact upon our society, and what we can do about them—will be our concern in this book.

It must be stressed at the very outset that our war against extremism is a two-front war: against extremists of the Left and of the Right. On both fronts, we have ranged against us those who want to change the character of our society by splitting it down the middle into mutually warring camps.

We in America—having given extremism, as it were, a constitutional right to exist—have been able to afford the active presence of a far Left and a far Right because we have been overwhelmingly a nation of moderates. Extremism of Left and Right, home-grown and imported, has been with us always. But the liberal-conservative, or conservative-liberal, center has been the native habitat of the vast majority of our people.

A certain proportion of those who belong to the center have recurrently, under the impact of abnormal conditions, felt the pull of the left or right extreme and have moved away from their customary standing place; but not, as a rule, for keeps, or even for long. The danger now is that too many of us will move too far and too permanently away from the moderate center. To the extent that we do so, we give the extremists among us a more disruptive power over our common life than we can afford to let them have.

This two-front war in which we are engaged may well outlast our century. It seems certain to outlast our generation. Yet most of us, up to now, have scarcely begun to gear our efforts to its two-front character. Rather—sometimes by reason of circumstances, and sometimes by reason of personal slantings of mind—we have focused on only one front, or on only one front at at a time. The aggressive force at the other extreme, meanwhile, has thrived on being ignored or on being accepted as, perhaps, not too bad after all.

Much of the evidence to this effect is an old story. Thus, when Stalin was our ally against Hitler, we so far credited him with having a code of alliance similar to our own that the Soviet Union was able to grab for itself a satellite empire before we learned the score.

In the first years after the war, this unwariness continued to mark a host of good-willed groups. Bent upon one or another reform, and reluctant to admit that victory had not brought peace to the world, they designated right-wing elements as the enemy to be opposed—while keeping in mothballs their suspicion of the far Left. Communists, accordingly, found it possible to move in on one situation after another. They pretended to make common cause with the reformers, but used to their own advantage the chance to maneuver without being scrutinized. While their incautious allies were trying to solve problems or rectify injustices, they concentrated on publicizing these and on implanting enough hostility to make a solution impossible. And while we have put our verbs, here, in the past tense—speaking of the postwar period—the design of Communist effort remains the same.

But a similar design is operative, also, at the other extreme. During recent years, anxiety about Communism has fostered both the growth of right-wing extremism and an unwary tolerance of it. Such tolerance has expressed, in part, a reluctance to criticize those who say they are anti-Communists. In other part, it has expressed a feeling that such extremism is so much the lesser of two evils that concern about it can be postponed till the greater evil of Communism has been dealt with. Not least, however, it has expressed a hope on the part of many conservatives that they could, with respect to certain issues, make common cause with right-wing extremists without letting their influence get out of hand.

This might be called the reverse side of the coin of hope; for it matches almost point for point the hope of many liberals, through the years, that they could, with respect to certain issues, enter into a united-front effort with Communists without endangering the non-Communist character of their cause or their own organizations.

But surely the time has come to recognize that it is of the nature of extremism to go in for protective coloration. For the Communist, the most useful disguise that can be donned is that of the anti-imperialist, the peace-lover, and the seeker after social justice. For the Radical Rightist, it is that of the anti-Communist.

Wearing this guise, the Radical Rightist can often achieve a remarkable freedom to practice his special type of legerdemain: that by means of which he converts into a Communist or pro-Communist anyone with whom he disagrees on domestic or foreign policies. Most far-right action-programs are, in plain fact, as gigantically irrelevant to the real threat of international Communism as Communist action-programs are to the cause of freedom, peace, and justice.

"In order to fight an enemy you must know him," wrote Ernst Cassirer, in *The Myth of the State*. This would seem to be rudimentary wisdom. Yet we have been laggard learners, almost all of us, where twentieth-century extremism is concerned. The aims and tactics we have needed to understand have not been concealed from us—except in so far as we have permitted propaganda to hide them. They have been clearly spelled out by those who have needed to communicate them to their followers, and who, not without reason, have trusted the rest of us either to ignore the word on the printed page or to be blocked in our comprehension of it by our own psychocultural makeup.

Thus, even a sampling of what Lenin made plain in print is enough to make us ask, wonderingly, "Where were our minds when the foundations of Communist power were being laid?"

In 1902, in *What Is To Be Done?*, Lenin gave the design for both Party structure and conspiratorial tactics.

In 1913, in *State and Revolution*, he licensed the Party to make its own dictatorship total and permanent, while calling it "the dictatorship of the proletariat."

In 1917, in *Imperialism, the Highest Stage of Capitalism*, he accomplished two things. He revised the theory of the class struggle to make it embrace the struggle between colonial powers and subject peoples; and thus made underdeveloped countries, not only industrially advanced countries, into proper sites for "Marxist" revolutions. And he provided the definition of *imperialism* which has, ever since, allowed the Communists to hold captive peoples in subjugation while calling themselves anti-imperialists. Only capitalists can be imperialists in the Lenin lexicon.

In 1920, hard-pressed to hold the power he had seized, he gave the international conspiracy its marching orders, in *The Conditions of Affiliation to the Communist International*.

And in various writings, in the last years of his life, he explained his New Economic Policy (NEP) as simply a plan whereby Western capitalists would be paid to build up the Soviet strength by which they would later be destroyed.

Lenin wrote; but few among us read what was written. For that matter, there were long crucial years when his words were not easy to come by. From the forming of the Comintern, in 1919, to the present, our minds have been constant targets for Party propaganda; but Lenin's *Selected Works* were not published in this country until 1943, and then by International Publishers, with a dominantly Communist clientele.

To be sure, this same publishing house, in 1932—when Stalin hoped to spark a violent revolution in the United States—put into circulation 100,000 paper-backed copies of *Foundations of Leninism*, at ten cents a copy. But this was a propaganda item: a tool for making converts. Americans at large did not even think of studying it as a key to what our country was up against. Only since World War II have public concern and responsible scholarship combined to bring into being what might be called a layman's library of basic information about Communism; and even today it is a rare thing to find a non-specialist who knows with any degree of accuracy what Lenin wrote.

Just as Lenin set down his aims and tactics, so did Hitler. But again we did not read what he wrote until after we had been caught off guard by what he did. Hitler moved into our national consciousness around 1933. From then on, we read news reports of his speeches, rages, and posturings. But these did not recommend *Mein Kampf* to us as a "must" book.

And where would we have got hold of it in the years when we most needed to read it? It was first published in this country in 1939: a year after Munich and Hitler's march into Czechoslovakia, and in the very year of his signing of the pact with Stalin and his invasion of Poland and Norway.

Even at that tardy date, moreover—as we can personally recall—its issuance by two American publishing houses, Reynal and Hitchcock and Houghton, Mifflin, was widely disapproved. Why should Hitler be paid such a tribute of respect? Would not the book's sales put money into enemy coffers? That the book's reading might put desperately needed knowledge into our own minds was strangely disregarded.

Our major thesis in this book will be that the mistakes we made, during crucial years, with respect to Communism and Nazism, must not be repeated with respect to extremism of the Right. Even while we carry forward that self-education about Communism in which we as a people have become tardily engaged, and which can never be completed because of changes in the Party line and the world situation, we must begin doing our homework with respect to the second front in our two-front war against extremism. Here, we do not have to cope, as we did with Lenin's and Hitler's writings, with the problems of translation. The materials we need to read are being published in our midst every day of the week. The problem we have to cope with is that of our own unawareness of the need to learn.

We recall two incidents so oddly parallel that they serve to underscore the point we are trying to make. One dates from the time when we were shaping up our *What We Must Know About Communism*. Talking with a friend, we tried out on him our plan for the book—only to encounter skepticism about the worth of any book for the lay public on the subject of Communism. "Well," we challenged, "if we write it, will you read it?" He hesitated, and then blurted out, "I detest Communism. Why should I read about it?"

The second incident took place in late 1955, in an office in downtown Dallas. An executive friend with whom we were visiting picked up from his desk a publication put out by a man who was then, and still is, a spokesman for the far Right. With measured contempt he read its title aloud: *Dan Smoot Speaks.* Then he asked, "But who wants to listen?"—and dropped the publication into the wastebasket.

It seemed, then, a good enough place for it to go. But in more recent years, we have been troubled by our common tendency to throw away *unread* materials that come from the Radical Right. And we have been deeply troubled, while working on this book, by the number of persons who have expressed surprise that we think these materials—including Robert Welch's *The Blue Book of the John Birch Society* and *The Politician*—worth bothering about. Much as the question was once asked with regard to *Mein Kampf,* we have been asked whether we are not showing too much respect for the Radical Rightists by taking their materials seriously.

To toss into the wastebasket or otherwise ignore that which offends our sense of truth and fairness may be a satisfying gesture; but it may also be a costly one. May we not, as a people, be repeating once more a type of folly for which the world has paid, in this century, an appalling price?

The Radical Right is by no means a mirror-image of the Communist Left. Its contempt for "reformism" is almost Leninist in character. To a striking degree, its organizations are built on the principle that wisdom resides in a leader or elite group, and that it must be dispensed to the masses in predigested, capsule form. It thinks in absolutes and conquers the complexities of problems by means of pat oversimplifications. Also, it borrows many Communist tactics and stratagems. But, for all this, it is by no means simply Communism moved over to the opposite extreme.

For one thing, and an important one, it is an indigenous movement; not part of an international conspiracy. Its roots are here; not abroad. Thus, it can best be understood, in many of its aspects, as an nth-degree exaggeration of traits common among us in many gradations.

For another thing, while a considerable machinery has developed for the exchange of materials among far-right groups and for the overlapping of their Boards, the Right extreme is still occupied by a host of organizations—each of these having its own leadership. There is no single form of discipline; nor is there any one "top" from which directives can be handed down.

Lastly, while Communism can be studied as a definable theory-practice system, it is often hard to draw the line between Radical Rightism and the farthest right type of legitimate conservatism. This line cannot be drawn, we think, on the simple basis of where people stand on this or that particular issue. If we start cataloguing complex problems as ones about which there can be no legitimate differences of opinion, we play the extremist game—and out goes the baby with the bath.

Hence, we will discuss issues in this book only where they are combined to form the program or platform of groups that are shown to be extremist by the methods they employ. Our stress will be upon methods, and upon the view of man in society which these methods reflect. It is, we believe, in the area of tactics and stratagems that extremists, of Left or Right, most clearly show where the line is drawn between themselves and those who occupy the moderate center.

It is in this area, also, that liberals and conservatives must draw the line. One good reason, in fact, for studying the methods of extremism is to remind our liberal or conservative selves that we cannot make common cause with everyone who happens to be on our side of a particular issue. Some bedfellows are just *too* strange.

One final point must be made in this Introduction: namely, that we must not try to contain the influence of Radical Rightists by curtailing their civil liberties. We stress this fact because members of the Communist Party are, today, trying to spread confusion with respect to this point.

Thus, at the very time when Communists were protesting, as an infringement of their rights, the Supreme Court decisions that required Party members to register, Gus Hall, Executive Secretary of the CPUSA, was asked by a reporter, "Do you believe the Bill of Rights should cover the John Birch Society?" Hall gave a Communist answer; not a free man's answer: "No, the John Birch Society is out to destroy the Bill of Rights." (1)

Similarly, Herbert Aptheker, editor of the Communist journal, *Political Affairs,* when he was asked in Berkeley, California, about his stand on free speech, said that he favored free speech "for everyone except racists, fascists, and others with unscientific ideas." (2)

Coming from spokesmen for a Party that has destroyed civil liberties wherever it has seized power, while exploiting them everywhere else, such statements have a grisly humor. But they can be dangerous; for they comprise a theme in the current Party line that is expressly tailored to reach those who have become thoroughly exasperated with the Radical Right and who have never thought their way through to a basic understanding of what freedom of speech means.

It is not only that small virtue resides in opposing right-wing extremism by Communist methods. The matter goes deeper. It goes down to the bedrock paradox of freedom: namely, that our society can afford the presence of extremists only so long as the vast majority of us keep in mind the fact that we are obligated to defend their constitutional rights as we would defend our own. The acknowledgment of this obligation is what holds a free society together. If we forget it, or reject it, we help the extremists to split our society into mutually warring camps.

In the book of Matthew, Jesus warned his followers not to make self-satisfaction out of their power to love those who loved them: "do not even the publicans the same?" In parallel fashion, we come far short of proving ourselves to be defenders of freedom if we defend only the rights of those whose opinions we want to have spread abroad: Do not even the extremists, of both Left and Right, do the same?

The stress throughout this book will be upon the printed materials by means of which far-right groups work to shape the minds of their members and of the general public. Part I will concentrate on the John Birch Society. Part II will deal with a representative sampling of other Radical Rightist leaders and movements. Part III will attempt to interpret the practical consequences of what Part I and II reveal.

The Conclusion—*The Task Ahead of Us*—will return the problem of extremism to those who must ultimately solve it. The extremists will not solve it. Those who must do so are men and women who, in their personal lives, and through their involvements in society, affirm the values on which a free society must rest. The problem must be solved, in short, by those who are able to make a balanced outlook and a strict adherence to fair, aboveboard methods into an active, creative, dedicated way of going at the gigantic tasks by which we are confronted.

PART I

The John Birch Society

ONE

MONOLITH ON THE RIGHT

O UR personal awareness of the John Birch Society developed slowly. The first chapter of the Society was established in January 1959, in the wake of a founding conference in December 1958. But the organization did not, at the outset, draw attention to itself; and we went abroad that summer without having heard of it.

Shortly after our return in the late fall, however, a woman in Los Angeles who had read our *What We Must Know About Communism* wrote to ask whether we thought the new society would be a good one for her to join. We could only reply that we knew nothing about it, but would be interested to learn.

We meant that, about being interested. For several years, we had been urging upon some of our friends in adult education the need to encourage at the community level a responsible study of Communism. If, then, as this woman's letter suggested, a group had been formed to promote such learning, we wanted to be in on it. But we heard nothing more from her, and nothing more about the Society, for several months.

We were reminded of it, then, by a second letter from California—this one from a worried woman. She had gone with an acquaintance to a Birch Society meeting, and had been shocked by the atmosphere of apparent secrecy: "If they're out to educate the public, why don't they want the public to know what they're doing? It's almost as though they were planning to put something over on people." We asked her to send us materials about the group. But she had none to send; and the subject again slipped away into a corner of our minds.

It must, we think, have been in September or October 1960 that a man in one of our lecture audiences lingered to ask what we thought of the Birchers, and to put into our hands some clippings from a Milwaukee paper. These reported that Robert Welch, founder of the John Birch Society, had written and privately circulated something called *The Politician* in which he charged that the Eisenhower administration had been Communist-controlled. We did not believe that any considerable number of Americans could be brought to doubt President Eisenhower's loyalty. Welch, we felt, had merely exposed his own capacity to perpetrate nonsense. We were not impressed.

But 1961 and 1962 became years of cumulative learning—for us, and for many other people. At the beginning of 1961, Welch was able to announce that chapters of the Birch Society existed in thirty-four states and the District of Columbia. One hundred chapters were in California alone. It was not by reason of its growing membership, however, but by reason of the growing impact of its pressure-tactics, that the Society began to be more than a vague presence in the American scene.

Congress was suddenly bombarded with letters demanding the impeachment of Earl Warren. In response to this bombardment, and to Welch's impugning of Eisenhower's loyalty, members of Congress began to speak up—and thereby put themselves on the receiving end of Bircher denunciations.

On March 8, 1961, Senator Milton R. Young of North Dakota, discussing Welch's attack on President Eisenhower, drew the attention of his colleagues to a peculiar fact about the Birch Society. It names Communism as its target and draws only a vague line between Communists and liberals. Yet: "Strangely enough, most of its criticism is leveled, not against liberal public officials, but against the more middle-of-the-road, and even conservative, Republicans.

"They have accused me of being about every kind of scoundrel, including a Communist or pro-Communist."

Thus, Senator Young opened up the question of what kind of anti-Communism the Birch Society is designed to promulgate. Why does it spend conspicuously less time denouncing Communists than it spends denouncing *as* Communists or pro-Communists those who, like President Eisenhower, stand where most Americans have always stood: at a point well removed from both extremes?

By late March 1961, there was shaping up in Congress a conviction that some type of investigation of the Society would be in order. Senator Thomas Dodd of Connecticut said that he would raise the question with the Senate Internal Security Subcommittee. Representative Don L. Short of North Dakota called for an inquiry by the Justice Department. On March 30, Senator Thomas H. Kuchel of California proposed that the Senate Government Operations Committee question Welch about the aims and methods of his organization.

On April 3, Senator Stephen M. Young of Ohio brought up the subject of the Birchers' divisive tactics at the community level. The Society's "vigilantes," he said, were "practicing character assassination without regard for the truth, threatening merchants with boycotts, threatening college professors and school principals with dismissal"; and generally spreading "fear, hatred, and suspicion."

Two members of the House, Edgar W. Hiestand and John H. Rousselot, both of California, identified themselves as Birch Society members. Both defended the organization, while expressing their willingness to have it investigated. Hiestand dissociated himself from the attacks on Chief Justice Warren. Rousselot—who later, after being defeated for re-election, became West Coast organizer for the Birchers and is now the Society's National Public Relations Director—said that the Society's chapters, as he knew them, were "basically study groups."

All this Congressional back-and-forth, converted into news, contributed to our own growing knowledge about the Birch Society—a knowledge still made up of bits and pieces. More and more often, for example, we heard of the Birchers' infiltration of local PTAs and their disruptive tactics within these. We heard, too, of their calling child-guidance clinics brainwashing centers; and of their efforts to censor textbooks —in Phoenix, Arizona, for example.

Sometimes we were ourselves the target. Thus, several program chairmen of organizations to which we spoke told us of efforts—which they believed to be of Birch Society origin—to force them to cancel our lectures. Again, various individuals who had put our books on recommended reading lists became targets for letters of protest—samples of which they often sent on to us. And in certain school districts, notably in the Los Angeles area, the use of our *What We Must Know About Communism*, in classrooms or for reference, was denounced by the Birchers.

Because a couple of the bombarded schools were in the Congressional district of the late Clyde Doyle, we talked with him one day about what was happening: talked with him, that is, in his capacity as friend; not to try to involve him as a member of the House Committee on Un-American Activities. His comment was, in effect, that he would move over to make room for us: "They're after me, too."

Thus, the bits and pieces accumulated—like parts of a jig-saw puzzle not yet fitted together. But finally, within the span of a single month, one friend sent us copies of certain key pages of Robert Welch's *The Blue Book of the John Birch Society* and another sent some fairly long quotes from *The Politician.* Having read these, we took steps to get hold of both books; worked our way through them; and decided that they had been neglected all too long by all too many people.

Quite simply, these books provided a context into which to fit, and within which to judge in their aggregate, a host of evidential items that had seemed to us to represent more of a nuisance than a threat to freedom so long as we had viewed them separately. Also, they defined the Birch Society's brand of anti-Communism—which seemed to us more likely to hinder than to help our country's effort to cope, for as long as need be, with the world-wide realities of Communism.

We have summarized this learning process for two reasons. First, we think we are enough like most people that our experience underscores a general fact: namely, that free citizens can accept in theory the obligation to be eternally vigilant and yet be slow to recognize a development that calls for vigilance. In particular, it is never easy to determine the point at which an extremist movement, of Left or Right, has gone so far that a rallying of counterinfluences is called for.

When such a movement has developed to a point where

we are virtually forced to regard it as dangerous, we may feel like saying that it should have been nipped in the bud. But if we were to start nipping movements in the bud, before their actions had made their character unmistakably clear, we would both impoverish our society and nip freedom itself to pieces, bit by bit. The decision, then, that something must be done to counteract the influence of an extremist group is always one that has to be made, as it were, late in the game. This is part of the hazard of freedom; and part also, paradoxically, of its program for self-continuance.

In the second place, by recalling our own learning process, we gain a chance to re-emphasize our common need, today, to educate ourselves about the aims and methods of both extremes; not just one or the other. From the early 1950s to the present, we have personally been absorbed with the study of Communism. But during these same years, until the most recent two, we had merely *coped* with Radical Rightism as an incidental nuisance, where it had seemed to be getting out of hand at one point or another. We had not *studied* it. It took *The Blue Book* and *The Politician* to make us add to our personal curriculum the subject of right-wing extremism.

If Communism and Radical Rightism were truly the opposites which they claim to be, even a minimal study of both might seem like too much for anyone to undertake. But they are not. They denounce each other, while coming up to their attack on the liberal-conservative center from opposite directions, to compete for mastery of it. But they have so much in common that an earned intimacy with the aims and methods of either yields a large dividend of recognition when we turn to the other.

The California Subcommittee on Un-American Activities states in its 1963 *Report* that it does not find the John Birch

Society to be subversive. Attorney General Robert F. Kennedy gave a similar judgment in less formal language, in April 1961, when he replied to inquiries about the Society by saying that its members had not "broken any laws." (1)

Having found the Society to be non-subversive, however, the California Subcommittee proceeds to say in its *Report,* pp. 16-17, that anyone "familiar with the organization and techniques of the Communist Party must immediately note the close similarity between the two implacable enemies."

It then specifies some of the resemblances between the two: "Each has a monolithic structure in which authority gravitates from the top down through the various echelons to the rank and file membership. Each employs front organizations which it controls from behind the scenes. . . . Each operates bookstores and reading rooms through which it spreads its ideology. . . . Each movement operates through small units scattered throughout the country. The Communists call them clubs, the Birchers call them chapters. Each publishes a monthly list of directives that establish the current line of activity. The Communists call theirs *Political Affairs.* The Birchers call theirs the *John Birch Society Bulletin.* Each is geared to unleash a barrage of invective and attack against the other, and to bring to bear every pressure and device available."

We would ourselves go along with the conclusion that the Society is not subversive. The term is not one to be attached as a derogatory label to any group we happen not to like. In its *Guide to Subversive Organizations and Publications,* 1961, the House Committee on Un-American Activities relies on the categories established by the Attorney General; and the rest of us might well do the same.

The Committee lists, at one extreme, Communist and Communist front organizations—the determining characteristic here being a group's subservience to the dictates of a foreign power. At the other extreme, it lists organizations which the Attorney General has catalogued as totalitarian; as fascist; or as having adopted a policy of advocating or approving the commission of acts of force and violence to deny others their rights under the Constitution of the United States. In this last category, for example, we find the American Christian Nationalist Party, the Association of Georgia Klans, the Ku Klux Klan, and the Silver Shirts of America.

A group's being non-subversive does not mean, however, that we must remain indifferent to the amount of influence it exerts among us. If its aims and methods appear to be singularly inappropriate to a free people, we cannot passively allow it to capture public opinion—or our own minds.

The emphasis that is now being put upon education about Communism expresses a faith that the American people, by and large, would want nothing whatever to do with the kind of thing *Communism is* if they could be brought to understand its true character. It seems equally certain that they would overwhelmingly reject Radical Rightism if once they could be brought to educate themselves about what it stands for and how it operates. It can exert an influence potent enough to constitute a danger only so long as it can disguise itself as patriotism, as an indispensable form of anti-Communism, and as a staunch upholder of what is best in our political, moral, economic, and religious traditions.

To our minds, the John Birch Society does not help us either to defend our country against Communism or to carry forward the enterprise of freedom. On the contrary, and in spite of its being verbally aggressive in its anti-Communism, it renders, however unintentionally, a seven-fold service to the international Communist movement. Here, we can only state our conviction to this effect. But throughout the rest of Part I we shall be examining the bases of this conviction.

First, then, the Society creates confusion by its loose and irresponsible resort to derogatory labels.

Second, it fosters the belief that a totalitarian form of organization, with directives handed down from the top, is inherently stronger than one that operates by what Welch calls "debating society methods."

Third, it works to persuade people that the only part of the world-wide Communist threat about which they really need to be concerned is that of internal conspiracy.

Fourth, by labeling as Communist-inspired or Communist-controlled a host of indigenous American efforts to solve pressing social and economic problems, it acts as a brake upon social ingenuity at the very time when we most need to find American ways of coping with colossal forces of change.

Fifth, while it is specific about what it is against, its program for dealing with our twentieth-century complexities is limited to generalized platitudes.

Sixth, it encourages its members to believe that they are acting like responsible American citizens when they echo a leader's stereotyped pronouncements and work hard at tasks set for them by this leader.

And seventh, it advocates dangerously oversimplified solutions to problems beyond our shores—as when it promotes the belief that "it would still take only a few companies of U.S. Marines" to drive "Castro and his Communists out of Cuba, by force if necessary." (2)

In brief, guided by a line that Robert Welch lays down for it, month after month, the John Birch Society operates to blur the meaning of the term *Communist;* to substitute facile stereotypes for hard realities; and to plant suspicion where faith is needed, and fear where we need to have confidence. In this period of crises, tensions, and vast problems, it clutters up the scenery. Therefore, it should be studied—

not to prove it subversive, but to render it innocuous in the open market places of the mind.

The Society can best be studied through its printed materials; for it is through these that Welch both gives directives to the members and shapes their opinions with respect to issues. We shall be focusing, then, on *The Blue Book* and *The Politician;* on the monthly *Bulletin,* also written by Welch; and on the journal, *American Opinion,* of which he is editor. But first we must take account of Welch's own biography as it is presented in *The Blue Book.*

He was born in Chowan County, North Carolina, in 1889. He attended the University of North Carolina and then, for two years each, the Harvard Law School and the United States Naval Academy. Most of his adult life, however, has been spent in the candy-manufacturing business, in Boston.

He has been a member of the board of directors of the National Association of Manufacturers, as well as Regional Vice-President of that body and chairman of its Educational Advisory Committee. In 1941, he published *The Road to Salesmanship.* "As of January 1, 1957, Mr. Welch gave up most of his business responsibilities—and most of his income —in order to devote practically all of his time and energy to the anti-Communist cause."

In December 1958, Welch invited into conference, in Indianapolis, eleven men who were to become the founding group of the John Birch Society; and he did a full-scale job of presenting to them both his reasons for regarding the Society as necessary and his plan for its structure and program. What he said forms, now, the text of *The Blue Book.* As "bible" and handbook, this serves as a guide to thought and action for the members at large. For the rest of us, then, it can also serve as a guide—to the labyrinth of Welch's logic and the Birch Society's practices.

The book makes it clear that the Society is not cast in any typically American mold. Far from being one more voluntary association of the type to which we are accustomed, it is different in kind. Calling for a body of "disciplined pullers at the oars, and not passengers in the boat," Welch made his bow, in Indianapolis, to Lenin's concept of "the dedicated few"; and he declared himself willing "to draw on all successful human experience in organizational matters, so long as it does not involve any sacrifice of morality in the means used to achieve ends." (3)

The Society, he stated, would be "a monolithic body," operating "under completely authoritative control at all levels." It would waste no time on "debating society" tactics. The power of decision would be vested in "a personal leader": himself. Even the Advisory Council could only advise: it would have to take his word as final.

Welch felt no need to apologize for wanting a "monolith" or for appointing himself as leader. He was certain, he said, that "every man in this room" would agree that democracy "in government or organization" is "merely a deceptive phrase, a weapon of demagoguery, and a perennial fraud." (4)

Further, should any differences of opinion "become translated into lack of loyal support, we shall have short-cuts for eliminating both without going through any congress of so-called democratic processes." (5) Not only the "monolithic" form, in brief, is *Leninist*, but also the means for preserving it: namely, the purge.

The application blank which each prospective member must sign contains the following: ". . . I agree that my membership may be revoked at any time by a duly appointed officer of the society, without the reason being stated, on refund of the pro-rata part of my dues paid in advance."

The first fact to pin down, then, with respect to the John
Birch Society is that while its professed reason for existing
is opposition to Communism, it is built on the pattern of the
Communist Party. While it is *in* the American scene, it is not
of it: certainly not in the relationship it defines between
leader and led. Here it is kin to a system which fosters not
only dictatorship but the cult of personality.

We shall return to *The Blue Book* in the next chapter. But
first, to round out our introduction to Welch's viewpoint,
we turn to *The Politician*—which, compared with *The Blue
Book,* has had a stormy, ambiguous career. Welch wrote it
in its first form in 1954, which means that it antedated the
founding of the Birch Society by four years. He did not
write it, however, for public consumption, but as an extended
"letter" to a few intimate associates. Later, he added to the
original text, bringing it up to date, and gave it a somewhat
wider, though still ostensibly private, circulation.

It was talked about, however; and some copy of it became
the source, in mid-1960, of press comment and then of widespread controversy. The book could scarcely have failed to
arouse controversy; for what it amounts to is an elaborated
"proof" that Eisenhower, both as General and as President,
was "completely controlled" by Communist influences.

". . . these Communist influences made him put the whole
diplomatic power, economic power, and recognized leadership of this country to work, on the side of Russia and the
Communists, in connection with every problem and trouble
spot in their empire. . . . The explanation calls for a very
sinister and hated word, but one which is by no means new
in the history of governments or of nations. The word is
treason." (6)

Welch felt that the press comment which began in August
1960 amounted to a "smear"; that quotes were taken out of

context and so used as to misrepresent his full thesis. To put these quotes back into context, then, he published *The Politician*—on the advice, he said, of close friends.

He made a strong effort to prevent its being regarded as an official publication of the John Birch Society, asserting that it expressed only his own viewpoint. He could not wholly succeed, however, in separating it from the Society in the public mind. After all, he was the Society's undisputed policy-maker and virtually its self-appointed truth-maker; and in publishing *The Politician,* he described it, in the Prologue, p. xii, as "an always accurate presentation of events . . ."

The Birch Society has kept its affairs exaggeratedly private. But there are several out-in-the-open reasons for concluding that an unprecedented crisis developed around *The Politician,* and that it was not one that could be disposed of by a brisk resort to the purge. Small but significant clues suggest its having been one in which the judgment of influential members of the Advisory Council collided with Welch's judgment. If such a collision took place, it would appear that Welch emerged the technical victor.

We base this guess on three published items—two from that *Report* of the California Subcommittee from which we have already quoted; and one from the Birch Society's *Bulletin* of June 3, 1963. Taken together, these items suggest the unfolding of a curious drama in which the crisis of *The Politician* moved toward becoming a crisis of authority.

First, we turn to a statement made to the Subcommittee, in the spring of 1963, by Henri de La Chapelle—a leading member of the Birch Society who testified on its behalf. On the subject of *The Politician,* he expressed a certainty that ninety-nine percent of the members disagreed with Welch's "unfortunate comment about Mr. Eisenhower"; and he urged that this be taken as the purely personal comment which its author declared it to be. Thus, we can assume that a high percentage of the Society's more prudent and less extremist members did not agree with the thesis of *The Politician* and regretted the book's being published.

That their disagreement was more than passive is suggested by our second item. On page 6 of the *Report*, we read, as a comment by the Subcommittee itself, that "Welch has recently been quoted as saying that he is trying to withdraw each copy and get it out of circulation as quickly as possible."

The Chief Counsel of the Subcommittee, Richard E. Combs, tells us that the material of the *Report* was completed by mid-May 1963. Hence, we can assume that the above statement was believed at that time to express Welch's intention. Yet we must also conclude that it was not a heartfelt intention; and it may well have reflected the fact that, for one brief period, the Advisory Council almost succeeded in making its judgment authoritative; almost—but not quite.

This brings us to our third item of evidence. In the June 1963 *Bulletin,* we suddenly discover that what had begun to look like a dead albatross around the Birch Society's neck has turned out to be a prize bird in hand. Welch spends a good part of this *Bulletin* telling the membership about *The Politician.* He speaks of how valuable it is "as an aid to recruiting"; and, on p. 9, he surveys "what some of you good people might want to do to make *The Politician* the largest selling book in all history that failed to make the 'best seller' list."

Moreover, in spite of his earlier expressions of reluctance to publish the book, his effort to dissociate it from the Society, and his statement that he wanted to withdraw it from circulation, Welch declares in this *Bulletin* that *The Politician* has been victimized by a "conspiracy of silence." He suggests that members, to break this "conspiracy," buy from six to eighteen copies each—those who can afford to do so—and give them to their local drug stores, to be displayed and sold;

and that they pay for advertisements of the book in their local papers, and write letters about it to friends and editors.

He even suggests a wording for these letters: "If you would like to make sense out of what the Kennedy Administration is doing, you need first to understand what the Eisenhower Administration really did. This almost incredible but carefully documented chapter of history you can learn from *The Politician.* Read it—and judge for yourself." (7)

The final nine pages of the September 1963 *Bulletin* are likewise devoted to *The Politician:* chiefly to reprints of favorable comments and reviews. But here we again meet the claim that the book has suffered from a "conspiracy of silence"; and the source of this "conspiracy" is said to be "Comsymp influence in the American press." Here, also, we meet again the assertion that the book "is not a part of the official material of the John Birch Society in any way . . ."

We do not know by what standard an item becomes part of such official material. But at a different point in this same *Bulletin,* on p. 29, we read that *The Politician* "has now proved to be by far the most effective single help to our recruiting efforts."

On the evidence of *The Blue Book,* then, the Birch Society is designed as a monolith in which all decisions move from the top down. We may guess that in the Society, as behind the Iron Curtain, nature has shown signs of abhorring a monolith. But the story of *The Politician* seems to indicate, first, that Welch will not willingly share power with anyone; and second, that the current mass membership drive is designed to consolidate his position as leader.

By calling *The Politician* an unofficial item, he makes a token bow to those members who cannot accept its thesis. But by making it his chief recruiting tool, he virtually guarantees that, as time goes on, the more prudent and realistic portion of the Society's membership will become an ever smaller minority. Or to put the matter in reverse, an ever larger majority will be made up of persons who can believe that President Eisenhower was a traitor—and that John Foster Dulles, Milton Eisenhower, Allen Dulles, and General George Marshall were all part of the same "conspiracy."

HOW WELCH IDENTIFIES COMMUNISTS

IN his Foreword to the fourth printing of *The Blue Book*, dated February 22, 1961, Robert Welch writes, "We are fighting Communists—*nobody else.*" The italics are his.

In the next paragraph, he portrays "the apathy of the American public" as largely induced by "the incessant cackling of the Communist chorus: 'There ain't nobody here but just us Liberals.' " Thus, he frees himself from any inhibition which his first statement might seem to impose. He can dedicate himself to both the principle of fighting nobody but Communists and the practice of identifying as Communists-called-Liberals those whom he wants to fight.

Being freed to this extent, he soon forgets, it would seem, ever having said that *only* Communists are to be the object of attack. In the Footnotes for the same fourth printing, he designates a target group called "hazy characters"—one of the authors of this book being included therein. He has not,

he says, charged "that any of these people are Communists";
but he intends, nonetheless, to continue turning his "search-
light" on "their even hazier activities." (1)

To all this we can add the fact pointed out by Senator
Milton R. Young, of North Dakota: namely, that a high
percentage of those whom Welch attacks are "middle-of-the-
road, and even conservative, Republicans."

Welch, in brief, in both *The Blue Book* and *The Politician*,
tacitly promises to make clear the nature and extent of the
danger we face—and forthwith becomes an agent of enor-
mous confusion. Pronouncing, as it were, an authoritative
Let there be light, he envelops our national landscape in
smog.

In the September 1963 *Bulletin*, he further demonstrates
his quite remarkable capacity to reduce distinctions to a
general blur. On the subject of the effect that changes of
signal had upon dogs in Pavlov's experiments, he writes that
"by far the greatest usefulness of the diabolic system, to its
copyright owners in the Kremlin, will be its help toward making gibbering political idiots out of the American people.

"To this end you are going to see men who are recognized
by informed students as Communists suddenly taking some
strong anti-Communist line; projects that will damage the
Communists being promoted by Communist agencies; men
who have built up a sizeable following as anti-Communists
coming out at long last in support of Communist positions. . . .
The ultimate grand design is to reduce all groups and divi-
sions of the American people to a mental state where they
do not have the slightest idea of whom to believe, or what
to believe, *about anything*."

Welch offers no shred of evidence—much less, proof—
that such a Pavlovian campaign of confusion is being planned
or enacted. He states it as a fact. He often does this sort of

thing. Karl Marx, we would recall, first declared his all-embracing theory to be proved true by its "inner coherence," and then set out to gather evidence with which to convince the less inspired. When Welch gets the feel of a "grand design," he is similarly above the need of proof. If more earth-bound souls require it, he dumps into the hopper, so to speak, whatever he can find—and then, as in his reference to *The Politician*, declares his theory to be "carefully documented."

Thus, it would be irrelevant to demand proof in the present instance, or to point out the rather striking difference between the conditions in Pavlov's laboratory and those in an open society. What is relevant, however, is to ask how this odd application of Pavlov's principle fits into Welch's own mental economy. Why has he manufactured it at all?

He is not, we must assume, trying to reduce the more susceptible Birchers to "gibbering political idiots" by presenting himself as a dubious character: as a man who, having built up a sizable following as an anti-Communist, may come out "at long last in support of Communist positions."

We suspect, quite simply, that he has found in Pavlov a license to add to his list of suspects a whole range of anti-Communists: persons who, he has felt all along, could not be genuine because they do not stand at his end of the opinion-spectrum on domestic and foreign policy. Why should he not, then, take Pavlov's experiments and so "adumbrate their significance"—a phrase he likes—that the unaccountable is accounted for? Why not assume that persons who appear to be anti-Communists, but who hold wrong views, will "at long last" justify his suspicion of them by turning out to be part of a gigantic plot?

We are not blindly guessing this to be the inspired idea that Welch gleaned from Pavlov. We have been privileged to encounter a practical application of his theory. In May

1964, a man in one of our lecture audiences rose at the beginning of the question-and-answer period and put to us a
question so patently derived from Welch's interpretation
of Pavlov that we wanted to laugh. It went to this effect:
"Would you say that people who have pretended to be anti-
Communists in order that they could, later, attack true
American patriots, are hypocrites?"

Having read Welch's article, we by-passed his question and
asked, "Are you saying that we are Communists?" He said
that he was. We asked for his name and address, indicating
our readiness to sue for slander. He declined to give them.
The audience joined in asking for them. He still declined,
but said we would get them later—a statement not confirmed
to date. Then he walked out of the hall.

This was one case, incidentally, where the Birch Society
made known its presence. When people went out to the
parking lot, at the end of the evening, they found under the
windshield wipers of their cars reprints of an article which
first appeared in the October 1959 issue of the Society's
magazine, *American Opinion*. Written by Edward Janisch,
it is called "What We Should Know About Overstreet"; and
it purports to prove that our *What We Must Know About
Communism* adheres to the Communist Party line. We note
that the copy which we have in our file came from the
American Opinion Book Shop in San Diego; but reprints
are available from the Society's headquarters in Belmont,
Massachusetts.

Anti-Communists and also ex-Communists whose current
political and economic views do not match his own have
always seemed to be a problem to Welch; or they were, at
least, until he discovered Pavlov. For the most part, he has
dealt with them by affixing to their names the term *so-called*,

or some other term that would bring their integrity into question.

Thus on p. 227 of *The Politician* he names David Dubinsky and J. Lovestone as "both admitted Communists but claiming to be anti-Stalinist Communists." When was Dubinsky a Communist? When did he admit to being one? His known record as a tenacious anti-Communist goes back so far as to make both Welch and ourselves look like the newest of newcomers in the field. *Current Biography,* June 1957, says of him, "Since the 1917 Bolshevik Revolution in Russia he has been a foe of Communism."

William Z. Foster, who was in the CPUSA from the beginning, and who was for years its top man, published in 1927 a book called *Misleaders of Labor.* One of the men thus designated was David Dubinsky, then vice-president of the International Ladies Garment Workers Union.

George Morris, who became Labor Editor of the *Daily Worker* and the *Worker* in 1935, and who still holds this post with the latter publication, certainly does not view Dubinsky as a comrade. In his *American Labor—Which Way?* he names the ILGWU, with Dubinsky at its head, as a major source of financial support for the anti-Communist drive within the trade unions.

The operative leader among this disruptive "gentry," writes Morris, "was Jay Lovestone, the professional anti-Sovieteer . . ." Lovestone was a Communist in the 1920s; collided with Stalin; was expelled from the Party, on Stalin's orders, in 1929; and has for more than thirty years been an active anti-Communist.

But the fascinating thing about Welch's application of Pavlov's principle is that it exempts him from having to attach any importance to evidence of the above type. By making his "grand design" of conspiracy large enough, he can embrace within it, as actors in one plot that will eventually come to light, Dubinsky, Foster, Morris, Lovestone, and Stalin.

In plain fact, it would probably be impossible for any Radical Rightist to fight Communists—with the term responsibly defined—and *nobody else*. It would be as impossible as for a Communist to fight imperialist exploiters—with the term responsibly defined—and *nobody else*.

Certainly it is axiomatic among the Right extremists that those who are selling America down the river are far more numerous, and far more devious, than any save a beleaguered few—themselves among these—have even begun to realize. Thus, in December 1958, Welch said that he had been studying the problem of Communism for almost nine years, and practically full-time for three years. "Yet almost every day I run into some whole new area, where the Communists have been penetrating and working quietly for years, until now they are in virtual control of everything that is done in that slice or corner of our national life." (2)

Those who are convinced that Communists are almost everywhere, and also that they themselves are uniquely sensitive to the presence of these Communists, and hence able to identify them, are not prone to leave to duly authorized bodies the investigative jobs that are to be done.

J. Edgar Hoover, who deals with the actualities of the Communist threat and knows how hard these are to determine, has repeatedly warned against the dangers inherent in amateur investigations. Thus, he has urged, "Do not circulate rumors or draw conclusions from information coming to your attention. The data you possess may be incomplete or only partially accurate. . . . It is just as important to protect the innocent as to identify our enemies.

"Refrain from making private investigations. Report the

information you have to the FBI and leave the checking of data to trained investigators." (3)

The Right extremists fervently quote Mr. Hoover on the dangers of Communism, but heed him not at all on the dangers of amateur investigations. For one thing, they seem to feel that his style is impossibly cramped by legal restrictions, a quixotic concern about the innocent, and even by Communist pressures—so that they must stay on the job because of what he cannot do. And for another thing, they simply do not see themselves as amateurs.

At the founding session of the John Birch Society Welch presented himself, in fact, as a person endowed with a singular capacity to distinguish friend from enemy in the war against Communist conspirators. He could, of course, he said, make mistakes; but he knew from the frequency with which his opinion of "various characters" had coincided with that of J. B. Matthews that he had "a fairly sensitive and accurate nose in this area." Further, he had the benefit of "J.B.'s" files, memory, and judgment.

Matthews, we would recall, was appointed by the late Senator McCarthy as staff director of the Senate Government Operations Committee. Later, the Senator reluctantly let him go because of a furor over an article, "Reds in Our Churches," which Matthews published in the July 1953 issue of *American Mercury*. In this, Matthews stated that some seven thousand Protestant ministers had "been drawn during the past 17 years into the network of the Kremlin's conspiracy."

Welch, having qualified himself as an expert in the identifying of Communists, stated that, even though he might make an occasional mistake, he did not intend "to be frustrated by indecisions" or to let the Birch Society members be thus frustrated. He would undertake to say with authority, and without hesitation, "Help this guy, or let him help you, but stay away from that one . . ." (4)

Actually, Welch sees himself as so far from being an amateur that he feels qualified, when need be, to rebuke the FBI for going off on a tangent. This was made plain by *American Opinion*'s response to a speech which Assistant Director William C. Sullivan, head of the FBI's Division of Domestic Intelligence, made to a student audience in Salt Lake City, on August 15, 1963.

Among other things, Mr. Sullivan said that one way to combat Communism is to make a constructive approach to the problems of ignorance, poverty, materialism, social injustice, and political corruption. He added that extremism, because it too often equates honest dissent with Communism, "tends to weaken, divide, and confuse us." Declaring it to be "not enough to be against Communism," he said, "What we must be for is freedom under law"—a concept which he amplified to cover "freedom of expression, of inquiry, of dissent, of experimentation and education."

Mr. Hoover has said all these things. But Mr. Sullivan was not Mr. Hoover; so *American Opinion*, in its issue of November 1963, pp. 51-52, moved in for the kill. Mr. Sullivan wanted to "remove" such causes of Communism as ignorance, injustice, and poverty. But, asked *American Opinion*, "How about just removing the Communists?"

Mr. Sullivan wanted Americans to be done with extremism, and to be for freedom under law. This, it would seem, was just too much: "When the Assistant Director of the FBI starts sounding like Robert McNamara, Earl Warren, and Dean Rusk all rolled into one, we begin to wonder about the future of the FBI. . . ." Perhaps, with his views, Mr. Sullivan should "apply for transfer to the Department of Health, Education, and Welfare"—which the Birch Society has marked for liquidation.

Welch's attitude toward Congressional investigating committees is simple. He is *for* them, because they can expose Communists in public hearings. But since they have not exposed more than the smallest fraction of those whom he sees as Communists, he concludes that they are under the thumb of the "Communist bosses" within our government.

"Their files are already bulging with important evidence about individual Communists which has not been used and is unlikely to be used. The Communist political pressures have been so strong and so devastating, the Supreme Court's decisions have so hamstrung the actions of these committees that they hardly dare even *go through the motions* of hearings of this kind any more." (5)

All in all, our duly constituted authorities, as portrayed by Welch, are exceedingly frail reeds to lean upon. In *The Blue Book*, p. 21, he even says that "all really effective exposure of . . . espionage rings and agents" has "now been stopped." Since exposures have, in fact, continued without interruption, we recommend, as an antidote to this statement, a report by J. Edgar Hoover which the Senate Internal Security Subcommittee issued in May 1960. Entitled *Exposé of Soviet Espionage*, it can be secured from the U.S. Government Printing Office, Washington, D.C., for 15¢.

In the letter which he suggested that Birchers might want to send out to advertise *The Politician*, Welch described this book as "carefully documented." For a sampling of the type of documentation which he calls *careful*, we turn to his Chapter XVI: "Associates and Appointments."

The chief purpose of this chapter, Welch states, is "to turn the spotlight on the general run of appointments which Eisenhower has made since he became President, and to adumbrate their significance." While Eisenhower could not "dodge" the necessity of appointing "some good Republicans and sound

Americans" to his first cabinet, his later appointments showed his true colors. And these, according to Welch, were "almost invariably" dictated by a wish to weaken the conservative wing of the Republican Party, to get support for "socialistic measures," or "to put actual Communists or Communist sympathizers into influential positions . . ." (6) To support this thesis, Welch devotes pp. 221-248 of *The Politician* to the "documented" records of forty appointees.

Milton Eisenhower: "In my opinion the chances are very strong that Milton Eisenhower is actually Dwight Eisenhower's superior and boss within the whole Leftwing Establishment." The proof? Milton's "leftist" position is shown by his having been "an ardent New Dealer" and by his having supported "Owen Lattimore, and others like him, at Johns Hopkins." And the improbability of his really being Dwight's subordinate is shown by the fact that he is the more "intelligent" of the two brothers.

John Foster Dulles: "For many reasons and after a lot of study, I personally believe Dulles to be a Communist agent who has had one clearly defined role to play; namely, always to say the right things and always to do the wrong ones."

We pause, here, for *tactic* identification; for the trick Welch uses against Dulles is an extremist favorite. When a person with a clear record of anti-Communist statements is to be liquidated, what he has said is offered as a proof of how subtly Communist purposes can be disguised.

Welch speaks of having done "a lot of study" before reaching his conclusion about Dulles. What did he study? He names only one article, authored by former Senator William E. Jenner, which appeared in the April 1956 *American Mercury*; and, in a footnote, one book: Edgar C. Bundy's *Collectivism in the Churches*—of which we shall have more to say in Part II.

What proof does Welch offer to show that Dulles was a

Communist agent? He mentions, without elaboration, the "Japanese peace treaty, the Austrian peace treaty, and his very definite doublecrossing of the British government on the Suez affair . . ." He says that Dulles helped to persuade Thomas E. Dewey to support "the pro-Communist foreign policies of the Roosevelt and Truman Administrations"; that he was a friend of Dean Acheson; and that he was "a prominent and much publicized member" of the founding session of the World Council of Churches, in 1948. That appears to complete the record.

Welch undertakes to derogate, also, Ellsworth Bunker, Ambassador to India under President Eisenhower. Since he claims to have known him and worked with him in earlier years, he can scarcely have failed to know that, prior to 1951, when he resigned to take an ambassadorial post in Latin America, Mr. Bunker was Chairman of the Board of the National Sugar Refining Company: a fact that would have counted in his favor with the business-man reader to whom *The Politician* was first addressed.

Interestingly enough, however, Welch makes no mention in his "carefully documented" book of this part of Mr. Bunker's record—even though, in *The Blue Book*, he refers to his own "lifetime of business experience" as a valuable part of his preparation for detecting the fallacies of Communist theory.

Instead, he describes the Ambassador in terms calculated to make business men view him with distaste: as part of "the striped-pants and tinsel world of diplomacy"; and as a man with a "smooth and charming front." As for Mr. Bunker's record, "we cannot help mentioning at least one bag of bones somebody found in his immaculate-looking closets." This "bag of bones" turns out to be the fact that Mr. Bunker had been a member of the board of trustees of the Institute of International Education.

When Mr. Bunker was awarded a Presidential Medal of Freedom on December 8, 1963, his citation was as follows: "Citizen and diplomat, he has brought integrity, patience and a compassionate understanding of other men and nations to the service of the Republic under three Presidents."

In many cases, instead of directly attacking an individual, Welch denounces a policy or organization—thus giving himself a license to attack, at his own convenience, all the people who have been connected with it. In *The Blue Book*, for example, on p. 27, he says that our foreign aid program "was planned by the Communists." And in *The Politician*, p. 118, he describes NATO as the "most gigantic hoax in all history." It was, he says, cunningly devised to bankrupt America and to foster mutual hostility among the Western allies. By such pronouncements, he gives himself a virtual *Who's Who* of individuals who can be shown to have had dubious connections.

Again, in *The Politician*, p. 187, he declares both the Crusade for Freedom and Radio Free Europe to be servants of Communism; and proceeds forthwith to describe General Lucius Clay, first President of the Crusade for Freedom, as one of the men who helped Eisenhower "to mess up the Berlin situation so favorably for the Russians."

When we came upon this statement, we had a strong impulse to ask Robert Welch, as Joseph N. Welch asked Senator McCarthy, "Have you no sense of decency, sir, at long last? Have you left no sense of decency?" For it was General Lucius Clay who created and maintained for almost a year that brave, well-nigh incredible air-lift which finally, in May 1949, broke the Soviet blockade of West Berlin, saving that beleaguered city from starvation and Communist takeover.

In founding the John Birch Society, we would recall, Welch said that he did not object to borrowing Communist methods so long as his doing so involved no "sacrifice of morality." To study his manner of documenting the records of persons whom he wants to render suspect is to be left wondering what he would regard as a "sacrifice of morality." It is to be left wondering, also, how he can fail to see that an individual who chooses to employ innuendo and unproved assertions as substitutes for objective evidence describes himself by this choice.

THREE

A READING LESSON

ONE of Sandburg's early poems, *They Will Say*, begins thus: "Of my city the worst that men will ever say is this." Every so often, in the course of our reading of Communist and Radical Rightist materials, we have borrowed the form of this line to pose a problem to ourselves. Of extremism the worst that men will ever say is this—is *what*? What is the deepest evil that resides in this approach to the human scene?

Our tentative answer is that the worst that can be said of extremism is that it pronounces a death sentence upon honest communication. This is the death sentence which has, in our time, been antecedent to the well-nigh countless death sentences pronounced upon individual lives.

Nothing is more distinctively a mark of the human than is the power to use language both to build bridges of understanding across gaps of separateness and to capture and hold the nuances of personal experience. But where extremism prevails, language is allowed to perform neither of these functions. It is turned into a slave of the absolute answer and the irreconcilable cleavage. Its menial tasks become those of affirming the correct line and of identifying and deceiving the enemy.

A study of Communism has to be, in singular measure, a study of how words are used by propagandists and ideologues; for what is meant has continuously to be dug out from under what is said.

Upon a whole battery of familiar-sounding words the ideology itself imposes meanings that are not at all those to which we are accustomed: words like *peace, liberation, progress, negotiation, internationalism,* and *self-determination.* The Communist meanings of these words are ideologically fixed. No Party member can change them. Hence, they can be learned. But unless we learn them, there is nothing to prevent our being endlessly deceived by Communist propaganda.

We do not, however, by learning these words, exhaust the study of the Communist use of language. If the reader of Communist materials is to translate them into their meanings as he goes along, he must become familiar, for example, with the Party's ritualized methods of interpreting events. Thus, the Party can never acknowledge a setback *vis-à-vis* "the capitalist-imperialist enemy." If a setback occurs, it has to be converted into a triumph for the Marxist-Leninist cause. To fail thus to convert it would be to make the "fated" one-directional course of history somewhat less than fated.

We all remember, for example, the tense moment when Khrushchev and President Kennedy stood "eyeball to eyeball" over the surreptitious planting of Soviet missiles in Cuba; and when Khrushchev backed down and agreed to remove them. An article called "On Cuba, China and the U.S.S.R.," which was published in the February 1963 issue of *Political Affairs*—organ of the CPUSA—turned defeat into triumph in these words: "Catastrophe was averted by the firm policy of peaceful coexistence flexibly and correctly applied . . .

". . . World peace was saved; peaceful coexistence and peaceful competition were vindicated . . . Premier Khrushchev stood forth as one of the great statesmen of our times . . ."

Again, there is the language of polemical indirection. The Sino-Soviet conflict was conducted in this for as long a time as Mao and Khrushchev were trying to conceal the extent of the rift between them—and not only to conceal it, but to repair it. Mao, wanting to attack Khrushchev, attacked "certain people"; and Khrushchev, wanting to denounce Chinese policy, denounced that of Albania. By this language token, a new stage in the conflict was reached in the fall of 1963, when Mao denounced Khrushchev *directly*, and Khrushchev replied in kind.

It is significant that Stalin did not bother to use the language of indirection when he attacked Tito in 1948. He had no reason to do so, for he meant the break to be decisive. He thought he could eliminate Tito and put a man of his own choosing at the head of the Yugoslav Party.

Then there is the ritualized language of home-front propaganda. This contains the stereotypes in which the collapse of capitalism is predicted; and those in which the people are told that they own all the means of production; and those in which writers are told that they are most creatively free when they adhere to the tenets of socialist realism.

Again, there is the monstrous, polysyllabic language in which failures to fulfill plans are concealed and in which non-achieved successes are "achieved." It would take a book to encompass just one type of verbal maneuverings: those that have attended the repetitive postponements of the Soviet Union's surpassing of the West in per capita production.

For all its rigidity, Communist language can be stretched to cover what must be covered. Thus, it has been absorbing to follow the Soviet Union's verbal efforts to cope with the breaking up of the monolith and the return of nationalism to Eastern Europe. Here, we encounter the language in which the Soviet Union, probing unpalatable new dimensions of reality, seeks to discover what can be saved by persuasion where coercion cannot be used; and to discover how the unavoidable can best be portrayed as the always intended.

When we turn from the Communist Left to the Radical Right, we again face a problem of interpreting what we find on the printed page. Again, we must find our way around in a world of dogma and black-white thinking; of innuendo and invective. But there are striking differences between Communist and Rightist usage.

For one thing, the Communist use of language is related to a supposedly inevitable "great day" that lies somewhere in the future; but the Radical Rightist use of language is related to a sense of impending disaster. To borrow a term from James Thurber, the outlook to which it is geared is "doom-shaped."

Again, Rightist outpourings are marked by an anarchic quality that Communist discipline forbids. Within the frame of Marxist-Leninist ideology and the current Party line, Communist statements make sense: which is to say, can be comprehended. But within what conceivable frame does it make sense to say that a UNESCO plot was responsible for removing the McGuffey Readers from American classrooms?

When we came upon this charge—in UNESCO Tract, 1962, issued by the Cinema Educational Guild, Hollywood, California—we asked Congressman Lionel Van Deerlin, of San Diego, to check up for us on when the McGuffey Reader was last used in California. He reported that while no records were readily available for titles used before 1900, a sampling of books used earlier would suggest that McGuffey had gone out around 1885.

Again, each person who achieves a leader-role on the far Right appears to be a unit of self-dramatization, while spokesmen for the Communist Party line are more like interchangeable units in a propaganda machine.

This right-wing manifestation of ego is not to be confused, however, with the exercise of individuality. Publications of the far Right are, in some respects, almost as stereotyped as are the products of "socialist realism." While there is no one leader to dictate to all other leaders, the rules of the enclave prevail. No Radical Rightist leader could either hold his following for long, or remain in the good graces of his fellows, if he deviated too far from the standard pattern of "againstness" or undertook to qualify established dogmas.

One fixed dogma, for example, goes to the effect that liberalism leads to socialism, and socialism to Communism. It would go hard with any leader who pointed out that no country to date has come under Communist control by this prescribed course; or that the term *socialism* does not mean the same thing to Communists and non-Communists.

In Communist parlance the term is ideologically defined; and applies to the stage of development that follows the Communist Party's seizure of power and prepares the way for full Communization. This fact was oddly emphasized in the winter of 1963-1964, when Chou En-lai, on a good-will tour of Africa, refused to make the slightest concession to the Western meaning of the word—which has become also the African meaning. He would not apply the term *socialist* to the government of either Ghana or Guinea.

Some far-right publications are so blatantly extreme that no one with a modicum of moderation in his make-up would be likely to be misled by them. Thus, we have before us the November 1963 issue of *The Thunderbolt*: a newspaper of the States Rights Party. It announces itself to be a vehicle for "The White Man's Viewpoint." But we can only conclude that the type of white man who would feel that his viewpoint was represented by it would be, in Edwin Arlington Robinson's phrase, the "wrong man to meet on the wrong road at night."

Welch's *The Blue Book* and *The Politician* are of a different order—as are the various books and magazines that we will deal with in Part II. It takes more than a hasty reading of these to pinpoint the tactics by which the unwary could be confused.

In these books, facts and non-facts stand side by side, equally grave with portent. Documents cited to establish beyond doubt the pro-Communist connivings of persons in high places turn out to be magazine articles by other Radical Rightists. The reader is asked to credit exact statistics from no known source, and to be impressed by quotes from unnamed authorities.

And not least among the things that make for tough going is Welch's way of utilizing historical events the details of which have become vague in the reader's mind—if, indeed, he ever knew them. Since, however, we are recommending that people read these books, we wish in the rest of this chapter to illustrate certain key reasons why they should be read *with care*.

One good example of how Welch uses history is his handling of the U-2 affair and the subsequent break-up of the Summit conference in Paris, in 1960. Everyone "remembers" these events. But—speaking for ourselves—we had to go back and do our homework before we could cope with even this one small fraction of Welch's "proof" that President Eisenhower was a dedicated servant of the Communists.

In the Epilogue to *The Politician*, Welch says of the U-2 affair that "*everything* about it appears to have been handled in the manner that would best suit Soviet interests, no matter what the intentions of some of those involved may have been."

Of the events in Paris, he says that "it was arranged that Eisenhower would meekly sit still for a tongue-lashing from Khrushchev over the U-2 affair"—all this being simply "part of the scenario" which was designed, with President Eisenhower's collaboration, to raise the prestige of the Soviet Union and lower that of the United States. (1)

He simply discounts, in brief, the well-nigh unanimous verdict of the non-Communists present in Paris, and of the non-Communist press around the world, to the effect that Khrushchev's tantrums and boorishness contrasted very badly with President Eisenhower's dignified patience.

Elaborating the above theme in the July-August and September 1960 issue of *American Opinion*, Welch writes that "*all* available evidence indicates that the pilot of our famous U-2 must have purposely landed his plane in Russia; and that objectives of those who planned the incident must have been (1) to give the Soviet a model to duplicate; (2) to provide the American Communists with an excuse for getting reconnaissance over Russia suspended; and (3) to postpone the 'Summit conference' with a maximum disgrace to the United States."

When Welch, or any other Radical Rightist, says that "*all* available evidence" proves something or other, but offers *no* evidence, doubts are in order—as they are when he says that "the best-informed authorities agree," but names no authorities. Not even the absurd can be ignored, however, when its author is the official truth-maker for an organization bent on shaping public opinion to fit its own purposes. Hence, it seems worth while to pin down certain facts.

The number one fact is that the Francis Gary Powers flight of May 1, 1960 was the first one to fail in a flight-program which, at that time, extended back over a four-year period. President Eisenhower—Welch's "traitor"—ratified this program after the Soviet Union rejected his "open skies" proposal.

While Khrushchev must have found these flights galling, it was not until the capture of the Powers plane, with its photographic plates still intact, that he learned the scope and type of information which our government had been successfully accumulating. His resultant perturbation was obvious.

Once he knew these facts, there was no longer a security reason for withholding them from the American public. On June 1, 1960, therefore, Secretary of Defense, Thomas S. Gates, Jr., issued a statement to the press, saying, "From these flights, we got information on airfields, aircraft, missiles, missile testing and training, special weapons storage, submarine production and aircraft production . . ." (3)

Welch's thesis would require us to believe that it raised the prestige of the Soviet Union to have the whole world know that its security system had been thus breached—not on a single occasion, but continuously for four years.

Certainly, there was public confusion in the wake of Powers' capture, and President Eisenhower might fairly be called the author of this confusion. First, in line with established protocol in matters of espionage, he misrepresented the nature of the flight, saying that a plane gathering weather-data had strayed from its course. Then, abruptly he admitted the plane's character. But we must recall that his misrepresentation took place before he knew that the photographic plates were in Khrushchev's hands. He reversed his stand after this fact was known. What profit—or mitigation of loss— could he logically have hoped that this reversal might yield?

Even to make a good guess at an answer, we must keep two facts in mind. First, the U-2 incident took place at a time when our government had been unsuccessfully trying to persuade the Soviet Union to agree to a program of on-site inspections, as a basis for a test-ban treaty. And second, even before Powers' capture, "American officials had discussed but rejected the idea of privately showing Khrushchev some U-2 pictures in hopes of persuading him to agree to ground inspection because so much already had been photographed." (4)

In what position, then, did the President find himself? It was too late to prevent Khrushchev's knowing what the flights had netted us. But might it not be, for that very reason, the time to lay our cards on the table and say, in effect, "All right, Premier Khrushchev. We already know more about your strategic installations than the on-site inspections we have proposed could possibly teach us. You have repeatedly said that you want a test-ban treaty. Your excuse for holding back has been removed. Do you, or do you not, want one?"

Khrushchev's conduct after the break-up of the Paris conference was scarcely that of a man enjoying a propaganda victory. His intricate footwork during the weeks that followed made him look more like a man on the spot: he kept advancing to threaten, but side-stepping to avoid collision.

From Paris, still flaunting his rage, he went directly to East Berlin; but instead of precipitating a real crisis by making good on his oft-repeated threat to sign a separate peace treaty with Ulbricht, he urged upon that disappointed leader a policy of patience. In the course of the summer, he threatened a missile defense of Cuba if the United States practiced "aggression"; but left himself free to define *aggression*. He threatened, likewise, to bomb our bases in Europe, and to breach the neutrality of Austria. Any step toward the carrying out of either threat would have precipitated war. But he took no such step. On many counts, in brief, he acted far less

like a man who had triumphed than like one who was working
to repair, with minimum risks, a damaged image of strength.

We have chosen to explore this particular instance of how
Welch handles history because, at this writing, our U-2 flights
are continuing over Cuba. Out of the multitude of flights, one
could fail. Hence, it is just as well for Americans to realize
that for the extremist mind, geared as it is to a conspiratorial
interpretation of history, any failure can appear to be treason.

Another feature of Welch's writing for which the reader
must be prepared we will call a monumental carelessness. If
it is not this, it can only be called a monumental callousness
in matters where other people's reputations are at stake.

One simple example will show what we mean. On p. 93 of
The Blue Book, writing about Americans for Democratic
Action, Welch says that "the ADA, whether a lot of members
know it or not, is the same as an arm of the Communist Party."
Thus, he virtually instructs Birch Society members to view
with alarm, and warn others against, those who belong to
the ADA.

Yet on p. 109 of *The Politician*, he writes, "Now it is per-
fectly all right for a man to be a Democrat, even an A.D.A.
Democrat, if that school of political philosophy expresses his
honest beliefs." It would be understandable if even the Birchers were, at times, confused by his directives.

Again, many of Welch's quotes turn out to be singularly
elusive affairs. On p. 26 of *The Blue Book*, for example, we
find him discussing a "plot" to make America, by gradual
stages, so like the Soviet Union that its final conversion to a
"police state" can be effortlessly achieved. He states that the
"best way to explain the aim here is simply to quote the
directive under which some of the very largest American
foundations have been secretly but visibly working for years.

This directive is 'so to change the economic and political structure of the United States that it can be comfortably merged with Soviet Russia.' "

Here, he states, in brief, without equivocation, that he is *quoting* a directive. But in *The Politician*, p. 268, he develops a similar theme, but speaks more vaguely of *directives*; and after giving a version almost identical with that in *The Blue Book*, he adds "or to that effect."

Thus, what a reader of the two books has to interpret is a charge, offered without evidence, to the effect that certain unnamed foundations are working under either a precise directive or vague directives from an unidentified source. It would seem to be the better part of wisdom to ignore the whole charge—at least, until Welch is ready to do a more responsible job of backing it up with explicit evidence.

Another sleight-of-mind tactic which Welch seems to favor is based on the phrase "nobody will ever know." It consists in using this phrase with the implication that *what nobody will ever know* would be appalling if it were known. But not a single fact or figure is offered to show that the *unknown* is not simply the *nonexistent*.

Thus, in *The Politician*, p. 227, we find a passage designed to prove that Allen Dulles, as head of the CIA, was serving the Communist cause. In a sentence heavy with ominous possibilities, Welch writes, "How many millions of dollars of American tax-payers' money Allen Dulles has turned over to Walter Reuther's stooge, Irving Brown, to promote Communism in fact while pretending to fight it (through building up the leftwing labor unions of Europe), nobody will ever know."

This same formula is then repeated several times over, with different "pro-Communist" recipients in each case. Thus, there is built up a passage which, read in a resounding voice, might make good theater; or good demagoguery. But it is not good documentation.

It is not even morally responsible documentation; for there is not one word in it to indicate that Allen Dulles actually handed over CIA funds to the persons named in any amount whatever; or to show that the persons named were, in any instance, serving the Communist cause. Yet on the basis of evidence as flimsy as this, Welch calls Allen Dulles a "protected and untouchable supporter of Communism." How Welch can think that no "sacrifice of morality" is involved in his resort to this type of documentation "nobody will ever know."

The CIA seems to be almost equally a target for the Radical Rightists and the Communists. It is also a target for various persons and groups that might better be called muddled than extremist. Hence, we would strongly urge that as many Americans as possible read a speech which Senator Thomas Dodd, of Connecticut, made in the Senate on February 17, 1964—entitled "The Dangerous Game of Baiting the CIA." Reprints of it can be secured from the Senator's office in the New Senate Office Building, Washington, D.C.

One policy would seem recommended by Welch's record of proving what he wants to prove—by means of appeals to unnamed authorities, quotes for which no source is given, insinuations, and charges unsupported by evidence. We hope that many persons will undertake a *careful* reading of the Welch books. But we recommend that those who do should erect in their own minds a warning sign: DANGER: SLIPPERY WRITING AHEAD.

FOUR

SCHOLARSHIP LIMITED

IN the fall of 1963, Jack Bass of the Columbia, South Carolina, *Record* made a study of the John Birch Society in that state: a study first serialized in the paper on November 6, 7, and 8, and then issued in reprint form.

Among the persons with whom Bass talked was William M. Tindal, section leader for chapters in the Columbia area, who said that he was interested in the Birch Society because its aim was to "get the American people to educate themselves on the menace of Communism." Later in the interview, after he had expressed basic agreement with the thesis of *The Politician*, Bass asked him whether he thought there might be some distortion of fact in Welch's writings. Tindal replied that he did not have enough background to be a judge of such matters. But: "Mr. Welch is a very well-read man."

This statement opens up one of the most fundamental of all the problems posed by today's brand of Radical Rightism. Not only Welch, but every leader of the far Right, has to establish himself as *a man who knows*; for he purports to deliver trustworthy facts and interpretations about complex problems which plain people have every right to want to understand, but about which they do not feel well enough informed to trust their own judgment. Such leaders, moreover, do not stop with delivering facts and interpretations. They invite people to "educate themselves"—by means of a program that will expose their minds only to such materials as give support to the far-right line on every issue of domestic and foreign policy.

When Welch met in Indianapolis, in December 1958, with the eleven men whom he had invited to collaborate with him in founding the John Birch Society, he went to considerable lengths to qualify himself as a man who indubitably knew whereof he spoke. What he there said on this subject is included, now, in *The Blue Book*—together with what he said about Communism, the type of organization the Birch Society was to be, and other matters that concerned him.

Thus, we find him reporting not only that he had studied Communism for some nine years, and "practically full time" for three years, but that he had talked or corresponded "with many if not most of the leading anti-Communists in this country and throughout the world." Further, he had "diligently studied . . . anti-Communist books and objective histories" of the events of the past two decades; and he had kept up with the Party line by a regular reading of Communist periodicals. (1)

To these specific qualifications for handling the subject of Communism, he added certain more general ones. Thus, by reason of his "lifetime of business experience," he could more clearly see "the falsity of the economic theories on which Communism is supposedly based" than could "some scholar coming into that study from the academic cloisters." Yet, he said, he enjoyed an advantage over "many business men" by reason of his "lifetime of interest in things academic, especially world history." (2)

Fortunately, we have a chance to study not only the quality of Welch's scholarship but also the uses he makes of it; for in each of two key sections of *The Blue Book*, he builds his argument squarely upon a documentary base. One of these sections he calls *Look at the Score*. In it, he undertakes to explain how the Communists have been able, in so brief a span of time, to take over so large a part of the earth's surface. In the other section, *But Let's Look Deeper*, he pits his scholarship against a trend in our country which he sees as both so dangerous and already so far advanced that, if it is not reversed, it will assure Communism's victory.

Our aim in the present chapter will be to appraise not only his argument in *Look at the Score* but also the documentation on which it rests. This section is singularly important; for it spells out the basic Welch thesis about how matters stand and what must be done. In the next chapter, we will make a similar appraisal of *But Let's Look Deeper*.

Two factors, according to Welch, account for Communism's chain of victories. One is a long-range strategic plan, first enunciated by Lenin and undeviatingly adhered to by the Communists ever since. The second is a conspiratorial cunning which has, on the level of practical implementation, provided support for the grand strategy.

"Lenin died in 1924," writes Welch. "But before he died he had laid down for his followers a strategy of this conquest. It was, we should readily admit, brilliant, farseeing, realistic, and majestically simple. It has been paraphrased and summarized as follows: 'First, we will take East Europe. Next, the masses of Asia. Then we will circle that last bastion of capitalism, the United States of America. We shall not have to attack: it will fall like overripe fruit into our hands.' To make doubly clear what he meant and how firmly he meant it, with regard to taking Asia ahead of Western Europe, and then using Asia as a stepping stone and base from which to conquer Western Europe and the rest of the world, the strategy was also stated that, for the Communists, the road to Paris lay through Peking and Calcutta. Today, you can easily see how that road to Paris is leading back from Peking through Calcutta, Cairo, Damascus, Bagdad, and Algiers." (3)

By thus presenting Lenin's long-range plan and the swift, accurate drive toward its fulfillment, Welch makes two points that are vital to his whole argument. One is that the Communists can think circles around us in the area of strategy. The other is that they have been consistently winning, all across the board—or across the world; and that the West has just as consistently been losing.

No matter how "brilliant, farseeing, realistic, and majestically simple" a plan may be, however, it is not self-fulfilling. It must be implemented: supported with know-how and with material resources. Also, its relative strength must be further enhanced by a conspiratorial weakening of the enemy.

With the theme of conspiracy thus introduced, Welch forges ahead with his argument—to the effect that the Soviet Union has been able to convert Lenin's strategy of conquest into a chain of actual conquests only because it has contrived, with conspiratorial cunning, both to borrow in almost limitless amount the know-how and strength of the West and to do a termite job of weakening the West's will to resist.

No one, it seems to us, could reasonably disagree with Welch's contention that borrowing from the West—by means of theft, purchase, and espionage, as well as by imitation—has been a major factor in the growth of Soviet power. Such borrowing took place even under the Tsars. Lenin introduced it on a grand scale, in 1921, by means of his New Economic Policy (NEP). Stalin and Khrushchev have continued it.

At the time of Lenin's NEP, our Secretary of State, Charles E. Hughes, wanted no part in any build-up of Soviet strength. But as Werner Keller points out in *East Minus West = Zero*, "America's system of free enterprise enabled the American industrialists to make private agreements with the Soviet Union. . . . From 1921 to 1925 alone, thirty-seven million dollars' worth of machinery and equipment was pumped into the USSR by American industry." (4)

Nor was this the end of the matter. Stalin's First Five Year Plan could not have got off the ground without his borrowing from the West. His plan, for example, called for a swift build-up of the automotive industry; and on May 1, 1930, a Soviet representative got Henry Ford to sign on the dotted line a contract that called for his providing the Soviet Union— for the sum of $30,000,000—with "patents, licenses, technical assistance and advice, and the supplying of spare parts." (5)

There has been no time since 1921 when Western strength has not been a major factor in the build-up of Soviet strength —with the tactics of purchase, expropriation, theft, and espionage all playing their part. Welch is quite right in specifying that the Soviet Union is not a self-made power.

In like manner, we must grant a large measure of truth to his "termite" theme. Four decades and more of concentrated propaganda effort and conspiratorial infiltration could scarcely have failed to make some dent; and it would be overoptimistic to assume that the denting process has ended.

Beyond these points of agreement, or semi-agreement, however, Welch goes his own singular way; or his Radical Rightist way. The path he takes and on which he hopes that at least a million Americans will follow him is that of identifying our own government—no longer ours, as he sees it, but a virtual Communist outpost—as the enemy that has made it well-nigh impossible for the Soviet Union to fail or for ourselves to succeed. By taking this line, he licenses himself to recommend an alternative guardian of our common defense: namely, the John Birch Society.

"As I see it," he told his Indianapolis audience, and continues to tell all readers of *The Blue Book*, "you have just two alternatives. Either you and tens of thousands like you come into the John Birch Society and, without giving it the whole of your lives, still devote to its purposes the best and most you can offer, with money and head and heart as well as hands; or in a very few years you will, by force, be devoting all to the maintenance of a Communist slave state." (6)

Most Americans, we would guess, see our government as one that has made its quota of blunders and wrong judgments in dealing with the Communists, but that has basically tried to serve our national interests and those of freedom. Welch, in contrast, presents it as the *willing donor* of whatever the Communists have lacked in their own right and have needed for their execution of Lenin's master strategy.

The "door of betrayal" in Washington, we read in *The Blue Book*, p. 19, "is known to be wide open, and nobody—in Congress, in the executive branch, in the Pentagon itself—nobody even dares to try to close it." And in a supplement to the *Bulletin*, entitled *The Time Has Come*—not specifically dated but bearing a 1964 copyright—we find that the above theme, set forth in 1958, is even more strongly stated: "Washington has been taken over!

"By which we mean that Communist influences are now in full working control of our Federal Government."

Here, we discover the key to the Birch Society's—and, more broadly, the Radical Right's—brand of anti-Communism. It is a brand that presents as unnecessary, or downright harmful, most of America's around-the-world activities and involvements. It is an anti-Communism which contends that, if it were not for treason and conspiracy in high places, we could, on our own—without the high costs of entangling alliances and big defense systems—make things happen as they ought to happen, all around the world. We could do so by pulling back out of the world, as it were, and simply cleaning up the mess in Washington. What we might need to do abroad, in military terms, could be done by a well-placed bomb or a regiment of Marines.

Communism's advance would be stopped in its tracks—so the argument runs—and Communist regimes would be toppled by the uprisings of suppressed peoples, if our government, directed by "Communist bosses," could be forced to stop underwriting Lenin's grand strategy with our tremendous resources of materials and know-how.

Welch says that he is not advocating revolution "in any technical sense." He thinks the John Birch Society can do what needs to be done "without building barricades in the streets." Yet what he advocates might be called psychological insurrection. In this period of grave national crisis, he wants at least a million Americans to withdraw their trust from our duly constituted government and to reinvest this trust in a private, monolithic organization that will not, he states, make its action-program wait upon "parliamentary procedures and a lot of arguments among ourselves." (7)

As we have noted, Welch presents himself as carefully schooled in the subjects he talks about; and he makes his pronouncements as one having authority. Many minds, we must conclude, find convincing the thesis outlined in this section of *The Blue Book*. It is a terrifying thesis. Yet it brings a kind of order out of chaos; and it provides anchorage for a host of grievances and anxieties, by making explicit the *why*, *how*, and *who* of all our national troubles.

Nonetheless, what he asks people to believe and to do is so serious—so destructive of confidence and national unity; so out of line with our historic methods of meeting crises; and so irrelevant to the problem posed on a planetary scale by international Communism—that it makes us turn back to take another look at his credentials.

When we do thus turn back, we realize that the first fact to be underscored is that *there is no record whatever of Lenin's ever having laid down that "strategy of conquest" on the existence and success of which Welch builds his whole argument.*

Furthermore, such a strategy would have been very much out of line with what Lenin did write. True, around 1919, when hoped-for revolutions in Hungary and Germany failed to materialize, Lenin began to evince active interest in the Asian countries and to encourage the forming there of Communist Parties. Also, he wrote, in 1923, that in "the last analysis, the outcome of the struggle will be determined by the fact that Russia, India, China, etc., constitute the overwhelming majority of the population of the globe"; and he noted with approval that this majority was becoming more and more interested in its own emancipation. (8)

But this statement, written a year before his death, falls so far short of enunciating any grand, explicit strategy that it emphasizes the implausibility of such a strategy. Certainly, it maps no road to Paris through Peking and Calcutta.

On the evidence of his own writings, Lenin's hopes were focused during the last years of his life on the Comintern—the Communist International—and his New Economic Policy. The Comintern, made up of Communist Parties in Western countries, was given the task, in 1920, of sparking revolutions in these. The NEP was a plan to make concessions to

Western industrialists in order to get them to build up the productive strength of the Soviet Union.

A piece that he wrote in 1921—*The Food Tax*—shows how these two interests met in his mind. In this, he tells his fellow Bolsheviks that certain conditions would have to be fulfilled before the USSR could again try, after its first disastrous experiment, to make a transition to a fully socialist economy. His first condition was massive and widespread electrification. For this, he allowed ten years, adding that this period could be shortened "only if proletarian revolution is victorious in such countries as England, Germany, and America." (9)

When we came across the passage in Welch's *Blue Book*, we leafed through Lenin's *Selected Works* to confirm our conviction that nothing of the type appeared there. Then we sought help from persons who have read the *Complete Works*, in Russian. Research scholars at Stanford, we learned, had looked for the "strategy" in vain. So had the Curator of the Slavic Room of the Library of Congress. In *The Communist Line Bulletin* of March-May 1959, Louis F. Budenz calls this particular "quote" one of the "many questionable quotations from Lenin and Stalin that are floating around in ill-informed anti-Communist circles."

Welch did not invent it. It has, apparently, been "floating around" for some years. But his use of it as the very foundation of his argument about the source of Communist strength suggests two things: first, that he has not read Lenin thoroughly enough to know how at variance with his stated hopes this "strategy of conquest" would be; and second, that "the leading anti-Communists" with whom he has talked and corresponded have not been the persons usually rated as top scholars in the field.

If Welch ever gives a precise reference that enables anyone to find this "quote," or even a close approximation of it, we and other searchers would gladly credit him with unraveling a mystery. To date, we have not heard of his giving such a reference; but we have been told of queries addressed to him.

An item in the July-August 1961 issue of *American Opinion*, p. 53, would almost suggest that he is keeping the "strategy" as too valuable to relinquish, but trying to dissociate it from the name of Lenin. The item begins, "Basic Communist strategy for conquest of the world, as laid out forty years ago and relentlessly followed ever since . . ." The pattern, then, as it unfolds, is the same as the one in *The Blue Book*; and his calling it Communist, instead of Leninist, does not make it any more convincing. For who other than Lenin was drawing up grand strategies for the Communists forty years before 1961?

The fact is that when we take a second look at Welch's carefully spelled-out qualifications, they begin to seem very odd. While he says that he has "diligently studied . . . anti-Communist books," he makes no mention of having read Lenin, or Stalin, or Mao; and aside from his reliance on Lenin's tactics, which he could have come across in any of a host of places, his books show no sign of his having done so.

Surely, these men—plus Khrushchev—have been Communism's prime movers and shakers; and the world, in all too many of its parts, has been moved and shaken. Yet, curiously, their major writings may well have lain quite outside Welch's area of interest; for they lend slight support to his determined thesis that conspiracy in high places, here at home, is well-nigh the only aspect of Communism we need to worry about.

Again, Welch reports that his diligent study has embraced "objective histories" of the past two decades. Yet at point after point, his account of events seems strikingly subjective. He flatly states, for example, that no real break between

Stalin and Tito ever took place: that the appearance of one was a ruse to deceive the West. But he neither supports this statement with any evidence nor explains away the documentary evidence by which it is contradicted.

He does not even tell his readers about the Cominform Resolution of June 28, 1948, which expelled Yugoslavia from that body. He does not tell them about Stalin's economic blockade of Yugoslavia; or about his effort, when this failed, to bring about Tito's downfall by splitting the Yugoslav Party.

The oddest feature of all, however, about *The Blue Book* and *The Politician* is one that escapes the reader at first—because it seems so improbable. This is the fact that these books, in spite of all pretensions to the contrary, are not really about Communism. One could, so to speak, read them till doomsday without gaining any specific, accurate knowledge about the ideology or its revision through the years; about the structure of the Soviet system; about the international apparatus; about the factors involved in the power-struggle after Stalin's death; about relationships within the orbit; or even about the specifics of the current Party line in this country.

The more one studies these books, the more clear it becomes that Welch's self-appointed task is far less that of educating people about Communism than it is that of insuring that pressure will be brought to bear where he wants it to be; and that of exposing as Communists or pro-Communists those whose influence he wants to liquidate. For his purposes, he may well find accurate scholarship less useful than his "fairly sensitive and accurate nose."

FIVE

SPENGLER ACCORDING TO WELCH

IF extremism has produced any odder piece of documentation than that in Section Two of *The Blue Book—But Let's Look Deeper*—we have not come across it. Welch gets off to a promising start. Communism's rapid spread, he tells us, points both to the shrewdness of its own tactics and to weaknesses in the Western body politic. We would not quarrel with this statement, nor with Welch's conviction that our political weaknesses need to be understood.

It does seem a tall order when he goes on to assert that to understand them "we have to go deeply into both the political history and the philosophical history of the human race." (1) But once he is launched on this journey of exploration, he makes clear the fact that what he means by a deep analysis of human history is an acceptance of "a cyclic theory of cultures"—particularly as set forth in Spengler's *Decline of the West.*

No sooner have we assimilated this surprise than we meet another. The "so-called liberal scholars of the world," we are told, made a concerted attack upon the Spengler book—only to find that its truth could not be downed by spurious arguments. Finally, to divert attention from Spengler, these scholars cast another man—"a meretricious hack named Arnold J. Toynbee"—in the role of most distinguished historian of our time. This tactic, executed by "the international socialists," relegated Spengler to obscurity.

This is not how we remember the book's reception. At the time it was published in America, in the late 1920s, we were both involved in what Welch calls "things academic"; and we seem to remember a period when anybody who was anybody, so to speak, carried around with him a copy of *The Decline of the West*. Certainly, it was dissected: its portentousness invited to argument. But for many persons who had, in that decade, parted company with the theory of automatic progress, the swing to a theory of cultural doom was a compensating gesture.

Out of curiosity, we wrote to the American publisher, Alfred A. Knopf, to ask how *The Decline* had really fared, and whether he had ever been aware of a liberal conspiracy against it. In a letter dated October 30, 1963, Mr. Knopf answered this latter question with a firm negative. As for figures, the unabridged edition—which runs well over nine hundred pages—has sold, he reported, more than forty thousand copies, and continues to sell at the rate of about four hundred a year: ". . . there has been no increase in this average sale since the foundation of the John Birch Society."

This sales record does not argue *The Decline's* having been relegated to obscurity by the very part of our population most likely to struggle through nine hundred pages of involuted analyses. Among European intellectuals, moreover, the book has had a far wider reading than in this country.

All this opens up an interesting question: why did Welch feel that his cause would profit by his portraying "so-called liberal scholars" as enemies of Spengler? The most logical answer appears to lie in the use he was preparing to make of what he presents as Spengler's theory. "This theory," he writes, "is absolutely fatal to the acceptance of socialism or any form of collectivism as a forward step, or as a form of progress in man's sociological arrangements. For in Spengler's view collectivism is a disease of society, concomitant with decay, and remarkably similar to cancer in the individual." (2)

Spengler, in brief, is being conscripted to serve as Welch's theoretician in his war against socialism; and any author to whom this role is assigned must, in Welch's argument, be one whom the liberals—or "so-called liberals"—would view with alarm.

The paragraph that follows this unequivocal setting forth of Spengler's theory contains, however, a curious statement: "It has been many years since I read Spengler, so I do not know how far I am wandering from his own specific or exact thinking, in trying to present his central theme. There is certainly more of Welch than there is Spengler in what follows."

That last sentence is strikingly true; and it marks a watershed in the argument. In what leads up to it, Welch is providing himself, it would seem, with a majestic ally in his struggle against what he defines as the enemy in our midst. Yet from this sentence on, he goes it alone, shaping his own analysis.

Spengler, we might say, is kept on stage just long enough to show the type of intellectual company in which Welch moves, and is then retired to the wings. He is no longer needed. Worse, his continued presence would be an embarrassment; for what Welch presents as Spenglerism, with a bow to the fact that he may wander a little from the precise theory, is so far removed from what Spengler actually says as to be, on certain counts, almost the opposite.

We feel it to be in order, then, to bring Spengler back on stage, to speak for himself. We do so not because we want to present him as a prophet for our age—which we do not— but because there is no reason why he should be dragooned into doing forced labor for the Radical Right.

First, however, we must recall Spengler's reason for writing this mammoth text; for it is easy to forget that *The Decline of the West* was designed as a guide to the right exercise of political authority. Being, as its author proudly said, *German*, it does not deal with those practicalities of power politics which absorbed Machiavelli in *The Prince*; but with the mystic concepts of soil, blood, fate, and a "soul"-relationship between leader and led.

By 1911, Spengler was certain that a war was in the making. He was convinced that Germany would emerge from it as a majestic imperial power; but he was not sure that its political leadership would handle wisely the greatness which its military leadership was about to deliver. Hence, giving up his post as a teacher, he undertook to inspire to greatness Germany's postwar leaders.

What troubled Spengler was his country's lack of a civil elite as carefully disciplined as was the Prussian Officers Corps. Germany had never provided, as Britain had, for the training of civil servants who could rule as if to the manner born: civil servants who could remain "in form" anywhere in the world and under any impact of circumstances.

By a political leadership's being "in form," Spengler meant its being so imbued with the spirit of its culture that its exercise of authority would be a second-nature enactment and affirmation of this spirit. To try to insure, then, that Germany's postwar leaders, with a vast and various empire to administer, would remain *German* to the core, Spengler worked out his theory of cultures. He portrayed each culture as being, so to speak, a separate "cosmos"—fated, indeed, to go through its own cycle of birth, growth, decay, and rebirth, but not subject to corruption unless it allowed its separateness to be breached.

Nothing turned out, of course, as Spengler had anticipated. His book was first published in 1918, the year of Germany's military collapse: the year that ushered in that chaos out of which Hitler eventually emerged as a living caricature of Spengler's blood-and-soil leader.

In various translation, however, his culture-centered text moved out around the world. And in 1958, its fortieth anniversary year, Robert Welch announced that *The Decline of the West* provided the exact theory needed to validate the John Birch Society's war against socialism and collectivism.

What, then, does Spengler actually say? He says that each culture takes on its identity at a stage of intimate contact with rural landscapes and realities: "the *landscape-figure* dominates man's eyes. It gives form to his soul. . . . The village, with its quiet hillocky roofs, its evening smoke, its wells, its hedges, and its beasts, lies completely fused and embedded in the landscape. . . . It is the Late City that first denies the land. . . . And then begins the gigantic megalopolis, the city-as-world, which suffers nothing beside itself and sets about annihilating the country picture." (3)

The villain of Spengler's piece is the City—brought into being and made ever larger, not by "collectivist" governmental forces, but by economic forces armed with "cause-and-effect rationality" rather than "soul-knowledge." To cast his theory as "absolutely fatal to the acceptance of socialism or any form of collectivism as a forward step" is nonsense. His thought travels on an altogether different track:

"The stone Colossus, 'Cosmopolis' stands at the end of the life course of every great culture. The Culture-man whom the land has spiritually formed is seized and possessed by his own creation, the City, and is made its creature, its executive organ, and finally its victim." (4)

The "sterility of civilized man" becomes evident at this stage. With man no longer able to be creative within the megalopolis which his own acquisitiveness has created, the cultural pyramid "crumbles from the summit, first the world-cities, then the provincial forms, and finally the land itself, whose best blood has incontinently poured into the towns . . ." (5)

What "wisdom" was Spengler thus urging upon Germany's leaders? This is where Welch's solemn praise of *The Decline of the West* becomes downright funny. Spengler was warning them not to stake Germany's hopes for imperial grandeur on the rationalistic theories of David Hume and Adam Smith, or on the machine-centered, money-based economy to which these English theories gave rise.

Against English Capitalism, Spengler pitted a concept that *"all economic life is the expression of a soul-life."* This, he said, was "a new, a German outlook upon economics, an outlook from beyond all Capitalism and Socialism—both of which were products of the jejune rationality of the eighteenth century . . ." (6) Marxism, in his view, was simply Capitalism with a new set of owners put into control "through a new kind of accounting," but neither better nor worse than the original from which it derived.

Although neither Spengler himself nor Robert Welch appears to have grasped this fact, there are striking similarities between Marxism and Spenglerism. Each of the two German philosophers made Capitalism a mighty protagonist in the drama of history; and each—Spengler no less than Marx— portrayed it as fated to overreach itself and bring on a climactic conflict in which it would be destroyed.

In Marx's *linear* drama, the productive and acquisitive forces within Capitalism are propelled into conflict at the point where the impoverishment of the proletariat leaves no one to buy what a machine-economy produces. The machines grind to a stop—but not for long. The silence of stagnation explodes into the uproar of revolution. The dictatorship of tho proletariat replaces that of the bourgeoisie.

In Spengler's *cyclic* drama, the productive and acquisitive forces within Capitalism are also brought to a point of con- flict. For a long time, money and machines cooperate to build the City, and to build it larger and larger. But as the stage of "Cosmopolis" approaches, the technical thought of the engineer is further and further inhibited by "the dicta- ture of money." It stands in real danger of succumbing to this stronger power. "But with this, money, too, is at the end of its success, and the last conflict is at hand . . ." (7)

For Spengler, however, unlike Marx, this terminal conflict —the one that brings down the whole City-system, and re- turns the culture to the soil for a fresh start, after an interval of Caesarism—is "the conflict between money and blood."

Welch talks as if Spengler were, in a general way at least, co-author of his thesis that if America wants to rid itself of the cancer of collectivism, two things must happen. American forces and resources must, to the greatest possible extent, be pulled back within our national boundaries. And government must be made to pull back to within its original boundaries of authority, leaving the economic domain alone.

Perhaps he derived the first part of this thesis from an imprecise memory of Spengler's wish to keep German cul- ture impregnably *German*. But we are at a loss to know from what he could have derived the second part of the thesis; for Spengler's attitude was not anti-governmental.

It would seem that Welch must have utterly forgotten what the German philosopher said about "the *private* powers of the economy"—for which he had little respect. "The *private* powers of the economy," he wrote, "want free paths for their acquisition of great resources. . . . They want to make the laws themselves, in their own interests . . ." (8)

Welch may have recalled that Spengler disliked democracy, as he does himself. But Spengler's reason for disliking it was not Welch's reason. Spengler defined democracy as a "tool" to be used by the private money-interests to create a "subsidized party": a party through which, scorning the principles of law and "true rulership," they could manipulate the government to their own advantage.

We hold no particular brief for Spengler's theory; and our taste for grandiose cosmologies of blood and fate is limited in the extreme. But we do hold a brief for Spengler's being given a fair hearing. If Welch felt the need for a theoretician, he picked the wrong one. Spengler according to Welch is not even a kissing cousin to Spengler according to Spengler.

For all its oddness as an example of scholarship, Welch's way of bringing in Spengler is revealing. One element that is repetitively made manifest in Welch's writings is a taste for grand designs, all-embracing theories, and orotund phrases. On this count, we must grant that Spengler was a natural for him to choose as a theoretician—just as Lenin's "strategy of conquest," even though not Leninist, was a natural foundation for him to choose for his analysis of Communist victories. It may well be that one reason why Welch talks such elaborate nonsense about Communism, when he might so usefully talk sense, is that he cannot resist the appeal of the pseudo-impressive.

OF STATISTICS AND PERCENTAGES

WELCH's manner of guiding the Birchers toward the conclusions he wants them to reach is an extraordinary blend of the folksy and the erudite. Month after month, by means of *American Opinion* and the *Bulletin,* he keeps them persuaded that he recognizes them as the salt of the earth and is educating them for a great mission; that whatever he asks them to do will be relevant to their country's need; and that he is, in his grasp of affairs, more than a match for a conspiracy designed by intellectuals.

This is no slight accomplishment; and one key to Welch's success is his remarkable power to use the tools of scholarship without letting them cramp his style. Among the many tools that he thus employs, statistics and percentages seem to occupy a favored place. In this chapter, therefore, we wish to examine two quite different, but equally characteristic, examples of how he uses figures to give authority to the points he wants to make.

The first example, and the more formal of the two, is what Welch has named the *American Opinion Scoreboard*. This is presented each year as a document heavy with portent; and this is even more true than usual, perhaps, in the case of the 1960 Scoreboard. This appears as an insert in the July-August and September issue of *American Opinion*; and the entire 99-page issue—said to hold "fifty thousand words of warning"—is built around it.

A page of explanation begins thus: "On the following pages we present *American Opinion*'s third annual *Scoreboard*, which shows the status of the International Communist Conspiracy in 107 countries of the world on the first of June, 1960. As before, the table is a composite of estimates made *independently* by highly qualified and expert observers on four continents—each a long-time student of the techniques of Communism."

Further down on the same page, we find a statement of what Welch claims to have done with these estimates: "We measure the degree of *effective control* that the International Communist Conspiracy exercises *over everything of political or economic importance* that is done in each country—the degree to which the conspiracy can prevent whatever it does not want and can induce or impose whatever it does want."

The first four words of that sentence are worth noting: "We measure the degree . . ." Both *measure* and *degree* are words that imply some precision of technique. Actually, on the *Scoreboard*—except for the countries of the Communist orbit, where control is set at a uniform 100 percent—each percentage has a built-in latitude of 20 points.

Thus, that of Spain is 0–20—which, translated into words, means that the Communists may have no effective control whatever over the political and economic life of that country or may control as much as one-fifth of it. This latitude by itself, of course, takes most of the meaning out of the phrase,

"We measure the degree," for the position of the Communists in a country where they have no bases of economic or political action under their control is different *in kind* from their position in a country where they can effectively use one-fifth of the economic and political instrumentalities of power as a means to the further extension of their power.

Other countries to which Welch assigns the percentage of 0–20 are Australia, Ireland, New Zealand, and Portugal. So far as the United States is concerned, the Communists are said to exercise a 40–60 percent *control over everything of political or economic importance that is done*; and a plus is added to show that the degree of control may be even higher. Apparently, in Welch's mind, the need for this plus has been confirmed; for the 1963 *Scoreboard* jacks up the estimate to 50–70 percent.

For other countries—to take a bare sampling—percentages are as follows: Great Britain, 50–70; Iceland, 80–100; France, 30–50; Norway, 50–70; India, 60–80; Italy, 50–70; and so on.

The *Scoreboard* is followed by a section headed RECAPITULATION: PROGRESS OF CONSPIRACY, 1 June 1958–1 June 1960. Here we are told that in 1958, 16 countries were "relatively safe"; but by 1960, only 5. In 1958, only 12 countries were "sliding into the abyss"; by 1960, 28 countries. In 1958, 25 countries were "under Communist slavery"; by 1960, 32 countries.

At this point, the already impressive ambiguity of the *Scoreboard* goes up, we might say, to 80–100 percent. The countries to which percentages of 70–90, 80–100, and 100 are assigned add up to 32. Hence, we can assume that these are the ones which are said, without qualification, to be "under Communist slavery." But this means that the Birch Society's "experts" make no distinction, so far as category is concerned, between, say, the Soviet Union and Bolivia; or between Red China and Tunisia. When, in brief, we try to put exact meanings into the terms in which the *Scoreboard* is framed, even their semblance of meaning drains away.

More important, however, than the question of what particular terms may mean is the fact that the whole *Scoreboard* —set up to look impressive, and presented each year as an important document—is an elaborate form of nonsense. If Welch were a different type of man, we would call it a hoax. But as we have worked our way through his output of printed materials, we have become ever more certain that he is his own most convinced follower. His words may seem to inhabit a plane where *No Trespassing* signs have been set up against any intrusion by unwanted facts. But they do not have that "oiliness" which makes us feel that some of the Radical Rightist leaders, with a shrewd eye on the market, are peddling anti-Communism as a form of merchandise.

No trained and experienced investigator has ever pretended that he could, with reference to even one country, and even with a 20-point latitude, reduce to a percentage a vast imponderable like "the degree of *effective control* that the International Communist Conspiracy exercises *over everything of political and economic importance.*" Yet Welch asks the Birchers to credit the assertion that "highly qualified and expert observers on four continents" have made estimates on the basis of which percentages of this sort can be assigned to 107 countries spread out over five continents and Oceania.

No trained and careful student of Communist affairs would say that the Party hierarchy in the Soviet Union, or in any country of the orbit, enjoys a 100 percent power to "prevent whatever it does not want" and to "induce or impose whatever it does want." Yet Welch asks the Birchers to credit a *Scoreboard* that assigns to every country of the orbit, plus Yugoslavia, such a 100 percent control. This means, we would note, that Khrushchev has wanted, and has been able "to induce or impose," the black-market operations, the theft of state property, the colossal mismanagement, the hoodlumism, the peasant apathy, and the intransigence of writers and artists against which he has been inveighing for years.

We wish we had space to quote many of the *American Opinion* items about the countries for which percentages are given; but we will limit ourselves to the case of Venezuela. It is a country that has been much in the news during the past two years or so, because of Communist sabotage; Betancourt's resistance to this; his urgent appeals for OAS help; and the orderly transition, for the first time in its history, from one administration to another by free election. These factors lend special interest to Welch's description of it as "the Communist puppet-state of Venezuela"; and to his listing of it among the 32 countries that are categorically stated to be "under Communist slavery."

The *American Opinion* item says that "some recent bickering between Castro and Betancourt suggests that our State Department may be planning another 'Tito' operation, to supply the Communist conspiracy with American weapons and munitions at the expense of American taxpayers under the ludicrous pretext that one of the Kremlin's branch-managers is 'anti-Communist' . . ." And it says that no "rational and informed man" can doubt "that Romulo Betancourt has been for all his adult life, and is today, a cunning, vicious, and utterly ruthless agent of the international Communist conspiracy . . ." (1)

All of this brings us back to his "highly qualified and expert observers." Who are they? Not one of them is named. Each is said to have been "a long-time student of the techniques of Communism." Where does he stand in the company of trained research scholars in the field? Is he also a long-time student of the techniques for gathering data in highly complex and ambiguous cultural fields? How well does he know each of the countries about which he has made an estimate?

Did these "experts" whose estimates are used to "measure the degree" of Communist control in 107 countries start from any agreed-upon procedures and definitions that would make it even remotely rational for their findings to be reduced to a single table of percentages? By what methods did they guard their conclusions against the influence of what scientists call the *personal equation*: the tendency of the observer's eye to see what it brings to the seeing?

This last question is highly pertinent. Nowhere in his writings do we find Welch characterizing as an *expert* any-one whose viewpoints contradict his own. The role of the expert, indeed, in Welch's frame of reference seems to be chiefly that of providing him with authoritative support for what he "knows." If, then, these observers were chosen as experts, and were still rated as experts at the end, we are left wondering whether their observations had any appre-ciable effect upon their judgments.

Further, there is a striking correspondence between what they have reported about various countries and what Welch has been saying about these countries all along. Thus, for example, Egypt is assigned a percentage of 80–100, and is thereby classified as "under Communist slavery." In the item that analyzes Egypt, we read that Nasser "was probably a conscious agent of the international Communist conspiracy at the time that the U.S. Central Intelligence Agency financed and encouraged his rise to power." No evidence is offered to show that the CIA ever performed any such role. This, in brief, would appear to be a Welchism, pure and simple. Edwin Arlington Robinson speaks of "our inch-rulings of the infinite." Do these solemnly presented *Scoreboards* amount to anything more than Welch-rulings of the imponderable?

At one point in our study of them, indeed, we were forced to wonder whether Welch himself knows what he thinks they mean. We also felt like asking, after the manner of *The New Yorker*, "Which Birch Society publication do you read?"

In 1958—the year the Society was founded—the first *Scoreboard* set the degree of Communist control over our national life at 20–40 percent. The sixth one, which appeared in July 1963, set it at 50–70 per cent. By *Scoreboard* standards, in brief, the situation became staggeringly worse during this span of years. Yet the September 1963 *Bulletin,* in an item designed to prove the usefulness of Bircher activity, declares that our country's chances of being saved from Communism have greatly improved during exactly the same span of years.

In 1958, we are told, before the Birch Society got on the job, our country's chances were only one in a hundred. By 1963, thanks to the Birchers, the situation was so much better that these chances "would be rated by a coldblooded book-maker as about one in four."

If we try to put together the implications of the *American Opinion Scoreboard* and the item in the *Bulletin,* dated only two months apart, we find that Welch's percentages can be taken to mean almost anything—and hence, had best be taken to mean almost nothing. On the basis of the data he provides, for example, there is no reason why we should not say that Communist control over all the important political and economic aspects of our national life has been rapidly increasing ever since the Birch Society was founded.

Our second example of how Welch uses percentages dates from October 9, 1961, and a speech that he then gave at

Garden City, Long Island. In this, he said that "the most trustworthy estimates" indicate that "about three percent of the Protestant clergy could now be described as Comsymps." He volunteered no parallel estimate for the Catholic priesthood. Asked about this, however, during the question period, he said that his guess would be that the Comsymps who are priests would not yet come to "more than one-half of one percent of the total—as against three percent among Protestants."

To his mind, as he explained later, he was complimenting the priesthood. But Monsignor Francis J. Lally, Editor of *The Pilot*—newspaper for the Boston diocese presided over by Richard Cardinal Cushing—took it upon himself to be a spokesman for the common-sense fact that a percentage does not exist in its own right. To have any meaning at all, it must be capable of being translated into a figure.

In an editorial entitled "One half of One," and dated October 14, 1961, he wrote, with amiable irony, "It is going to be a tough pill to swallow, but after so many others from the same source, we might as well open up and take it. Mr. Robert Welch has in effect declared that there are 273 Catholic priests in the United States who are Communist sympathizers. In his own words he made 'a long-range guess' that one-half of one percent of the U.S. Catholic priests are 'com-symps.'

"We would like to go along with Mr. Welch and make him a sporting offer. We will print the names of any fifty of these priests that he can produce and along with it, as space allows, whatever evidence he has to support his charges . . ."

In response to this "sporting offer," Welch did not name even one Comsymp priest. Instead, in a long letter which was published in full in the October 21 issue of *The Pilot*, he expressed his complete surprise that anyone would expect him to do so. The percentage which he had "pulled out of a hat" was not, he explained, intended to refer to any specific list of priests who could be identified as Comsymps; nor was it intended to imply that he could "substantiate" his guess.

He had, he said, simply chosen this percentage as a reasonable one with which to suggest the probable difference of degree of Communist infiltration into the priesthood and into the Protestant ministry. The figure he had applied to the latter was not "any wild surmise." It "was based on what such authorities in this area as Herbert Philbrick and Dr. J. B. Matthews have been saying for years; on the work of other students in the same field; and on the results of some very thorough, extensive, and *professional* surveys made for and at the expense of a good friend of mine who is an outstanding Protestant layman. And there are thousands of Protestant ministers . . . who thoroughly agree with these estimates."

This 3 percent estimate with respect to Communist sympathizers among Protestant clergymen was apparently first made by J. B. Matthews in 1953; but it has become, for Radical Rightists, a standard propaganda item. The figure of 7000, supposedly equivalent to it, is almost as standard.

Yet the oddness of all this is glaringly apparent. Three percent is a definite percentage. Seven thousand is a definite number. There would seem to be no way in which a leap could be made from the exposure of a few ministers, or even from the exposure of several hundred, to the precise conclusion that 3 percent of *all* Protestant ministers are Comsymps.

And what about the "thousands" of ministers to whom Welch refers? Have they, separately or as a group, made any independent survey of the Communist sympathizers in their own profession? If so, when, and by what method? Their faith would obligate them to see each fellow minister as an individual—and not, after the manner of the Communists, as part of a "mass." How have they made their appraisals, now of this minister, and now of that one, until they have totted up enough individuals to be equivalent to 3 percent of the whole?

Again, moreover, the matter of the *personal equation* has to be taken into account. What proportion of these "thousands" belong to that segment of the profession that has ranged itself against the "social gospel" and the Councils of Churches? Would those who have taken this doctrinal stance hold to the same definition of *Communist sympathizer* that would be used, for example, by the FBI? What does the term mean in their lexicon?

We ask these questions because we have recently read an article called "The National Council of Churches," which appeared in the December 1961 issue of *The Spearhead*, Wichita, Kansas. It is authored by Dr. Charles Poling, a retired Presbyterian minister who frequently speaks for Billy James Hargis's Christian Crusade; and it appears to be derived from one of his speeches.

Dr. Poling begins by urging Protestant laymen to take the initiative because the ministry has failed to lead a crusade "against the Godless forces of Communism and to part company with the National and World Councils of Churches." He says, "Practically all of our National Council leaders" have been "following the Communist line." And he declares, "Personally, I find it impossible to play on the same team with an organization that joins forces with Communism."

It turns out that what he means by "following the Communist line" is being on the same side as the Communists with respect to certain issues. His whole argument is built on the pattern of "parallel positions"—as though we were to prove him to be a Comsymp by saying, "Stalin wanted Hitler to be defeated—so did Dr. Charles Poling." This statement would patently be both silly and unjust—but scarcely more so than the case that Dr. Poling builds up against the Council.

Out of a various record, for example, he selects instances in which the National Council and the Communists have been on the same side of an issue. Then, ignoring all negative instances, he proceeds to prove by means of these that the Council has "joined forces" with the Communists. He gives no weight to differences of motive, or to the fact that, in most cases, the stands taken are not actually the same. They appear to be so only because Dr. Poling imposes upon every issue an either-or pattern.

Again, he does not say what other elements in our society were, with reference to this or that issue, on the same side as the Communists and the Council. He says, "The Communists are against the Bricker Amendment—so is the National Council." But he does not say that Congress failed to pass the Amendment—which fact would not argue that body's being for it. He says, "The Communists are opposed to the Connally Reservation—so is the National Council." But he does not say that the American Bar Association, albeit by a slender margin and after intensive debate, also took this stand.

Further, he does not show, or even attempt to show, that the National Council has in even one instance, through the years, *changed sides* on any issue when the Communist Party has done so. Yet this is the crucial point to which trained investigators give weight. The trained investigator does not contend that individuals or groups are proved to be pro-Communist by their being simply, with respect to various issues, on the same side as the Communists. But it is a different story if their record shows that their graph of zigs and zags matches that of the Party line. The Council's record shows nothing of this type.

We come back, then, to the "thousands" of ministers. Are

they free of the type of bias which Dr. Charles Poling exhibits? And further than this, did they arrive at the 3 percent estimate only after this had been put into circulation as an authoritative estimate? In other words, if, back at the beginning, Matthews had specified a different percentage—say, 2½ percent or 4 percent—could they, at that time or at any time since, have set him straight, saying, "We have concluded that 3 percent would come closer to the truth?" If not, in what sense does their agreement with the 3 percent estimate serve to validate it?

A further oddness is worth noting. We cannot think, off hand, of a single other area in our society where a percentage arrived at in 1953, and arrived at by unspecified methods, would still be quoted as accurate in the 1960s. But this particular percentage seems always to be as good as new. What bestows upon it, in this changing world, its singular durability? The total number of Protestant ministers in the country has changed, has grown considerably, since 1953. How does the Party manage to prevent any change in the *percentage* of them who are Comsymps?

In any case, Welch explained to Monsignor Lally that this 3 percent estimate was "trustworthy." He then explained how he had derived from it his estimate with respect to Comsymps in the priesthood. It takes longer, he noted, to train a man for the priesthood than for the Protestant ministry. Thus, it would cost the Communists more for each planted trainee; and they would also run a longer risk of his becoming a defector before his training was finished. Moreover, they could use only men who were willing to accept the condition of celibacy. Taking these factors into account, Welch explained, he had decided that his "trustworthy" three percent should, to fit the likely number of Comsymps in the priesthood, be scaled down to one-half of one percent.

Between April and October of that year, he reported, he had "made this same speech . . . twenty-seven times," using the same percentages when occasion arose. "Now honestly, Monsignor Lally, what is wrong with all of that?" We are left wondering why his "lifetime of business experience" can show him the fallacy in Communist economic theories but cannot answer this question for him.

The issue of *The Pilot* that carried Welch's letter carried also Monsignor Lally's response. Even after weighing Welch's explanation, he wrote, "we will have to continue to ask for the evidence. Where are the 'masquerading' priests? . . .

"Undoubtedly, Mr. Welch has a good deal of trouble with statistics and this is not an uncommon difficulty; but we should insist that facts and figures are very important when one sets out to organize an effective anti-Communist movement."

Here, Monsignor Lally turns from figures to logic; and he puts his finger on a fallacy which accounts for much of the injustice done to individuals and groups by Radical Rightist arguments. In these arguments, it is well-nigh standard practice to say that the Communist program has called for the infiltration of the churches, or the schools, or the government; and then to conclude, with no offering of evidence, or with the offering of only one or two dramatic cases, *that infiltration has actually taken place to this or that specified degree.*

"It is possible," writes Monsignor Lally, "that Communists could penetrate the ranks of the Catholic clergy, but actually where is the evidence that makes this possibility a present reality? It is also possible that Communists might wish to infiltrate the ranks of the FBI. Are we to conclude therefore that there is some small percentage there? They might even wish to penetrate into the central office of the Birch Society.

Have we a right to say, then, that they are there? The world of possibles is far away from the world of existing realities; to fail to make this distinction is to live in an unreal world."

Coming back, then, to Mr. Welch, he concludes, "We would be pleased to accept him as a companion in the vital effort our times demand against Communism were he not so uncertain an ally. His good will we have never called into question, nor his zeal; but for the rest we will continue to remain in agreeable disagreement."

SEVEN

OF MEN AND METHODS

S O far, we have talked chiefly of Welch's own manner of operation. Here, we wish to move beyond what he does to what he recommends that others do. In Section Four of *The Blue Book—And So, Let's Act*—he outlines a ten-point action-program for Birch Society members.

By studying this program, which is kept up to date through the medium of the *Bulletin,* we can learn two things: first, how our American culture is being impinged upon by Bircher influences; and second, what types of activity Welch rates as appropriate for a Society which he describes as made up of "men and women of good character, good conscience, and religious ideals."

"If I were the 'man on the white horse' on our side in this war," Welch writes—and proceeds to say what he would do if he had resources enough, and enough authority "over one million dedicated supporters" that he could coordinate their activities "with some degree of the positiveness and ef-

ficiency that Communist leaders exercise over their members and fellow travelers." (1)

The Communists, of course, achieve their degree of
"positiveness and efficiency" by ruling that no one answers
back and everyone does what he is told. Welch claims—and,
we feel sure, believes—that he stands for individual responsibility. But the type of responsibility which he asks the
rank-and-file Birchers to assume is not that of being keepers
of their own minds. Rather, the whole program outlined in
And So, Let's Act seems geared to the vision of a million
Americans dedicating themselves to the task of translating
Welch-made directives into social and political action.

First, then, the program calls for the establishment of
reading rooms—which would also be lending libraries—"in
just as many of the cities, towns, and villages of this country
as may be possible." By March 1964, according to the *Bulletin*
of that month, the number of these libraries was "almost
but not quite up to two hundred units."

"How many books each of these reading rooms will have,
especially which books, and under what conditions, would
of course be tightly controlled from headquarters." Why
"of course"? The answer is as obvious by Bircher standards
as it would be by Communist standards. Welch says that
such control would be necessary to prevent Communist
sabotage. But another reason for it is made obvious by the
first list of books, one hundred in number, that he approved
for the libraries. Speaking of this list, he says that "for any
good American who really wants to know the true history
of events and developments of the past two decades, these
books alone or even a majority of them will constitute a
complete education in the field." Significantly, there is no
book on the list that would contradict his own view of the
character and dimensions of the Communist conspiracy.

To put the matter another way, no one of these books would challenge his thesis that "our danger remains almost wholly internal, from Communist influences right in our midst and treason right in our government . . ." (2)

The Society's reading rooms are not designed, in short, to encourage any all-around study of Communism. They are indoctrination centers. Here, then, is the first things that Birch Society members are tacitly asked to do. So far as complex problems of Communism and American domestic and foreign policy are concerned, they are asked to take themselves out of the American tradition of education, and into an indoctrination system, where the "truth" that is to be their truth is handed down from above.

Second, the program calls for the putting of "conservative periodicals" into places—such as barber shops and doctors' offices—where people will pick them up for casual reading. So far as doctors' offices are concerned, Welch warns that little cooperation could be expected from the American Medical Association: it "has now been 'took,' to the extent that we could not count on any direct help there . . ." (3)

For fraternity houses and other places where academic minds can be reached, he recommends the *National Review;* for places where the audience would be the general public, *Human Events, American Opinion,* and *The Dan Smoot Report.*

Third, Welch calls for the encouragement and support of such radio and TV programs as those "of Fulton Lewis, Clarence Manion, and dozens of more localized broadcasters . . ." We can assume that his approval of the printed *Dan Smoot Report* would extend to the same *Report* on radio and TV; and a further key to the type of program he recommends is to be found in the May 1961 *Bulletin.*

This *Bulletin* names sixteen organizations and movements to the programs of which the Birch Society gives support, but with none of which it is affiliated. Among these are several that feature radio programs: Billy James Hargis' Christian Crusade, for example; and Carl McIntire's 20th Century Reformation Hour.

Fourth, the program calls for "organized planning and control to make full and effectively coordinated use of the powerful letter-writing weapon that lies so readily at hand." Welch says that the Communists' claim to being able to "land fifty thousand individually written letters in Washington in a space of seventy-two hours" should be made to "look like peanuts" by the Birch Society.

This letter-writing tactic deserves more space than we can give it here. Hence, we will pass it over for the time being and devote the next chapter to it.

The fifth point in the Welch program is frankly Leninist: "We would organize fronts—little fronts, big fronts, temporary fronts, permanent fronts . . .

"This front business, like a lot of techniques the Communists use, can be made to cut both ways." (4)

Lenin called such fronts "transmission belts" because the Party could, by means of them, reach vast numbers of people who would balk at accepting the Party itself as a guide. And fronts could be used, also, in reverse—as "belts" by means of which to move non-Communists into the Party by gradual stages.

There is no mystery about why a conspiratorial body, working to mislead people into serving its purposes, should find such fronts invaluable. But why does Welch need them? He insists in *The Blue Book*, p. 130, that while he and those who work with him are "opposing a conspiracy," they are not "making use of conspiratorial methods." Then why borrow from the Communists a method that has never been other than conspiratorial?

The most durable of the several fronts upon which Welch bestowed life as soon as the Birch Society came into being was *A Petition to Impeach Earl Warren.* He recommended this to the founding group of the Society in 1958. In the October 1963 *Bulletin,* we find him saying, "If, during the fall and winter, we could get one million Americans to read carefully the whole *Warren Impeachment Packet,* we would actually be able to get the Chief Justice impeached during the next session of Congress." And the February 1964 *Bulletin* devotes two pages to suggested tactics for stepping up the campaign. One of these is to tie in the impeachment movement with Warren's appointment to head up the Commission to investigate the assassination of President Kennedy.

Welch recommends that the Birchers, in connection with their front activities, also use the related Communist stand-by: mass petitions. "Goodness knows the Communists have proved their subtle value and effectiveness. We ought to outdo the Communists at least two to one at that game . . ." (5)

Ought they? If so, why? The very essence of the mass-petition technique has been that of persuading Americans in multitude to sign documents which they have not studied and often have not even read. By what standards of value should an anti-Communist body join the Communists, even as opponents, in encouraging Americans to go in for this sort of mindless signing of their names?

The right of petition is a deep and vital part of our heritage. But was this right established on behalf of the sort of tactic which the Communists employed, for example, in the case of the Stockholm "peace petition" of 1950? Was it not, rather, established to affirm the right of free and responsible individuals to make known their common viewpoint with respect to one or another issue?

The mass petition is a travesty upon this honorable invention of free men. The only value it attaches to a person's name is that of lengthening a list. It is geared to the assumption that "the masses" can always be manipulated in the service of policies determined at the top.

Innumerable loyal Americans were caught by this Communist tactic—caught once, or twice, or more than twice—before they began to recognize its character; and a new generation of the inexperienced has come on the scene, now, to be vulnerable to it. Moreover, Bircher appeals would be specifically directed to persons on the conservative side of the liberal-conservative center; and they have had less chance than have persons on the liberal side to become immunized by painful experience to the mass-petition technique.

Since, therefore, Welch talks of setting petition-goals that range from one hundred thousand names to ten million, it seems worth while, even at this late date, to recall the process by which the Communists undertook to get five million names on the Stockholm "peace petition." Their multiple petitions in behalf of causes dear to the Party have all fallen into the same general pattern.

The text of this "peace petition," adopted at the Communist-controlled World Peace Congress, held in Stockholm in March 1950, was addressed to "all people of good will." Those who circulated the petition at vast open-air "peace meetings," or passed it down the rows at religious gatherings, or offered it to workers pouring out of a factory, described it merely as being for "peace" and for "the outlawing of atomic weapons as instruments of aggression." But the implications that were subtly woven through the text were to the effect that the United States was sole author of the cold war, and aggressive arch-enemy of all peoples everywhere who hunger for peace.

Virtually no one who signed the petition had a chance to study it. Few had a chance to read it even hastily. To reassure those who might run their eye over the page in search of a clue to its character, a quote from the Secretary General of the United Nations—on the subject of peace—was printed at the bottom. The set-up gave the impression that this statement had been made in support of the petition. It had not. It had been lifted out of an altogether different context and used without the author's consent.

In the end, the petitions signed in this country found their way to a numbered lock-box in a New York City post office; and thence to Moscow—there to be put with other petitions that had been similarly circulated by Communist Parties all around the world. Thus, there was added to the Kremlin's arsenal of propaganda weapons "documentary proof" that millions of human beings regarded the United States as an aggressor and an enemy of peace.

If Welch wants the Birchers "to outdo the Communists at least two to one" at this kind of game, he should, we feel, explain how his method of circulating a petition would differ in kind from the Communist method. How would he make sure that each person who signed his name had, first, been given a chance to study the document carefully?

He suggests, for example, that the technique could be used to prevent any American President's attending a summit conference. "Just as soon as the wind of such a forthcoming summit conference started to blow, we would launch the gathering of one of the most gigantic petitions of all time. . . . It is just possible that we could get ten million signatures . . ."

We can think of a number of good reasons for not being enthusiastic about summit conferences. They seem to provide Khrushchev with a chance to exhibit, rather than enact, a will to negotiate. We feel, too, that they tend to downgrade those persons at the ministerial level who must, in the end, do the slogging work of negotiation. And, not least, they put our President at a disadvantage. He cannot act with the decisiveness of a dictator. Hence, he can all too easily be maneuvered into a position where he seems, with all the world looking on, to be holding back from a step toward "peace" which Khrushchev can show himself eager to take— because he knows that he will not have to take it.

Does our feeling on this score mean that we would want to sign a Welch petition? It does not. Recalling Welch's fixed idea that our government is run by "Communist bosses" and traitors, we very much doubt that we would want to set our names to the *implications* that would be woven into his Bircher document. This matter of *implications* is what the American public needs to understand with respect to the whole mass-petition technique—regardless of which extreme uses it. The time has come, we would say, for Americans strongly to reaffirm the integrity of their own names by not signing anything that they have not studied.

The sixth point of Welch's action-program calls for the "exposure" of enough "Communists" to provide a shock for the American public—with *American Opinion* to be used as the medium for such exposures. And here Welch gives a concrete example of the type of thing he has in mind.

The head of one great educational institution, he says, is a man "whom at least some of us believe to be a Communist." Hence, this man's exposure should not wait upon proof: "Even with a hundred thousand dollars to hire sleuths to keep him and his present contacts under constant surveillance for a while, and to retrace every detail of his past history, I doubt if we could prove it on him." (6)

Yet five hundred dollars, he says, would be enough to

let him satisfy himself as to whether "our guess had been correct" and to "get all the materials needed for quite a shock." He would then publish in *American Opinion* an article "consisting entirely of questions to this man, which would be devastating in their implications." They would not be so couched that an innocent man could clear himself by giving honest answers. Their "devastating implications" would be so built into them as to lodge in the reader's mind, whether or no—to nudge that reader, gradually, toward doubting the man's innocence and, in the end, toward believing him guilty.

Here, Welch abandons all pretense that he is acting within our moral code: "The question technique, when skillfully used in this way, is mean and dirty. But the Communists we are after are meaner and dirtier, and too slippery for you to get your fingers on them in the ordinary way . . ." (7)

Quite apart from the fact that the man was, in this instance, to be exposed without having been proved to be a Communist, the way Welch rationalizes his resort to an immoral tactic needs to be evaluated. Stripped of its trimmings, what it means is that if we regard an enemy's behavior as "mean and dirty," we should not only model our own behavior upon it but urge other Americans—a million or so—to do likewise.

Welch's seventh point also calls for the use of loaded questions—to be directed, in this case, at a platform speaker who is to be "exposed." The trick, he indicates, would be "to send about three people to his 'lectures' (but a different three each night), have them sit apart and show no connection with each other, and let each of them ask a question during his question-and-answer period." (8) The question-askers, in brief, would not let the content of a lecture influence their reaction: they would come with their questions prepared in advance. This again is a Welch application of an old Communist tactic.

We know American audiences fairly well after some thirty years of experience with them. They are not stupid; and they are not willingly unfair. Therefore, a speaker who has nothing to hide has nothing to fear from the above tactic—particularly if he has done his homework on *The Blue Book*. The success of the tactic depends upon his being caught off guard; upon his hesitating, and giving the impression that he is evasive, because he recognizes that the question is "loaded"; upon his starting, in contrast, to answer it before he recognizes the trap, and then becoming awkward in the process of trying to extricate himself; and, most of all, upon his distrusting his audience.

He can do any of several things—and no one of them will be rendered less effective by his relaxing and enjoying himself. If he has started to answer and has had to backtrack, or has otherwise given an impression that he is hiding something, he can simply explain his predicament to the audience, taking the question apart to show why it is unanswerable in the form given. Then he can ask that it be rephrased.

Or, if he judges the charge implied in it to be slanderous, he can go directly to this charge and ask whether it is intended. If the questioner says that it is, the speaker can and should ask that it be made explicit; and that the questioner provide his name and address.

Either of the above approaches, we would note, has the effect of turning the planted agent of the Birch Society into a morally and legally responsible individual, *whose words are his own*. If he is willing to enter into an American type of give-and-take on these terms, well and good. If he is unwilling to come out into the open, as an individual whose words are his own, the audience will not long remain blind to this fact.

As a matter of public education, the speaker may want, somewhere along the line, to explain how the tactic of the loaded question—used alike by the Communists and the Radical Rightists—is designed to operate. The one indispensable element in all this, we would emphasize again, is that the speaker himself must respect and trust his audience.

The eighth point in Welch's program has to do with the American Opinion Speakers Bureau. The first task of the Society in relation to a speakers bureau, Welch indicates in *The Blue Book*, would be that of lining up correct speakers who would be willing to appear before groups for small fees or none.

"Then we would go to work putting together the huge lists of church clubs, P.T.A. groups, and others who use such speakers, and start making known to them who was available on what subjects." (9)

A pamphlet called *A Frank Report,* submitted to the Birch Society members by the National Finance Committee, gives an account of the state of the Society's affairs as of July 1, 1963. It contains two items that give some indication of how the plan for the speakers bureau is working out.

Thus, we read, on p. 203, that the American Opinion Speakers Bureau has, "by an extensive registration system," built up a list of "several hundred able volunteer speakers"; and that these are to be provided—free or for a small charge— "to Service Clubs, Women's Clubs, P.T.A. audiences, and other groups in the twenty or more categories of such local organizations which hold weekly or monthly meetings throughout the United States."

The second item is a reprint of a letter in which one chapter tells Welch what it accomplished during 1961. It arranged engagements in its locality—the name of which is deleted in the reprint—"for over 30 anti-Communist speakers";

furnished nine speakers for out-of-town engagements; and elected seven of its members "to program chairmen jobs in various civic organizations."

It begins to seem as though groups that belong to our American liberal-conservative center are really going to have to cultivate the skill of looking in both directions at once; for the Communist Party, USA, is likewise in the business, now, of providing free speakers to community and campus groups. Its bureau is in New York, at the same address as the *Worker;* and it is engaged in an all-out effort to secure speaking engagements for top-ranking Party members—with student and church audiences as prime targets.

The ninth point has to do with a long-range hope on Welch's part: he hopes that the Birch Society will become, on the world front, a *body* in the sense that the Communist Party is one. By the term *body,* he indicates, he means a force "which can move and work and make itself effective as an entity."

Tenth: "Finally, and probably most important of all . . . we would put our weight into the political scales of the country, just as fast and far as we could." An awareness that Welch meant very literally what he said on this score, and that Birch Society members are dedicated to the fulfillment of his program, has been swiftly growing among us.

At this writing, for example, extremist elements in California—with the Birch Society, it would appear, the strongest among them—have captured the Young Republicans and the Republican Assembly, and appeared for a time to be well on their way toward gaining control of the State Central Committee. And Senator Thomas Kuchel, of that State, has been mincing no words in warning his fellow Republicans of what may lie ahead:

"The Republican Party faces one of the gravest dangers in its long history. In California all the odious totalitarian techniques of subversion and intrigue are now being used by a frenetic but well-disciplined few to capture and control our party, and to make it an antiquated implement of embittered obstructionism." (10)

If we take the ten-point program of the John Birch Society, and put with it the current Communist Party line as this is spelled out in the *Worker* and *Political Affairs*, we find ourselves to be confronted by a stark conclusion: *we are all targets now.*

EIGHT

LETTERS UNLIMITED

W ELCH, in proposing his plan for letter-writing campaigns, states that there should be "a continuous overwhelming flood of letters, not just to legislators or the executive departments in Washington, but to newspaper editors, television and radio sponsors, educators, lecturers, state legislators and politicians, foundation heads and everybody else whose opinions, actions and decisions count for anything in the ultimate total of actions and decisions." (1)

The first purpose which he assigns to this "outpouring of mail" is that of encouraging correct viewpoints and slowing down "the brazen advance of some of those on the other side." His second purpose has to do, not with those who are on the receiving end of the "outpouring," but with the Birchers themselves. Each campaign, he notes, gives "the members of our local chapters and volunteer groups just one more activity, one more thing to do."

This statement tells to what general "family" of organizations the John Birch Society belongs. It belongs—as does the

112

Communist Party—to the type in which the leader or the hierarchy looks at the rank-and-file member across a wide status-gap and sees him as a kind of perpetual child. Groups that want their members to act like mature, self-governing individuals discourage, rather than encourage, their making a sense of importance out of mere busy-work. But groups that want them to play follow-the-leader provide busy-work out of which they can make a sense of importance.

A program of ceaseless activity has been, in every country, one of the chief means by which the Communist Party has bound its lay members to itself, while alienating them from their environing society. Super-busyness with assigned chores keeps rank-and-file members in a "correct" relationship to those who hand down directives from above. Further, it rewards them for relinquishing their independent selfhood by making them feel usefully part of a vast historic process. And not least, it encourages the atrophying of their relationships with other groups: there is simply no time left for anything outside the Party. Frank S. Meyer, in *The Moulding of Communists*, pp. 22–25, gives a precise and vivid account of the rank-and-file activity that goes on within the Party.

Welch states that he does not, after the manner of Lenin, claim the right to absorb the whole of the Birchers' lives. We are sure that he means what he says on this count. Yet we are also sure that he knows—or intuitively feels—that a monolithic structure needs to keep its lay members extraordinarily busy, lest their minds choose their own directions of approach to problems and issues. What he says about letter-writing campaigns points to his awareness of this fact. So does the amazing range of activities recommended in each *Bulletin*.

The writing of a letter can be a highly individuated enterprise, one that engages hand, emotions, and intellect. But while Welch's plan provides abundant exercise for hand and emotions, it is hard to see how it provides any for the intellect. Decisions about both target and subject-matter are handed down from above. Nor is this all. Even the form that letters should take and the tone they should have are leader-determined. Finally, in Welch's own words, "the amount of promptness and participation" in each campaign should be "constantly checked and evaluated by a central headquarters or director." (2)

In the light of all this, persons and groups that find themselves on the receiving end of a Bircher "outpouring of mail" do well to realize that what has come to them, psychologically speaking, is just a letter from Robert Welch. While the fact that it arrives in hundreds or thousands of envelopes changes the weight of the mailman's load, it does not change the intrinsic weight of the message.

The October 1963 *Ladies' Home Journal* carried a story by James Clavell, called "The Children's Story." Clavell, we would recall, was the author of the 1962 best-selling novel, *King Rat,* a book that portrayed wartime conditions in a Japanese prison camp. The book was written out of his own experience: the rigors of such a camp had led to his being invalided out of the British Royal Artillery, with the rank of Captain, in 1946. He is now an American citizen; and "The Children's Story" is set in America.

The story, like George Orwell's *1984,* employs the literary device of placing its events *after* a totalitarian—and obviously Communist—seizure of power. Its setting is a classroom in an American elementary school. The aim of the story is to show the highly subtle methods by which a young Communist teacher, chosen by the hierarchy for her skill with children, contrives to alienate the students, step by careful step, from their parents, their country, and their religion.

If the story has a moral—and we would say that it both has a moral and is an intensely moral document—it is that the most fearful weapon in Communism's arsenal is not espionage, or the ballistic missile, or the machinery of terror. It is a deliberately cultivated skill in severing the bonds that unite the young with their parents and their culture.

Reading the story is, in fact, a fearsome experience; for Clavell puts the reader into a position where he has helplessly to watch a trained, dedicated, attractive young Communist teacher move a group of students over from one value-system to another. She does not frighten them. She wins them over by kindness and "logic": by making them feel how outmoded their parents' religious and patriotic views are. The reader can only watch, for example, unable to intervene, while she brings the children to a point where it seems to them to be quite all right to cut up the American flag and take the pieces home for souvenirs—because the flag is, after all, she has told them, only a symbol.

In the November 1963 *Bulletin* Welch exhibits his total lack of comprehension of the story. He tells the Birchers, "You are gradually given the impression, but *only* the impression without any outright statement, that this is an account of the wonderful conditions that will prevail when the Communists officially take over the educational system. . . . Though of course the word Communism and Communist are never mentioned. . . . In fact, this is about the smoothest, while at the same time being about the most brazen . . . piece of propaganda *against* God and country that I have ever read." Then he advises the Birchers to read it; and, giving them the name and address of the Editor-in-Chief of the Curtis Publishing Company, suggests their writing to him letters of protest.

An article called "A Report to Our Readers," in the April 1964 *Journal*, sums up the results of this Welch-made suggestion. From the time the story was published up through January 15, 1964, the magazine received 2,378 letters about it. "In better than half of the letters received, exact phrases from Mr. Welch's denouncement were parroted word for word. In many other letters they sang through the writers' own sentences in partial, piecemeal echo of the Birch bulletin." The editors of the *Journal* concluded that, out of the total of 2,378, as many as 2,000 letters had been written in response to "an inaccurate directive from a single person."

Oddly enough, the Birchers who wrote these letters may have felt that they were expressing their own views. Yet their parrot-responses suggest that if Welch had understood the point Clavell was making, and had put the story on the agenda as something to be commended, these same members would have larded their letters with his words of praise.

The psychological mechanism that works in such a case is one on which John Gates, former editor of *The Daily Worker*, has shed considerable light. After he broke with the Party, in the winter of 1957–1958, Gates wrote an article —published in *The Progressive*, March 1958—in which he defined the type of "freedom" that people enjoy when they do what someone at the top tells them to do.

Thus, he explained that the CPUSA's subservience to every zig and zag of the Moscow line was not, in the ordinary sense of the word, "a case of dictation from abroad." The American Communists, he said, were "eager to accept the word of the Soviet Communists as the final say." In like fashion, we can readily believe, a majority of the Birchers feel that they are exercising their own independent will when they follow to the letter a recommendation they find in the *Bulletin;* for they provide the eagerness with which Welch's word is accepted and parroted as final truth.

In the October 1963 *Bulletin*, we find the directives for another type of letter campaign. Here, the target is Mr. George R. Vila, President of the United States Rubber Company. The offense for which he is to be brought to account is that of having spoken well of the United Nations in his April 1963 letter to the Company's employees.

In his letter, which Welch reproduces in the *Bulletin* and describes as "the most blatant form of pressure on behalf of this Communist-controlled criminal monstrosity that we have yet seen," Mr. Vila makes no pretense that the UN is a perfect organization or that it has been able to fulfill the hopes initially invested in it. He expresses his view, however, that it is still worth supporting and worth trying to improve: "No other group is so organized as a world forum . . ."

Moreover, Mr. Vila says: "The UN is more than the members of the Security Council and the General Assembly. It is the agencies actively working to improve world health, science, culture, food supplies, and business economy."

Suggesting that this company president be, in effect, overwhelmed with a flood of protests, Welch instructs the Birchers as follows: "Make clear your understanding that—except as his own stockholders might object, Mr. Vila has a perfect right as President of the U.S. Rubber Company to write anything he wishes to the Company's employees; but that you and other members of the public have a perfect right to judge the Company by what he says in such a letter."

Having made this clear to Mr. Vila, the Birchers should send either copies of their letters or separate letters to the Company's local distributors; and, wherever possible, to its stockholders. Further, the Company should be bombarded with anti-UN postcards, bearing GET US OUT! stickers.

In what tone should this campaign of genteel blackmail-within-the-law be conducted? "Whether your letters are short or long," Welch tells the Birchers, "keep them polite, friendly, and well reasoned—without sacrificing any firmness in your opposition to such support of 'The House that Hiss Built.'"

In the following month, November 1963, Welch provided the Birchers with another target. Again, it was a large corporation: McDonnell Aircraft. And again the matter at issue was support of the United Nations.

"The United Nations crowd," Welch wrote in the *Bulletin*, pp. 13–15, "becomes more brazen and more aggressive all the time. But the top prize, for outstanding propaganda service to this instrument of international deception and brutality, must go as of now to the firm named above. They have just been boasting in print of their having, in 1958, made United Nations Day (October 24) the seventh paid holiday in their company. . . . That's like boasting of being the first company in the world to give a gold medal to a coldblooded murderer. Now the company obviously hopes that it is setting another precedent by offering its employees an opportunity to vote for April 4, as NATO day, to be the eighth annual paid holiday . . .

"Since it seems unlikely that this firm will want to stop with just eight paid holidays, however, we suggest that our members help them out by recommending others. One might be the birthday of Alger Hiss . . .; or, if the company wants to show its traditional Americanism, perhaps of Benedict Arnold . . ."

Members of the Birch Society are told that they need not follow any directive that goes against their conscience. Whether the reason be conscience, or good taste, or simple inertia, many members obviously do not carry through on every letter-writing campaign. While it is embarrassing to have two thousand supposedly free Americans denounce a story as Communist-inspired just because Welch missed the meaning of it, two thousand letters still fall very far short of being the fifty thousand which, in *The Blue Book*, he speaks of wanting to be able to deliver at a specified point within a period of seventy-two hours.

What interests us here, however, is the *fact* that Welch tells the members that they need not do anything of which their consciences disapprove; for this fact is in itself a reminder of how different in kind the Birch Society is from the host of voluntary associations to which we are accustomed. It would never occur to the leader of any typically American group to confirm in words the obvious fact that his own authority is of a lesser order than is that of a member's conscience.

It is in little ways like this, but with odd frequency, that Welch reveals the extent to which the Society is an outsider in the American scene. Thus, the first item on the October 1963 agenda, as set forth in the *Bulletin,* was recruiting; and the campaign to secure new recruits should, the text specified, be carried on "by all practicable means that are honorable."

Some things, it would seem, should be taken for granted. To have members employ dishonorable means of recruiting would plunge the average organization into a state of crisis. But the subject of holding to honorable methods would no more come up in the normal course of events than would the subject of one's personal honesty in a normal conversation.

Welch's statement, then, to the effect that the Birchers are individually free to obey the dictates of conscience does not so much reassure us as remind us of certain peculiarities of the Society he has founded: its monolithic structure, for example; its built-in provision for the purge; its leader's demand that personal loyalty to him be the organization's binding force; the high value it puts upon busy-work.

When we try to think of the individual member of such an organization as *free,* we find that the concept of freedom that comes to mind is less the American concept than the one set forth in a basic text of the world Communist movement: *Fundamentals of Marxism-Leninism:*

"While granting extensive rights to its members, the Party at the same time naturally demands loyalty to its programme, aims and ideals . . . Lenin wrote: 'Everyone is free to write and say whatever he likes, without any restriction. But every free union is also free to expel members . . .'

"Party discipline does not expect anyone to relinquish his own convictions if these convictions are not at variance with the principles of Marxism-Leninism."

But: "The Party has strict rules regarding those who do not obey its adopted decisions . . ." (3)

So has the John Birch Society. Many organizations, to be sure, have some provision for ridding themselves of undesirable and "deadwood" members. But so far as we know, the Birch Society is the only organization in our midst that both claims to uphold our American value-system and requires prospective members to sign an agreement that they can be ousted from the Society at any time, "by a duly appointed officer . . . *without the reason being stated* . . ." The italics are ours.

A further peculiarity of the Bircher frame of reference should be noted: namely, that those who inhabit it are never encouraged to weigh the possibility that they may be mistaken—about anything. Our society is based on a religious tradition which, disturbingly and redemptively, reminds the individual that he is fallible. He is told to get the beam out of his own eye before he starts probing for the mote in the eye of another; and that unless he can declare himself to be sinless, he had best keep the upper hand of his stone-throwing impulses. He is told that the never-rejected sacrifice is a humble and a contrite heart.

The gospel according to Welch, however, rarely expresses

any awareness that he may be mistaken. In the Foreword to the fourth printing of *The Blue Book,* for example, he says that he has been able "unhesitatingly" to ascribe most conservative criticisms of the John Birch Society "to nothing more serious than the normal jealousies and petty hypocrisies of mankind." As for criticism from the "Liberal Establishment," it can be dismissed as "a torrent of smears."

This Welch pattern of response to criticism appears to be orthodox for the members also. In the case of the campaign against the Clavell story, the *Ladies' Home Journal* answered every letter on which an address was given. Fifty-eight Birchers responded to these answers with further letters; and these letters were not only more hysterically vituperative than the ones written by these same persons on the first round, but they unanimously rejected any explanation of the story which might exonerate the *Journal* from the charge of being part of a Communist conspiracy.

Again, when Jack Bass of the Columbia, South Carolina, *Record* was making his study of the Society, he asked William C. Highsmith, Major Coordinator for the Carolinas, Virginia, and Tennessee, about the Society's critics. Highsmith answered with complete assurance that they fall into just three categories. They are "Communists, Communist sympathizers (Comsymps), or misguided conservatives." (4)

All this means that, within the larger frame of our American life, the Birchers—like the Communists, and like various other Radical Rightist groups—are encouraged to inhabit a psychological enclave. Within this, they are virtually secure against any stimuli that might move them to recheck their conclusions or ponder the moral implications of their methods. They can be expected, therefore, after the manner of insulated minds, to move further and further away from reality in their judgments, and from any live-and-let-live attitude toward fellow Americans with whom they disagree.

In addition to Welch's insistence that our government is the mainstay of the world Communist movement, there are a great many controversial issues and complex problems about which the Birchers are certain to disagree with a great many persons—whom they will then brand as Communists, Comsymps, dupes, or hazy characters.

The August 1963 *Bulletin* gives a catalogue of what the Birch Society is *for:* what its aims are. It might better have been called a catalogue of what the Society is *against.* Virtually all the items have to do with getting rid of something; putting an end to something that is being done. Not one of them represents an effort to tackle a complex problem, domestic or foreign, and shape up a workable solution to it.

Five items are dedicated to "getting the government out of"—education, "the welfare business," the "Communist-inspired 'civil rights' turmoil," religion, and competition with private industry. Others call for States' Rights; the abolishment of the income tax; a "Supreme Court that obeys the laws and the Constitution"; and for driving "Castro and his Communists out of Cuba, by force if necessary."

One item calls for "getting the United States out of the United Nations, and the United Nations out of the United States"; another, for "an immediate discontinuance of the so-called Alliance for Progress"; another, for a "rapid cessation of all foreign aid"; and yet another for "immediate abolishment of Radio Free Europe, Voice of America, United States Information Service, the Peace Corps, and all similar absurdities."

There are items on this list about which non-extremists would disagree; and items about which they would want to qualify their opinions, and even acknowledge their considerable ignorance. But taken *in its entirety,* and illuminated by what we have come to know about Welch-approved methods, this program makes strikingly clear the fact that *the John Birch Society is not a conservative organization.* It has tried to persuade conservatives that its cause is theirs; that it is carrying the banner for values they want to cherish. But it is not conservative. It is an exponent of anarchic radicalism of the Right.

Genuine conservatism holds to an organic concept of society, and of society's development within a time-span which embraces the past, the present, and the future. A conservative, for example, may be against federal aid to education; but he will not brush off the problems which the federal government has felt obligated to try to solve by means of this aid. He will put his mind on how these can be effectively handled at the state and local level.

He may, again, give a low rating to our foreign aid program, or to the Alliance for Progress. But in each instance, he will acknowledge our national need to find a way to deal with the problems at which these have been directed. Also, he will continue to discuss these subjects with persons with whom he disagrees; and he will refrain from converting these persons into agents of the Communist conspiracy.

The genuine American conservative, in short, like the genuine American liberal, puts his mind on problems. In both the material and the social areas, our country has, from the beginning, been a problem-focused and problem-solving country. The Birch Society is content to deal in stereotypes, oppose a ubiquitous "conspiracy," and let problems take care of themselves.

PART II

And Others

NINE

THE DAN SMOOT REPORT

W E shall not be building Part II, as we built Part I, around a single leader and his organization. But neither will we aspire to any total coverage of Radical Rightist groups. There are too many of them. Our plan will be to deal in such detail as we can with five men and the programs with which they are identified. By this means, and against the background of what we have already said about the John Birch Society, we can hope to combine some depth of treatment in each case with a gradual broadening of the picture of far-right extremism.

Later—in Part III—we can broaden this picture further by a survey of various other groups and programs. In the process of introducing these, we can explore some of the intergroup relationships that make it reasonable to speak, not simply of the Radical Right, but of a Radical Right movement.

If we begin with Dan Smoot, of Dallas, Texas, it is because his name has already been mentioned in Part I. Welch, we would recall, named *The Dan Smoot Report* as one of the publications that he wanted Birch Society members to place in barber shops and doctors' offices, for the general public to read.

Also, we have ourselves known Smoot's work for a longer time than we have that of any of the other persons we are writing about. His name became familiar to us, as it did to a considerable number of other Americans, by way of Facts Forum. This radio program, originating in Dallas, and sponsored by H. L. Hunt of that city, was on the air weekly from 1951 to 1955.

We used to listen to the Forum, now and then: most often, when we happened to be in Texas, or elsewhere in the Southwest, on some work-project. But for at least one year out of the four, we read the transcripts regularly—and thus began to get a first feel, as it were, of how Smoot handles materials.

And this is the essence, we believe, of what Americans must learn about each of the major Radical Rightist leaders and opinion-makers: how he marshals words, quotes, news items, definitions, and generalizations, and makes them prove what is to be proven. What is his characteristic way of attaching to persons and groups the labels that he hopes will stick? How does he draw mammoth conclusions from whatever scraps of evidence are ready at hand? Only familiarity with the style of a far-right spokesman can warn the reader that a certain statement had better be taken apart and examined; and that a certain quote had best be checked for accuracy.

During the years that he was with Facts Forum, Smoot, in his own words, "spoke to a national audience, giving *both* sides of controversial issues." This was what made the program so odd: so different from anything that is usually called a forum. While it provided equal time for the presentation of both sides of controversial issues, it did not provide for each side a speaker to whom the upholding of that side would come naturally; and as a spokesman for *both* sides, Smoot was an odd choice.

Both on the record, and on his own testimony, the type of mental activity that Smoot likes best is that of *taking sides*: upholding tho "truth"; being categorically "pro-American"— as he defines the term. There is not an iota of evidence to suggest that his spontaneous approach to any problem would ever be that of the impartial researcher; or of the judicial weigher of pros and cons; or of the generous explainer of people to people across lines of difference.

Moreover, he tells us—in a Special Anniversary Issue of the *Dan Smoot Report*, dated June 1961, and given over in its entirety to "The Dan Smoot Story"—that as far back as 1943, he had concluded that "the philosophy of communism is closely similar to the philosophy of 'liberalism' which has dominated the intellectual and political life of America since 1933." And in this same "Story," the two sides that he spoke for on Facts Forum are revealingly defined as "the socialist-liberalist point of view" and his own "constitutional-conservative opinions."

He reports that many listeners complained "that they could never tell which side he was on"; and that various "prominent liberals" complained of his "slanting" his presentations. We would settle for saying that we never had any impression that he would want to convert anyone to the "socialist-liberalist point of view."

In any case, he says that he received, in response to the Forum programs, "well over a hundred thousand letters, most of them from people who liked the nationalist, pro-American, anti-communist, anti-socialist, anti-big-government side of [his] broadcast." He liked that side, too; and in 1955, after leaving Facts Forum, he started his own "free enterprise" publication, "to give only one side—the side that uses old-fashioned American constitutional principles as a yardstick for measuring all important issues."

Every responsible maker of opinion and policy, of course, tries to operate in terms of these "constitutional principles." Every honest judge makes them his constant yardstick. Smoot has no corner on them. What distinguishes his approach is the unhesitating promptness with which he knows, with respect to even the most complex issues, which side these principles proclaim to be indubitably the right one. Many persons—including seasoned legislators, judges, and lifelong students of the Constitution—have to study issues more closely before they can be sure of what these very principles require.

Smoot's "free enterprise" publication, the first issue of which appeared on June 29, 1955, was called *Dan Smoot Speaks*: a title which, as we noted earlier, moved a Dallas friend of ours to ask, as he tossed a copy into the wastebasket, "But who wants to listen?" Some eight months later, Smoot himself realized that the name sounded, in his own words, "frightfully pompous"; and he changed it to *The Dan Smoot Report*. He calls this a "weekly magazine." It is composed of two unbound sheets folded together to make eight pages of print.

Since the spring of 1957, the radio-TV *Report* has been sponsored by D. B. Lewis of Los Angeles, a manufacturer of pet foods who, we are told in "The Dan Smoot Story," believes that "approximately 80% of everything the federal government is presently doing" is unconstitutional.

This 80 percent estimate may not differ much from Smoot's own. In the first issue of *Dan Smoot Speaks*, he warned his readers against "programs of government-planned and government-subsidized housing, health insurance, electrical power, or security in old age" that would "convert the nation into a prison."

And in the February 15, 1960 *Report*, he says that the reason some men want "federal aid to education" is to "get the schools under the control of the central bureaucracy in Washington." If they succeed, "there can be no turning back to fundamental education in the schools. The public schools will become propaganda arms of the centralized government, used for the primary purpose of brainwashing future generations into an acceptance of socialism—called, of course, 'liberalism.'"

Two items appear in the *Report* again and again; and these can help us to orient ourselves with respect to Smoot's background of experience, on the one hand, and, on the other, to the feeling he has about his own work.

One is called *Who Is Dan Smoot?* From it we learn that Smoot was born in Missouri, in 1913, and "reared in Texas." He got his BA and MA degrees at Southern Methodist University and, in 1941, went to Harvard to work on his doctorate. The war changed his plans. He went into the FBI, and stayed in it until 1951, when he left to take on the Facts Forum program.

The other recurrent item is called *What You Can Do.* It tells the reader that "Washington officialdom uses your taxes for programs that are creating vast cesspools of waste and corruption—and dragging our Republic into the quicksands of socialism." Then, after assuring the reader that he "can help educate and arouse the people," it continues: "If *The Dan Smoot Report* was instrumental in bringing you to the point of asking what *you* can do about saving the country from mushrooming big government, here is a checklist for you: Have you urged others to subscribe to the *Report?* Have

you sent them reprints of a particular issue of the *Report?*
Have you shown them a Dan Smoot film? Have you ever suggested a Bound Volume of *The Dan Smoot Report* for use by
speakers, debaters, students, writers? Have you read and
passed on to others any of the Dan Smoot books—*The
Invisible Government, The Hope of the World, America's
Promise?"*

If the reader does undertake thus to spread the word, what
will the word be that he is spreading? And how comfortably
certain can he be that it will cleave to the truth: that he will
not inadvertently, by means of it, mislead anyone—whether
about the facts of a situation or about the viewpoint of a
fellow human being?

Answers to these questions lie embedded in the textual
material of the *Report.* The more significant among them cannot be stated in a few words. We are going to give over the
rest of this chapter, then, to just three items: all of them
dating from the summer of 1963; two of them taken from a
single issue of the *Report.* We might have chosen others,
from issues spread out over a longer time-span. But it seems
to us that the very clustering of these items suggests the
extreme care with which *The Dan Smoot Report* should be
read.

In the July 15, 1963 issue, headed "More Equal Than
Equal," Smoot spells out his position on the civil rights issue.
The first page holds a 12-point civil rights platform "which
was announced by the communist party in 1928." Current
federal activities in the field are then so presented as to suggest their being a virtual implementation of this Communist
platform.

Our focus, however, will be on Smoot's presentation of
seven crimes of violence—all dating from June 1963, and all

involving whites and Negroes. From the way these cases were handled, Smoot draws the conclusion that "civil rights for negroes, in the eyes of politicians hungry for votes, means that harming a negro is a national disaster which requires federal action even when such action violates the Constitution; but negro violence against whites is a routine matter beneath the notice of federal authorities." He reports the cases as follows:

On June 12, 1963, Medgar Evers, negro field representative for the National Association for the Advancement of Colored People in Mississippi, was murdered in Jackson. The FBI investigated the crime as a federal case. FBI agents identified a suspect and arrested him under authority of civil rights laws, later turning him over to state authorities for prosecution on a murder charge.

On June 12, 1963, a white man was killed by a negro during a race riot in Lexington, North Carolina. Federal authorities showed no interest in this case.

On June 12, 1963, two white men were injured by shotgun blasts fired into their private places of business, during a race riot in Cambridge, Maryland. Federal authorities showed no interest in the case.

On the night of June 12, 1963, 6 negroes stabbed an 18-year-old boy and raped his 15-year-old companion in Cleveland, Ohio. Federal authorities showed no interest in this case . . .

On June 19, 1963, three white soldiers were dragged out of their car in Washington, D.C., and beaten by a gang of negroes. One of the white soldiers—Edward Betcher—was killed. The negroes ran over his body with their car, as they were leaving the scene. The FBI did not enter this case . . .

On June 19, 1963, a homemade bomb, thrown or placed by unknown assailants, damaged a negro church near Gillett, Arkansas. Newspaper accounts indicate that the FBI did enter this case.

On the night of June 26, 1963, dynamite bombs blasted the homes of two white police officers in Minneapolis. Prior to the bombings, both white men had received numerous threatening telephone calls from negroes. Federal authorities did not enter this case.

It does not take a lawyer to ask: What goes on here? Why does Smoot mention only one variable: that of race? Why, with his background, does he ignore the second variable: that of jurisdiction?

We asked a judge whom we know what we should study to learn about the jurisdictional aspects of the Medgar Evers case; and from the materials to which he directed us, we learned that the case came under Section 241, Title 18, U.S. Code: *Conspiracy Against the Rights of Citizens.* This section makes it a federal offense for two or more persons to conspire to prevent, by intimidation, a citizen's enjoyment of any right guaranteed by the Constitution. The determining legal factor in the case was not race, but evidence to the effect that the attack on Evers involved the element of conspiracy and that it stemmed from his having been active in voter registration, which is a constitutional right.

We were able to check facts locally about the handling of the Washington, D.C., crime. For information about the other cases, we wrote to the various Chiefs of Police. One reported that the case had not come under his jurisdiction and told us to whom to direct our inquiry. One did not answer; and there we turned to other on-the-spot sources of information. Our findings were as follows:

The Chief of Police in Lexington, North Carolina, knew of no killing on the date Smoot gives: June 12, 1963. But there was a race riot on the night of June 6, and a number of people, white and colored, were arrested. "In this riot," the Chief states, "Fred Link, white male, was killed. Joe Poole, colored male, was charged with murder"—and later pleaded guilty of second-degree murder. "The local police department with the assistance of the State Bureau of Investigation handled the case." As for the FBI: "They immediately, as usual, contacted the local police department, and we furnished them with all the information we had." Nothing in this information suggested a basis or need for federal action.

We were unable to learn anything about "shotgun blasts" in Cambridge, Maryland, on June 12, 1963; but on June 11, two white men were struck by shotgun pellets as they sat in a car on the outskirts of the Negro section. Neither man was seriously injured. Maryland State Police were on duty in Cambridge; and we find it hard to account for Smoot's apparent feeling that federal authorities should have wedged in on the case.

In the Cleveland crime, the Police Department started an immediate investigation, with more than fifty officers on the job; but again, no federal statute had been violated.

In the Washington, D.C., case, local police promptly identified and arrested the criminals. Terrible as the crime was, there was nothing in its nature, we are told, to bring federal authorities into it. And what should they have done—with the arrest already made? Interestingly enough, this is one of the two listed items for which Smoot gives his source of information. The crime took place on June 19. The AP report to which he refers in a footnote is dated June 20, and it makes plain the fact that the five suspects were already under arrest. Hence, Smoot's statement that the "FBI did not enter this case" seems exaggeratedly odd in this instance.

Bombing *per se* is not a federal offense. But a provision in the Civil Rights Act of 1960 prohibits interstate transportation of explosives "with the knowledge or intent that they will be used to destroy property or to intimidate persons." In the Gillett, Arkansas, case, the FBI offered to follow up some out-of-state leads; but its help was not felt to be needed. The Minneapolis police sent various items of evidence to the FBI Laboratory for examination. No one was injured in either case.

Smoot creates a strange ambiguity by the way he presents this crime list. As a rule, he is a strong upholder of local and state authority. Yet here he makes it seem that federal authorities were remiss, in case after case, in not moving in—we might say, barging in—where they had no jurisdictional right to be.

The July 22, 1963 *Report* contains a section headed *Where*

We Are. In it, Smoot declares that a "treacherous cowardice" now prevails among "intellectual and political leaders," manifesting itself in a wish "to abandon the national independence which our forefathers won with blood and valorous devotion to high ideals."

One item with which he documents this thesis is President Kennedy's speech in Frankfurt, Germany, on June 25, 1963: a speech in which, *according to Smoot,* he told "Europeans that Americans would risk destruction of their cities to defend Europe, because America cannot survive without European help."

In 1963, both Khrushchev and de Gaulle were trying to convince West Europe—and Germany, in particular—that the United States would, in a crisis, sell its allies down the river to save itself from nuclear destruction. Enough nervousness was thus being generated to pose the threat of an every-nation-for-itself scramble for nuclear weapons. Into this atmosphere of uneasiness, President Kennedy injected a note of reassurance which Smoot seems to have regarded as "cowardly."

What President Kennedy said can be checked by reference to the text of his speech, which is given in full in the *State Department Bulletin,* July 22, 1963, pp. 118-123. He deliberately drew attention to the fact that some people were saying that the United States would not "abide by its commitments." Then he declared that "such doubts fly in the face of history. For 18 years the United States has stood its watch for freedom around the globe. . . . But, in addition, these proved commitments to the common freedom and safety are assured, in the future as in the past, by one great fundamental fact— that they are deeply rooted in America's own self-interest . . ."

He urged the nations not to turn "the clock backward to separate nuclear deterrents"; and within the context of this call for a unified rather than an anarchic Western defense system, in an age of nuclear weapons and Soviet aggression, he said, "The United States will risk its cities to defend yours because we need your freedom to protect ours." He did not say that "America cannot survive without European help."

Here, as with the crime cases, Smoot leaves wide open the question of what he thinks should have been done. Is he saying that our membership in the Western alliance is inherently cowardly? Or is he saying that if he had stood in the President's shoes, his "devotion to high ideals" would have made him tell the Germans that Khrushchev and de Gaulle were quite right: that we would not, in a crisis, stand by our commitments, because we could get along all right even if Western Europe were destroyed or lost to Communism?

It seems worth recalling how Great Britain risked its cities, and brought on the blitz, by going to the aid of its ally, Norway, in 1940, when Hitler invaded that country. Britain was honest in its self-interest—which, in the face of Nazi aggression, it took to be inseparable from that of other free nations. Perhaps Smoot feels, and felt at the time, that this British policy of standing by its commitments meant a "cowardly" forsaking of its high ideals. But this has not, we think, been humanity's verdict.

We have stressed in these two instances the ambiguity that Smoot has left in the wake of his charges, because this is one thing that has to be watched for in his writings. All too frequently, after a bold strike at an opponent, he seems to find it prudent to remove himself from the presence of the complex problem with which this opponent has been coping.

To illustrate further, in this same *Report*, what he means by "treacherous cowardice," Smoot writes: "Note Walter Millis (in a formal study which cost American tax payers $20,000 and was prepared for the U.S. Arms Control and

Disarmament Agency) arguing for the necessity of a world so 'completely policed' by an international army that such uprisings as the American Revolution of 1776 would be suppressed, 'as was the Hungarian Revolution, with all the global forces of law and order cooperating.'"

What occurs, here, to a person who has read the Millis article is that Smoot has not. His footnote tends to confirm this. He is not quoting from Millis. He is quoting from an article by Edith Kermit Roosevelt, which was read into the *Congressional Record* of June 6, 1963, by Senator Strom Thurmond. Edith Kermit Roosevelt's column appears in various far-right publications. It is regularly featured, for example, in *The Independent American*, New Orleans, organ of the Conservative Society of America. This Society, founded by Kent and Phoebe Courtney, is a supporter of a far-right third party. We will be evaluating some of its programs and publications in a later chapter.

The six-man study to which Millis contributed one part, is called *Quis Custodiet?: Controlling the Police in a Disarmed World.* It was sponsored by the U.S. Arms Control and Disarmament Agency, under Grant ACDV/LR-8, and was published in April 1963. It is devoted, not so much to the question of how an international police force could control a disarmed world, as to that of how, in a disarmed world, such a police force could be kept from becoming an uncontrollable menace.

Millis's attitude toward revolution, which is set forth in Volume II of this study, pp. A-10ff., is almost the exact opposite of that which Smoot attributes to him. The part about the American Revolution of 1776 seems to have been inserted into the argument by Edith Kermit Roosevelt, as part of her singular interpretation of Millis' view; and Smoot carries it forward into the *Report.*

Millis states in plain black and white his conviction that, no matter what "pyramid of power" might be erected in behalf of international law and order, the right of revolution would have to be preserved. He says, ". . . the world cannot be denuded either of the weapons or of the ideas which make revolution possible. Revolution is, of course, an exercise of coercive power. . . . Yet a world in which a possibility of revolutionary violence did not exist would be repugnant to most Western ideas of freedom . . ."

Millis does, indeed, say that in a "completely policed world" a revolution like the Hungarian would be suppressed "with all the global forces of law and order cooperating." But he says it as part of his reason for seeing such a "completely policed world" as neither likely nor desirable.

If an uprising like the Hungarian took place, he says, under any "foreseeable system of demilitarization," the course of events would be open-ended, because "contiguous states would find their interests involved." Thus: "It is difficult to see all the complications that might arise . . . but it is even more difficult to believe that all could be dealt with by an international police force alone."

The chief guardian of law and order in a demilitarized world, Millis contends, should be "the national police forces rather than an international police force"; and he suggests a world-wide application of the principle embodied in Article II of our Bill of Rights. This reads: "A well-regulated militia being necessary to the security of a free state, the right of the people to keep and bear arms shall not be infringed."

Smoot quotes Millis as saying, "One cannot resist the conclusion that there must be a supranational autonomous police power, with veto-free sources of revenue . . . solely responsible to a supranational political authority"; and he so attaches this quote to his misquotation about revolution as to make it appear that Millis's "supranational autonomous police power" would be used to suppress revolutions like the Hungarian.

In the original, the above statement appears in an alto-gether different context. Millis, after making "the national police forces" into the "chief guardian of law and order," takes up the residual problem of how to prevent the internal crises of nations from getting out of hand, and spreading abroad, in areas where national police forces have not yet been reliably established. For the limited task of keeping the peace in these areas, without infringing the jealously guarded independence of any state, he recommends an international police force.

Here, then, is the "treacherous cowardice" against which Smoot inveighs. Our chief reason for giving as much space as we have to this example is that the U.S. Arms Control and Disarmament Agency is, according to Radical Rightist dogma, always engaged, one way or another, in a nefarious effort to sell American sovereignty down the river.

If we had had to go through *The Dan Smoot Report* with a fine-tooth comb to hunt out the examples we have used of odd crime-reporting, misleading paraphrase, and outright misquotation, this chapter would not have been written. All writers and speakers, including ourselves, have been inno-cently guilty, at times, of misreading the meaning of a pas-sage and therefore misreporting its author's viewpoint; and also of putting more trust in secondary sources than they have turned out to deserve.

But as we have noted earlier, our acquaintance with Smoot's materials reaches back into the days of Facts Forum; and it covers the period of *Dan Smoot Speaks*, as well as, intermittently, the period of *The Dan Smoot Report*. On the basis of reading what he has written, we have been virtually forced to conclude that he has a much too cavalier way of dealing with evidential items.

It is not that he makes errors of carelessness, under the

pressure of work. It is that all his errors, regardless of their subject matter, are singularly alike in character. There may not seem to be much resemblance between a statement that federal authorities "showed no interest" in a white man's being killed in Lexington, North Carolina, and the statement that Millis advocates a type of supranational police force that would make impossible a revolution like our own. But the resemblance is there.

Smoot's incidental errors are all subtly alike, we have come to believe, because they derive from two interlocked basic errors. One is his commitment to the idea that every issue, no matter how complex, can be sliced down the middle into a pro-American and an anti-American side, the way an apple is sliced with a knife. The other is his commitment to the idea that it is more *American* to decide in advance what is to be proved, and then prove it, than it is to let facts speak for themselves.

In the early summer of 1955, Smoot issued an undated flyer announcing his new publication, *Dan Smoot Speaks.* Comparing this project with Facts Forum, he said, "I will continue to furnish the same kind of factual, analytical discussions of controversial issues that I have been giving on the air—except that now I will give only one side: the anti-Socialist, anti-Communist, anti-big-government, pro-Freedom side."

Further: "Not having to devote time and space to the other side, I can do a better job than before. Anyone who has found my broadcast transcripts helpful in the fight for freedom and constitutional government will find my newsletter about twice as helpful."

This statement, it seems to us, contains the very essence of the Smoot approach; and it is one that has given him a very solid standing place among Radical Rightist leaders, even though he does not head up a membership organization.

This approach appears to be based on two assumptions: first, that no person who is soundly pro-American is ever baffled by the complexities of any problem; and second, that, so far as the support of freedom is concerned, it is "twice as helpful" for Americans to make up their minds about issues after hearing only one side as it is for them to hear and evaluate both sides, or several. We will have to admit, in conclusion, that the effect upon ourselves of a considerable exposure to Smoot materials has been to confirm us in our stubborn preference for doing our own thinking in the open market places of the mind.

TEN

CARL McINTIRE:
MAKER OF SCHISMS

IN our account of the back-and-forth between Robert Welch and Monsignor Francis J. Lally, we got somewhat ahead of ourselves and posed a question for which we had not yet laid any proper foundation. Welch told Monsignor Lally that "thousands" of ministers agreed with him that about 3 percent of the Protestant clergy are Comsymps. We asked, rhetorically, whether these "thousands" belonged to that portion of the ministry that denounces as pro-Communist not only the National and World Councils of Churches but also the concept of a "social gospel."

At that point, we were able to illustrate the outlook we had in mind by only one sketchy example: Dr. Charles Poling's effort to turn a list of "parallel positions" into a proof that the National Council of Churches has joined forces with the Communists. But one whole sector of the Radical Right is led by ministers who would applaud Dr. Poling's effort:

ministers who proclaim religious liberals to be well on their way toward atheistic Communism, and political and economic liberals to be well on their way toward Communist collectivism.

Moreover, these ministers enjoy the support of various like-minded laymen's organizations: the Circuit Riders, for example, of Cincinnati, Ohio; and the American Council of Christian Laymen, of Madison, Wisconsin. These groups undertake to weld the opinions of those who occupy the pews in our Protestant churches into a weapon with which to bring down any occupant of the pulpit or any official church body that does not hew to the exact line of the Radical Right's religious-political-economic orthodoxy.

For themselves, these ministers and laymen claim a maximum religious freedom. But like the Communists, they combine their demand for an untrammeled freedom to propagate the truth with a rigidly intolerant will to prevent the propagation of error: which is to say, of any doctrinal, political, or economic view that differs from their own.

It has been said of Stalin that, on the one hand, he revised Leninism to whatever extent his own version of expediency required while, on the other hand, he reduced this same Leninism to so rigid a set of formulated phrasings that he could identify "revisionists" by their slightest verbal deviation from these—and could proceed to liquidate them. These doctrinaire Rightists of whom we are speaking might well, in this particular sense, be called *Stalinist*.

The term would fit them more accurately, in fact, than does the all too carelessly applied term *fundamentalist*. It is true that they call themselves fundamentalists. It is also true that, for complex sociological reasons, the Rightists have been most successful in peddling their brand of anti-Communism in those parts of the country where religious fundamentalism prevails. But we ought not to jump from this

fact to the conclusion that religious fundamentalism and
Radical Rightism just naturally go tandem.

We might profitably recall here, indeed, an elementary
lesson in deductive logic. As college freshmen, we learned to
say in Logic I, "All men are mortal"; and then to deduce
from this categorical statement whatever further truth we
could. Thus, we learned that it is logically permissible to
say, "Socrates is a man. Therefore, Socrates is mortal." But
we also learned that it is not permissible to say, "X is mortal.
Therefore, X is a man."

Right-wing extremists constantly employ just this type of
fallacious logic. The Communists speak for peace. X speaks
for peace. Therefore, these extremists declare, X is a Communist. The Communists oppose right-to-work laws. X opposes right-to-work laws. Therefore, by extremist logic, X is
a Communist. The Communists have proclaimed their support of the civil rights movement. X supports this movement.
Therefore, X is a Communist.

If we resent this travesty upon logic when the extremists
use it, we had best be wary of using it ourselves. The doctrinaire Radical Rightists whom we are here discussing say
that they are fundamentalists. But this does not give us a
license to conclude that because X is a fundamentalist, he is
or is likely to become a Radical Rightist.

It would be more to the point to say that Christian fundamentalism is actually misrepresented by these Rightists. Their
doctrine is a highly selective blend of those aspects of the
New Testament that specifically relate to personal salvation
and those aspects of the Old Testament that give them permission to be exclusive and to hate their enemies.

We are not exaggerating. We have spoken above, for example, of the American Council of Christian Laymen—an
organization in Madison, Wisconsin, headed by Verne Kaub.
It serves as an outlet for many Radical Rightist books and

pamphlets—including those of all the men whom we will be focusing on in this chapter and the several to follow. Among the leaflets to which it has given wide circulation is one, now in its sixth printing, which is called "The Fatherhood of God and the Brotherhood of Man." It is written by a retired Methodist minister, Ebenezer Myers, of Lenoir, North Carolina. The text begins thus:

"The doctrine of the Fatherhood of God and the Brotherhood of Man has no foundation for its existence anywhere. It is not taught by the Bible; but on the contrary the Bible condemns it and teaches just the opposite . . ." This "opposite" is that "man is fallen, dead in sin, and lost without God's pardoning mercy." By uniting this theme with a text from the Old Testament—about "The children of men, and the sons of God"—Myers arrives at the conclusion that the "saved" are under no obligation to regard as "brothers" such of their human fellows as have not been "saved." These latter, the leaflet argues, are not "sons of God," but only "children of men." Hence, so far as the spiritually elect are concerned, they are strictly outsiders.

This type of doctrinal argument may seem altogether irrelevant to our present study. But it is not; for this is the type of doctrinal argument which, variously elucidated, provides the basis for attacks upon the "social gospel." Strangely absent from the books of these extremists who proclaim themselves to be Christian fundamentalists are any passages that stress the Golden Rule or that remind their readers of Christ's having said, "Verily I say unto you, Inasmuch as ye have done it unto one of the least of these my brethren, ye have done it unto me."

What we might call historic Christian fundamentalism does not reject the concept of human brotherhood or limit the field within which compassion is to operate. Neither, certainly, does it license its believers to proclaim—as the Radical Rightist doctrine does, in effect—that if people are really "saved" they will set their faces like flint against anything that bears the taint of internationalism or the "welfare state."

In this chapter and the three to follow, we will be considering the words and works of four men: Carl McIntire, Myers G. Lowman, Edgar Bundy, and Billy James Hargis. Each has his own organization through which to work. Each stamps upon his projects the trademark of his own make-up—and his own ambition. Yet they are all Radical Rightists whose attacks upon the Protestant ministry and the Councils of Churches reflect their readiness to demand that other people conform to the strict letter of both their religious doctrine and their political-economic doctrine—these two being treated as though they were inseparably one.

Three of the four men—McIntire, Bundy, and Hargis—are ordained ministers. Lowman is not: he is head of one of the laymen's groups mentioned above: the Circuit Riders. Not one of the three ministers, however, holds a pulpit in the church in which he was ordained. McIntire, as we shall note later, was dismissed from the ministry of the United Presbyterian Church for insubordination and malicious troublemaking. He now heads up a "splinter" church of his own founding. Bundy's ordination, in the Southern Baptist Convention, seems an isolated incident in his life—though he consistently speaks of himself as a Baptist minister. The ordination took place in a Louisiana church while he was in the Air Force. In his official biography we find no mention of seminary training; and he has never, so far as we could discover, served as pastor of any church. When he left the Air Force, he went into journalism, not into the ministry. He is now Executive Secretary of a layman's group, the Church League of America, Wheaton, Illinois. Billy James Hargis, head of Christian Crusade, was ordained in the Disciples of Christ;

but he has not, since 1957, been on that denomination's list of accredited ministers.

If the attacks these men make upon Protestant leaders, policies, and organizations were purely doctrinal in character, we would not be concerned with them here. We are concerned with them because all these men, in behalf of aims which they define as Christian, employ extremist methods. Also, their attitudes toward persons and groups whom they denounce is marked by an extremist will to demolish.

Further, the line which they lay down with respect to Communist infiltration of the churches and church councils has become a broad plank in the general platform of Radical Rightism. And still further, their assaults upon religious leaders and organizations can in nowise be disentangled from their assaults upon schools, community groups, labor unions, the government, and a whole range of international bodies. Finally, by calling their groups religious and their projects religious and educational, they all manage to enjoy a tax-exempt status. We might add that they are all self-revealingly touchy on this subject. Hargis fairly bristles at any suggestion that he is "talking politics"; and Bundy's group even reproduces in its brochure of information, "What Is The Church League of America," the letters from the Treasury Department which granted in the first instance, and then reaffirmed, the League's tax-exemption.

From this point on, we will, in this chapter, be focusing on Carl McIntire; and we put him at the head of our list of four men because he seems to typify to the nth degree two basic characteristics of the extremist—of the Left or the Right. The first of these is an inability to work comfortably, and as an equal among equals, in any group where divergent views are represented. The second is a tendency to adopt toward target persons and groups the attitude of the avenger: the avenger

whose arm is the elect instrument for striking down those
who have departed from the truth. McIntire could no more
linger at any point of cleavage to say to an erstwhile friend,
"Peace be with you," than Stalin could have said it to
Trotsky.

"Wherever issues are drawn between opposing sides," writes
McIntire, "there are always those who desire compromise and
a middle course. . . . But where one of the sides in the conflict has the eternal truth, as is the case of those of us who
embrace the great doctrines of the historic Christian faith,
to compromise in the slightest is to dishonor and destroy the
faith." (1)

Meeting this statement out of context, a person might think
that McIntire was refusing to seek a vacuous mid-point of
belief between Christianity and Communism; refusing to pretend, in the name of a relativistic tolerance, that differences
of belief about the nature of man, society, and the universe
are merely surface differences that do not really matter.

In fact, however, those with whom he is refusing "to compromise in the slightest" are not Communists. They are not
even the type of Christian who is commonly called liberal or
modern. Those whom he is denouncing are the theologically
conservative and fundamentalist groups that comprise the
National Association of Evangelicals. McIntire, in short, cannot tolerate even the doctrinal differences that separate him
from these orthodox fellow Christians. So far as he is concerned, those who do not exhibit a precise point-to-point
agreement with his version of "the historic Christian faith"
are outside the pale.

Our kind of society demands our being able to hold firm
convictions and yet grant to others a wide margin of freedom
to hold different convictions—denying to them only the right
to deprive others of their rights or to destroy the framework
of freedom. The strength of our culture is a flexible, live-and-

let-live strength: the kind Robert Frost speaks for in *The Star-Splitter*:

> If one by one we counted people out
> For the least fault, it wouldn't take us long
> To get so we had no one left to live with.

A society of creative balance can be destroyed by an excess of either rigidity or relativism. What it seems to call for is an interweaving of conviction and common sense.

The words of McIntire simply do not fit this pattern; and through his words, we seem to hear others coming from a distance—as we sometimes hear one radio program penetrating another. These background words are not those of the Sermon on the Mount or of the Bill of Rights. They are those of Lenin: "... *the only choice is:* either bourgeois or socialist ideology. There is no middle course. ... Hence, to belittle socialist ideology *in any way, to deviate from it in the slightest measure* means strengthening bourgeois ideology." (2)

McIntire's position, might, indeed, be described as that of the habitual dissenter who cannot tolerate even the slightest measure of dissent from his views; and as that of the habitual denouncer of others for whom all criticism of himself is manifest persecution. By what path of experience has he arrived at this position?

Born in Michigan, in 1906, McIntire spent his growing years in Oklahoma; got his AB degree from Park College, Parkville, Missouri, in 1927; and then entered Princeton Theological Seminary. There, he became an ardent admirer of Dr. J. Gresham Machen, an eminent fundamentalist scholar. When, in 1929, Machen broke with Princeton, and set up Westminster Seminary in Chestnut Hill, Pennsylvania, McIntire followed, and secured his degree from the new seminary in 1931. Soon thereafter he entered upon what might be called a life of schism-making.

He and Machen repudiated the regular Presbyterian mission board and set up the Independent Board of Presbyterian Foreign Missions. This group proved to be such a recalcitrant and ruthless trouble-maker that its officers were brought to trial before the Synod, in 1936. McIntire was found guilty on three counts; and the General Assembly of the Church, upholding the decision of the Synod, voted his dismissal from the ministry of the United Presbyterian Church.

This body states without equivocation that it took the only course left open to it "to exonerate the innocent ministers and lawful agencies upon which the offenders were heaping unmerited abuse and slanders." (3) McIntire contends—in a pamphlet called *Testimony to Christ and a Witness to Freedom*—that he was "suspended from the ministry and the communion of the church" for the "offense" of obeying God's word rather than man's. (4)

McIntire and Machen proceeded to found a new church: the Orthodox Presbyterian. But it soon developed that while they could *oppose* together, they could not *build* together. They split, before long, over seemingly minute doctrinal differences; and McIntire went on to found his Bible Presbyterian Church and Faith Theological Seminary. Of these enterprises, he writes, in the pamphlet referred to above, "There is no other gospel; there is only one . . ." That which has lain at the very heart of his motives has been, in this view, "this clear understanding of the eternal truth."

In 1941, his Bible Presbyterian Church and the Bible Protestants, another small denomination, formed the American Council of Christian Churches—to compete with the National Council. "God brought men from these churches together to form a council. . .

"Then the International Council of Christian Churches

came along in 1948 with a world-wide vision and mission . . ."
But this International Council did not just *come along*.
McIntire brought it into being, in Amsterdam, at the precise
time when the World Council of Churches was being formed
in that city; and he and his associates appear to have done
everything in their power, very deliberately, both to confuse
the public by the presence of *two* councils in the making and
to brand the founders of the World Council as *apostate*.

From that time to the present, the chief function of the
two councils—American and International—founded by Mc-
Intire seems to have been that of harassing the National and
World Councils. In Chapter 15 of his book *Servants of Apostasy* he reports with satisfaction that it has been his practice
to go to or to send representatives of his International Council
to any place in the world where international religious groups
of which he disapproves are scheduled to meet: there to challenge the authority of these "apostate" groups to speak for
Christian congregations.

This policy of harassment yielded him one 1959 victory of
which he seems oddly proud: that of splitting the Presbyterian Church in Korea. By this act, he disrupted in that
suffering land both the spiritual ministry and the relief program of one of the world's most effective mission churches.
On the home front, his American Council has served to unify
the efforts of those who are trying to set congregations against
their ministers and denominational boards, over the issue of
membership in the National Council.

All this complex program of disruption appears to reflect
two rigid assumptions on McIntire's part. One of these assumptions is made plain in the first chapter of *Servants of
Apostasy: The Dividing Line*. Here, we learn that his quarrel
with the National and World Councils stems basically from
the fact that these bodies seek to unite churches *in terms of
such beliefs and purposes as they have in common*, while

leaving precise statements of doctrine to the member denominations. To McIntire, this is apostasy: to be associated in any way whatever with bodies that call themselves Christian but that do not hew to the exact doctrinal line that he knows to be the one in which the "eternal truth" is expressed.

The second assumption that makes "irreconciable" his opposition not only to the National and World Councils of Churches but also to the leadership bodies of most Protestant churches is flatly stated in a small brochure called *What Is the Difference?* This brochure declares his Bible Presbyterian Church to be "in a definite sense a leader in the historic separatist movement of the 20th century"; and it declares, without qualification, that this Church "does not believe in the social gospel."

This statement marks the point at which McIntire's quarrel with fellow churchmen about matters of doctrine broadens out to include his quarrel with both governmental and voluntary agencies. Through the years, McIntire has, with singular consistency, put his views on record in three ways. He has done so through his pronouncements—in his books; in his newspaper, *The Christian Beacon*; and over the air, by means of his radio program, *20th Century Reformation Hour*. He has done so through his schismatic activities; his "splintering" operations. And he has done so through what might be called his guerrilla tactics of harassment and denunciation.

On the basis of his own spelling out of his position, it seems fair and accurate to say that he is against any type of authority by which he feels himself to be restrained or with which he feels himself to be in competition; that he is against any movement that seeks to unite people across lines of difference; and that he is against that which seeks to extend responsibility for human well-being beyond the "elect" in-group to the "unsaved," non-elect masses.

All this means that, under the world's present conditions

of conflict, he calls *heretical* or *apostate* that with which he disagrees in the doctrinal area, and calls *socialist, liberal, pro-Communist,* or *Communist* that with which he disagrees in the social-political-economic area.

Thus, for example, he does not say that consumers' cooperatives are *heretical.* He says, in *The Rise of the Tyrant,* that they are "little outposts of Soviet Russia." He does not say that UNICEF (the United Nations International Children's Emergency Fund) is *apostate.* He says that it is "helping to build the world welfare state and world government"; and that the " 'trick or treat' custom of Halloween could be used to help worthy agencies and causes which are not entangled with the Communist international conspiracy." (5)

This type of opposition to UNICEF—this type of identification of it with "the international Communist conspiracy"—is well-nigh standard among Radical Rightists. We would recommend, therefore, as an antidote to it, a speech called "The Facts About the United Nations Children's Fund" which the Honorable Walter H. Judd made in the House of Representatives on August 14, 1962.

Certainly, Walter H. Judd has had an unambiguous record of staunch anti-Communism. But he puts himself on record as counting it a "privilege" to have been in on the establishment of UNICEF. He says, "Through the 'Trick or Treat for UNICEF' project, boys and girls in the United States express their concern for needy children in other countries . . ." This project, to his mind, represents "the greatest effort made thus far by children to help children." And he urges all his "fellow citizens, young and old, to support UNICEF generously."

It would not do, in short, for us to pass over McIntire's interminable denunciations of Protestant ministers and Protestant bodies as though these were simply part of doctrinal disagreements. A basic reason why our society has been able to afford self-interest as a stimulus to initiative is that it has been equipped with a religious code whereby the consciences of men could be encouraged to do the policing of their self-interested drives toward acquisition and power.

No one would say that this policing job has always been reliably and excellently done. But the extent to which American history can be told as a history of reform and social evolution testifies to the fact that a yeasty force of Judaic-Christian conscience has been at work, within us and among us.

The Communists have, of course, directly challenged the very foundations of this conscience. By casting out the religious view that moral values derive from a source that transcends human classes and conflicts, they have given themselves a license to define differences as irreconcilable. Thus, in a letter to Marx, written on October 23, 1846, Engels told how, having been asked in a group to define Communism, and not having had time to go into any great detail, he had elected to stress just one thing: he had *"ruled out* peaceableness, tenderness or compassion toward the bourgeoisie." (6) In like vein, Lenin told the Young Communist League, "We say that our morality is entirely subordinated to the interests of the class struggle. . . . Our morality is deduced from the class struggle." (7)

But all of us who belong to the liberal-conservative center would do well to recognize the meaning in depth of the Radical Rightist assault upon the "social gospel." It is easy to miss this meaning if we focus on the Rightists' opposition to some particular act on the part of the National or World Council of Churches: some act which we, too, feel to have been ill-advised. It is easy to miss it, also, if we let ourselves become confused by the efforts of McIntire, Bundy, Hargis, and others to show that the church Councils work hand-in-hand with "liberalist-socialist-Communist elements" in the

United States Information Agency, or the State Department, or the Department of Health, Education, and Welfare.

But the two basic targets of attack in all this vast output of Radical Rightist propaganda are *the sense of human unity* and *the sense of mutual responsibility* as these have been traditionally instilled in us by religious influences. We dare not miss the fact that today's right-wing extremism is, in its very essence, a schismatic force: one that tries to identify Americanism with a kind of social atomism—each nation for itself; each race for itself; each class for itself; each man for himself. At many points, its use of anti-socialist and anti-Communist terminology seems little more than a convenience.

In striking measure, McIntire typifies this schismatic factor, this atomizing factor, in Radical Rightist dogma and practice. If we understand this, we can put into perspective his interminable assaults upon the reputations of other ministers and upon the programs of the Councils. One example will perhaps serve to show what we mean.

The National Council of Churches, at its 1963 General Assembly, which was held in Philadelphia, December 1–7, adopted a *Message to the Churches*. Among the problems which it weighed in this message were those attendant upon the coming of automation. "A responsible society," it stated, "must offer help to those who are victims of the social dislocations which mark a time of transition . . ."; and it went on to say that the churches, as well as public bodies and other organizations, must find ways of being of service—ways that no one, as yet, could clearly define.

McIntire's response to this appeared in the *Christian Beacon* of December 19, 1963. It was terse and categorical: "Here, of course, are the arguments to change America into a socialistic state . . ."

ELEVEN

MYERS G. LOWMAN OF THE CIRCUIT RIDERS

THE new Radical Rightists set great store by "fully documented" lists of suspect persons; and the most prolific list-maker of them all is Myers G. Lowman, of the Circuit Riders, Cincinnati, Ohio. He turns out, one after another, "compilations" of names, with "items of public record" attached to each name. He offers no key to a rational interpretation of these lists, claiming that the record "speaks for itself"; and the individuals who are listed are simply regarded thereafter as fair game by unofficial Communist-hunters.

Thus, Welch, for example, in *The Politician*, credits Lowman with having alerted him to the Communists' use of the Protestant ministry "as one of the most important channels of their propaganda."

The group now headed by Lowman, the Circuit Riders, was formed in 1951 by thirty-three Methodist laymen—to oppose "socialism and communism" in the Methodist Church. Most of the original members appear not to have been extremists, but simply persons who were troubled about the extent to which Communist influence was operative in the Methodist Federation for Social Action, and about the fact that the general public took this unofficial body to be an official part of the Methodist program. They wanted the Church to stop the Federation's use of Methodist buildings and its exploitation of the Methodist name. By focusing on this issue, the Circuit Riders enjoyed a rapid growth in membership during the first year.

At the 1952 Methodist Convention, however, most of the group's demands with respect to the Federation were met; and its membership, in consequence, rapidly declined. But the organization did not disband; and Myers Lowman, one of the original founders, converted what was left of it into something far more extremist than it was at first designed to be. Today, with just enough structure to qualify for tax-exemption, it appears to exist chiefly as an instrument of Lowman's purposes.

Lowman was not trained to identify Communists with any responsible accuracy. By his own account, as given in an interview which appears in the Denver *Post* of July 26, 1959, he gave up his business as a distributor of air-conditioning equipment to become Executive Secretary of the Circuit Riders. Yet he not only compiles his multiple lists, but gives lectures on Communism; takes on paid assignments to identify Communists, pro-Communists, and leftists in school systems; and passes judgment upon school textbooks.

He is a frequent speaker, for example, for Billy James Hargis' Christian Crusade. And on March 20, 1962, one of his fellow speakers for this organization, in Tulsa, Oklahoma, was Mrs. Harry Alexander, of Mississippi, who talked on

"Socialist and pro-Communist Propaganda in Textbooks." She reported that Lowman had given 136 addresses in Mississippi in behalf of the campaign which she represented: a DAR campaign to clean up textbooks.

In August 1958, the Atlanta *Journal* and *Constitution* alerted the Georgia public to an even more serious travesty upon legitimate investigation. Lowman, these papers reported, had been secretly hired for six months for $4500 by the Georgia Commission on Education—a public body—to do "investigation and research" into Communist influences in the Georgia schools; and to prevent any evidence of his employment from appearing on its public records, the Commission had channeled the money to him through a private segregationist group, the States Rights Council.

How did Lowman—trained neither as an investigator nor as an educator—get in on this Georgia deal? Governor Marvin Griffin—who said that he had "a mandate to preserve school segregation"—explained that Lowman had been recommended to him by segregationist leaders in Louisiana. In the Governor's judgment, Lowman had done "an excellent job . . . and earned his money"; and the attitude of the press toward the indirect manner in which he was paid was simply "carping." (1)

This Georgia story underscores an interesting fact: namely, that for Lowman, with his far-right clientele, it is an advantage rather than a disadvantage to lack disciplined training in the investigative field. Disciplined training in any field tends to foster a respect for professional standards; and professional standards can easily interfere with a man's doing an "excellent job" of documenting foregone conclusions and providing evidential support for a pre-defined mandate.

Khrushchev has been learning this. As the level of professional training has been raised among Soviet social scientists, for example, he has more and more often had to reproach them for putting other standards above those of strict adherence to the Party line.

For the job he does, and the audience to which he addresses himself, Lowman is doubly qualified as an expert. He has undeviatingly "correct" attitudes on all subjects that comprise the Radical Rightist line. And with reference to one aspect of the problem of Communism, he has developed a gimmick or formula that lends weight to his words: namely, the compilation of names and "items of public record."

This Lowman type of document can best be described as a scissors-and-paste job. It defies all efforts at exact interpretation. But this, too, is an advantage of sorts. By using it to create an impression that is never translated into any exact charge, the Right extremists can derogate the listed individuals and yet not make any overt statement for which they could be held to account.

Lowman's first list was "A Compilation of Public Records of 2109 Methodist Ministers." The first volume of this appeared in 1956; the second, not until 1961. Each volume is made up of multigraphed sheets stapled together. The white paper cover is dominated, in each instance, by the figure 2109 in huge black-faced type.

This practice of making the number loom large is standard for all the Lowman lists we have seen; and it can be taken, we think, as a clue to the type of impressiveness he aspires to for his compilations. Their weight is to be guaranteed by their length. The extent of Communist infiltration of the churches—and schools—is to be proved by scraping the bottom of the barrel for every name that will help to make the list just that much longer.

To date, in addition to the list of Methodist ministers, Lowman has published, under the imprimatur of the Circuit Riders, compilations of the "public records" of 614 Presby-

terian clergymen; 1411 Protestant Episcopal rectors—this specified to be 20.5 percent of the total; 660 Baptist clergymen;
42 percent of Unitarian clergymen and 450 rabbis; 30 of the
95 men who worked on the Revised Standard Version of the
Bible; and 658 clergymen and laymen connected with the
National Council of Churches. He has also published Volume I of a projected two-volume list of 6000 educators.

It would be an exercise in tedium to analyze all these basically similar lists. Hence, we will examine, briefly, only the
two that we find most frequently recommended by Lowman's
admirers: the list of Methodist ministers, and the list of
clergymen and laymen connected with the National Council
of Churches.

If we have counted correctly, Volume I of the list of
Methodists contains the names and itemized "public records"
of 545 ministers. Ostensibly, these all have three or more
items attached to their names; but 24 of them have, in fact,
only two. Volume II is devoted to one-item and two-item
listings.

If Lowman had any plan in mind for the total project
before he began totting up names and attaching items to
them, evidence to this effect is singularly lacking. Thus, in
any study of this type, we would certainly expect Volume I
to contain some introductory statement about aim and procedure, and to provide some key to the list's interpretation.
Yet when we open the cover, we are confronted directly,
without even a title page to break the abruptness, by a
crowded page of names with various items attached to each.
There is not one word of explanation to tell the uninitiated
reader what meaning he is supposed to draw out of what he
sees is front of his eyes: which may account for the fact that
most users of the list import into it whatever meaning they
want to find there.

Except for our calling the minister in question John Q.X., one entry on p. 1 runs as follows:

John Q.X.
Melish Brief Amici Curiae: Signer (Supreme Court, Jan. 11, 1951).
National Committee to Repeal the McCarran Act. Signer of open letter to Congress (Letter, January 19, 1951).
Statement endorsing Publication and Distribution of the Report of Seven Clergymen who Visited Yugoslavia: Signer. Press Release, Oct. 31, 1947).

Lowman likes to say of his lists, as we have noted, that "the record speaks for itself." Does it? If so, what does it say? Because of what they have been told about it, or have read about it, most of those who comprise Lowman's audience hear the record saying that John Q.X. is a leftist—or worse. But do the words on the page convey this message?

Here, we are confronted by the first glaring inadequacy of all the Lowman lists. They are put together as though Americans were born knowing both the character of all the indicated organizations and activities and how a particular individual's connection with one of these, or with half a dozen or more, should be interpreted.

It happens in the above case that all three of the projects named have been cited as pro-Communist or under Communist influence by governmental bodies. But this is by no means true of all the items that Lowman includes. The reader has no way of making distinctions without doing laborious research of his own. And when he has determined the status of a group, he still has not one iota of reliable evidence about why, or under what circumstances, an individual signed an appeal or attended a meeting.

By our count, which may be a few points off either way, 350 different organizations and activities are named in this two-volume compilation. Does Lowman seriously want to claim that each of these speaks up and identifies itself for the lay reader? Does he want to claim, for example, that the printed page informs the reader of a fact which we have determined by laborious checking: namely, that less than one-sixth of the 350 are cited as subversive on the Attorney General's list? Does it add the further fact that many of them are not mentioned in the *Guide to Subversive Organizations and Publications* of the House Committee on Un-American Activities?

In Volume II, we find that the only item under one man's name is "World Peace Appeal"; and that the only item under another man's name is "National Committee to Combat Anti-Semitism." Does this record which "speaks for itself" explain to the reader that the World Peace Appeal was one of the numerous channels through which the Communists conducted their drive for signatures on the Stockholm Peace Petition? And having spoken to this effect, does it go on and say that the National Committee to Combat Anti-Semitism is not mentioned at all on the Attorney General's list or in the House Committee's *Guide*?

It would not be so bad for the compilation to be inarticulate if Lowman would speak for it, making its meaning and purpose clear. But he does not. At times, indeed, he sounds as though he either has not decided what it means or does not want to commit himself. A press release that was issued when Volume I appeared said that the list indicated "in part" the "political, economic, and 'social gospel' activities" of the ministers named. But a Circuit Riders pamphlet, issued several years later, says that it tells how many times the names of these ministers have appeared "in connection with Communist-front activities."

When Volume II appeared, in 1961, it came trailing its own clouds of ambiguity. It contains the long-missing Foreword—which succeeds in clarifying virtually nothing. It assures the reader that "the vast majority" of the persons listed "would not willingly aid the Communist conspiracy"; but it offers no key by means of which the reader can distinguish those who belong to this "vast majority" from those who do not.

Was minister A wholly innocent in his intentions when he signed a certain petition? Was B, in contrast, deliberately serving the Communist cause? Lowman offers exactly no help whatever to persons who believe, after the manner of our religious and political tradition, that people should be judged as *individuals*. By his tacit repudiation of this tradition, he says, in effect: "Make any guess you want to about the individuals I have named. I am not concerned about what happens to individuals. I am out to prove that the Methodist Church has been 'soft on Communism.'"

The Foreword, moreover, does not say on what authority Lowman has classified as Communist fronts groups that have never been thus cited by any governmental body. And it gives no reason why the document should be at large at all.

This, to our minds, is the crux of the matter: this question of purpose. What function is the list supposed to serve in the public domain? Is it supposed to make people think twice before joining the Methodist Church? Is it supposed to make them wonder whether the individual ministers named are *currently* connected with conspiratorial Communism? So far as we have been able to discover, Lowman has never assigned a rational function to this or any other of his compilations. He has simply turned them loose in our society—there to be interpreted in any way that fear, ignorance, prejudice, and special interest may dictate:

> . . . mischief, thou art afoot,
> Take thou what course thou wilt.

The Methodist Church commissioned Dr. Philip Wogaman, a missionary candidate, to make a thorough study of this Lowman compilation: a study subsequently issued under the title, "The Methodist Ministry and Communism." Dr.

Wogaman devoted months to the job, trying to find out the truth about the relationships of the 2109 ministers to the listed organizations and activities. He visited such governmental bodies as the Subversive Activities Control Board, the U.S. Department of Justice, and the House Committee on Un-American Activities. He made use of the extensive files and records of Methodist Information; and he corresponded or talked with scores of the ministers. All this effort, we would note, was called for to make even approximately accurate sense out of a book offered to right-wing groups as one that "speaks for itself."

Dr. Wogaman found out, among other things, that only about 270 of the 2109 ministers named had had any connection with organizations on the Attorney General's list. Of these 270, 31 could not be found on any list of Methodist ministers; and 10 were already dead and 54 others retired at the time the list was compiled. In the end, he could find only 18 who had been active in any sustained way, or official way, in groups cited by the Attorney General. To put this number in perspective, we might note that the total number of Methodist ministers in this country at the time the list was compiled was over 27,000.

We ourselves, having found in the Circuit Riders pamphlet referred to above a statement to the effect that the names of the 2109 ministers "have appeared from 1 to 100 times each in connection with Communist-front enterprises," also did some counting—and then plotted a curve of distribution. One man, retired for a number of years, does indeed have 100-plus items attached to his name; and 12, a number of whom are no longer active in the church, have 25 or more items. At the other extreme, 1273 men, or well over half the total, are listed for one item each; 312 for two; and 192 for three. The connections Lowman indicates are, moreover, spread out over more than twenty years. The one-, two-, and three-item cases can well be said to tell nothing whatever about the leftward inclination of the Methodist Church—and they account for 1777 out of the total 2109. They tell a good deal, however, about Lowman's willingness to scrape the bottom of the barrel, and to put individual reputations in jeopardy, in order to make as long a list as possible: this to be used as a weapon against the current leadership and current policies of the Methodist Church.

The "Compilation of Public Records of 658 Clergymen and Laymen Connected with the National Council of Churches" appeared in 1962. It has an Introduction; and in this, Lowman states that the persons named have been "connected with the National Council of Churches and have also been affiliated in one way or another with the leftist movement of this generation." He states further that he includes in this "leftist movement" five categories of groups and activities.

One of the five is made up of "organizations, publications, and other projects which have been adjudged subversive by official agencies of government." Lowman does his own highly subjective defining of the other four categories. These are "militant pacifist organizations and projects whose aims and objectives abet, wittingly or unwittingly, the subversive apparatus of the Communists; one-world groups which are dedicated to the drastic abridgement or destruction of the sovereignty of the United States, thus seriously impairing our freedom and ability to act in our defense against the Communist threat; socialist organizations and group projects which openly agitate in defense of Communists and Communist causes"; and "popular-front type of action and organization in which Communists, Socialists, one-worlders, and pacifists openly work as a left-wing coalition against the interest and security of the United States."

On a number of counts, this compilation looks like a more professional job than does the two-volume list of Methodist ministers. It is a well-bound paperback. The pages are less crowded, and the type is better. Yet when we get down to essentials, we discover that all the old inadequacies remain.

Again, as with the earlier list, we turn to p. 1; and on it, we find the name of Earl Frederick Adams (American Baptist Convention), with a record of the posts he held in the National Council from 1950 until his death, in 1956. How does Lowman relate Dr. Adams to "the leftist movement"? In January 1938, he indicates, Dr. Adams signed a call to "New York State Model Legislature for Youth," sponsored by the American Youth Congress. This is the sole item listed.

The American Youth Congress was not started as a Communist front. Founded in 1934 by Viola Ilma, it was, at the outset, so far from being Communist that the CPUSA denounced it as Nazi. But since it competed with the CPUSA for the minds of American young people, it was promptly marked for take-over. At its second session, in 1935, the Young Communist League, by united-front tactics, began consolidating its hold upon the group. But the founders and supporters of the Congress did not thereupon turn the organization over, lock, stock, and barrel, to the Communists. They made a valiant effort to keep control of it; and it was not officially cited as a Communist front until exactly a year after Dr. Adams had signed the call.

As a rule, the argument that a person's affiliation with a group antedated the group's being cited as a front is highly unreliable as proof of his innocence; for no group would ever be cited as a front if no one in it had been serving Communist purposes before it was cited. But in view of the Youth Congress's history, of the fact that Dr. Adams has no other record whatever of a "leftist" affiliation, of the further fact that he did not apparently return for more after this one contact with the Congress, of the fact that the official citation of the group as a front did not come till a year later, and, finally, of the fact that Dr. Adams had been dead for six years when this compilation was issued, Lowman assumes, we would say, a very heavy burden of proof when he names Dr. Adams as having been affiliated with "the leftist movement of this generation."

This case, moreover, is not atypical. In spite of the fact that Lowman arrogates to himself the right to add four categories of his own defining to the one category determined by official bodies, 241 persons out of the 658 whom he names in this compilation are listed for one item only; and a further 108 are listed for two items. Such cases yield not one iota of reliable evidence that the National Council of Churches has a "leftward" inclination. But the fact that they are included tells much about how determined Lowman must have been to build up a "leftist" image of the Council.

The Introduction to this compilation contains a precautionary disclaimer. This warns the reader to "guard with the utmost care" against assuming "that these men and women of the National Council of Churches are Communists, Communist sympathizers, or Communist Party members." Does this mean that Lowman himself guards with the utmost care against letting any such impression with respect to them begin to circulate? We have one reason at least to believe that the answer is No.

On February 5, 1964, we attended a meeting, in Washington, D.C., of the American Coalition of Patriotic Societies. Lowman was both chairman and final speaker. Mrs. Harry Alexander preceded him on the platform—talking about Communist influences in textbooks. At the end of her talk, she held up to audience view this precise "658" compilation and described it in terms that made it seem to be a list of

Communists and pro-Communists connected with the National Council of Churches.

We wrote down her words; and, having written them down, looked across the room at Myers Lowman. He seemed to be listening. His mind may, of course, have been on something else—although people usually do listen when their own books are held up and described. In any case, we waited to see whether, when he went to the platform to speak, he would make the correction called for by his own disclaimer. He did not do so.

Is there any sound approach for a truth-seeking individual to make to Lowman's ambiguous compilations? We think there is. It is suggested by a statement once made by William James. Asked how a person could best work his way through a certain ponderous and turgid tome, James replied that the best way was not to go through it, but around it.

TWELVE

EDGAR C. BUNDY AND THE CHURCH LEAGUE OF AMERICA

EDGAR C. BUNDY, Executive Secretary of the Church League of America, was born in Connecticut in 1915; had his schooling in Florida, and got his AB degree from Wheaton College, Wheaton, Illinois, in 1938. He went into the Air Force in 1941, became an intelligence officer in 1942, and was honorably discharged with the rank of Captain in 1946. In 1947, he re-entered the service for one year, returning to civilian life in September 1948. He joined the Air Force Reserve and was commissioned as a Major in the Reserve on January 1, 1956. According to the Air Force, he has done several brief tours of Reserve duty, but has never been a "weekend soldier" and is not currently active.

In his official biography, which appears in a brochure called *What Is The Church League of America?* we read that in March 1942 he was "ordained as a Baptist minister in the Southern Baptist Convention . . . in the Emmanuel

Baptist Church of Alexandria, Louisiana." But when he left the Air Force, he became, not pastor of a church, but City Editor of the *Daily Journal,* in Wheaton, Illinois.

In addition to being, now, Executive Secretary of the Church League of America, he is also, according to his biography, its acting General Chairman and "a research analyst." He edits its weekly *News and Views* and writes most of the material for it. Further, he conducts "counter-subversive seminars," and lectures over the country. In 1958, he published *Collectivism in the Churches,* to expose "the alarming extent to which Communist propaganda has penetrated religious groups and institutions." While the Church League of America dates back to 1937, its policy can now be described as Bundy-made. Just as the Circuit Riders has become chiefly an outlet for Lowman's views, so the League has become an outlet for those of Bundy.

On two scores, Bundy invites us to have high expectations about how he will handle his materials; or perhaps we might better say, about the methods he will not employ, even to prove a case, because he knows how shabby they are. In the Foreword to *Collectivism in the Churches,* he firmly denounces the ancient and dishonorable *argumentum ad hominem:* the technique of attacking the person of an author whose work has, by its merit, proved invulnerable to attack. Again, in *News and Views,* August 1959, he says that the use made of the "smear technique" by Nazis, Fascists, and Communists has discredited it forever "for people endowed with intelligence and discretion."

This technique, he writes, can be "detected and identified by its looseness of documentation; by its obvious reflection of the speaker's own personal bias and emotions; by its motives which can usually be found by those who take the time to check; and by the subtle excitation of dislike and even hatred of others."

Having characterized the "smear," Bundy sets a standard to be observed by anyone who accuses "an individual or a group . . . of something unwholesome or improper." Any such accusation "should be supported by clear and conclusive documentation and not just the manipulated words of the accuser. The test of proof should be similar to what would be admissible as evidence in court."

This statement deserves applause. Its implementation would do much to restore among us an atmosphere of confidence and reason. This is why we find so regrettable Bundy's own repetitive resort to the very techniques which he deplores. He does resort to them, however—so often that his ways of doing so become, in effect, part of his style of writing. Hence, this chapter can be regarded as a "brief": *Bundy vs. Bundy*—Bundy, the analyst of the "smear technique," vs. Bundy, the user of it.

His "looseness of documentation" is made all the more interesting by the fact that the Church League, according to its official brochure, possesses files that contain nearly 400,000 3x5 cross-referenced index cards on individuals, organizations and publications "which serve the communist cause in the United States"—as Party members, fellow-travelers, party sympathizers or front-joiners, or dupes.

"There are not more than twelve files in the entire United States comparable to the Church League files."

This tax-exempt Church League is, in brief, setting up shop as an investigative body. Certainly this fact imposes upon Bundy an exacting obligation to abide by his own standard of proof: namely, that it should be "similar to what would be admissible as evidence in court." And this obligation becomes all the heavier with respect to statements made in his book *Collectivism in the Churches;* for this is described on its own back cover as "A Devastating Indictment, *Fully Documented!*" The exclamation point is Bundy's. The italics are ours.

On p. 49 of *Collectivism in the Churches,* Bundy announces his intention of listing "some of the prominent persons in the old Federal Council, together with their positions in the new National Council of Churches and the left-wing affiliations of a considerable number of them"; and here we again meet the name of Dr. Earl Frederick Adams.

Lowman, we recall, listed Dr. Adams as having been affiliated with "the leftist movement of this generation" on the sole basis of his having signed, in 1938, a "call" to a project sponsored by the American Youth Congress—taking no account of that struggle for control of the Congress to which no official body wrote *finis* till a year later.

Bundy, after noting the positions held by Dr. Adams in the Federal and National Councils, writes: "Communist-front association: American Youth Congress." Not one word is said about the date or nature of this "association." For all the reader can tell, it might have been an association in depth, and one that spanned years of Communist-front activity.

Should we conclude that the Church League's files are so inadequate that the 3x5 card on Dr. Adams holds no more information than Bundy here reports? Or should we conclude that Bundy, building up a case against the National Council, withholds information that was at his command? If so, on what basis does he advertise his book as "fully documented"?

Another man whom Bundy undertakes to derogate in the same section of his book is Dr. Luther A. Weigle, former head of Yale Divinity School and head of the translation committee of the Revised Standard Version of the Bible.

Six "leftist affiliations" are attached to Dr. Weigle's name: "Committee on Militarism in Education; Coordinating Committee to Lift the Spanish Embargo; National Religion and Labor Foundation; North American Committee to Aid Spanish Democracy; World Tomorrow poll which called for socialism (signer); War Resistors League."

Do Bundy's files show that only two of these six groups—those related to the Spanish Civil War—have been officially cited as Communist fronts? If not, what is wrong with the files? If they do show this, why does Bundy so present the six groups—the cited and uncited—that they all appear to the reader to belong in the same category? And, again, what about dates? And what about the nature of the "affiliations"?

From such research as we have been able to do, it would appear that Dr. Weigle's "affiliations" with the two Spanish War fronts consisted of his having signed one appeal for each—in 1937 and 1938. But why should the reader of a "fully documented" book have to hunt up such essential data for himself?

A second part of Bundy's derogation of Dr. Weigle takes the form of an attack upon the Revised Standard Version of the Bible. "Noted Hebrew and Greek scholars, examining the text, found that it was not a translation at all but an 'interpretation.'" Not one of these noted Hebrew and Greek scholars is named. Hence, the reader has no chance to weigh their qualifications against those of the scholars who worked on the Revised Standard Version. The biographies and scholarly records of these men are spelled out in a pamphlet called *The Truth*, published by the National Council of Churches.

Furthermore, Bundy gives no specifics about what his unnamed scholars found to be wrong with the text of the Revised Standard Version. Instead, he resorts to an *argumentum ad hominem*. The Revised Standard Version, he says, "was written by radical liberals of the International Council of Religious Education. Eight of these men have left-wing records, and one of the eight has more than twenty-five left-wing associations." But no data about these "left-wing" records are given. Hence, the reader has no chance to evaluate their significance.

To take one more example, Bundy lists Russian War Relief as the sole "Communist-front association" of another man on his list: Dr. Beverly M. Boyd. But on what authority does he call Russian War Relief a Communist front? It is not cited as such on the Attorney General's list; and we find no mention of it in the 1953, 1957, or 1961 editions of the *Guide to Subversive Organizations and Publications* issued by the House Committee on Un-American Activities.

Bundy's persistent "looseness of documentation" leaves us wondering, in fact, what he means by proof "similar to what would be admissible as evidence in court." He must, it would seem, have an odd notion of how our American courts operate; for the proof he offers in his downgrading of people is, often, strangely akin to the type that has been treated as admissible in rigged trials in the Soviet Union.

But such documentation is not the only aspect of Bundy's writings that calls for wariness on the reader's part. Another such aspect might be described as leaping logic; for Bundy has a way all his own of taking a broad jump from an initial statement to a conclusion that does not follow from it.

Thus, on pp. 25–26 of *Collectivism in the Churches*, he states that leaders of the Federal Council of Churches took the emphasis "off the teaching and preaching of Christian doctrine and put [it] on the Social Gospel, by which the material conditions of the world would be changed. It can be seen from this that the church was opening its doors wide for the entrance of the teachings of Karl Marx and his associates; for Marx was a materialist at heart and believed in changing the economic conditions of the world in order to bring in a better society."

But it can *not* "be seen from this." Is Bundy seriously asking us to believe that only Marxists have been interested in improving man's material lot? Is he also asking the world's hungry, crowded, underdeveloped nations to believe that if they want to change "economic conditions . . . in order to bring in a better society," they have no choice except to become Marxists?

On other occasions, Bundy's weapon is the out-and-out derogatory label. In the March 1959 issue of *News and Views*, for example, under the heading "Left-Wing Bias in the Religious Press," he gives about equal attention to *The Christian Century* and *Social Progress*. He has every right to dislike these magazines and to say that they veer to the left, if he believes this to be true. We are by no means implying that they should be immune to criticism. But the way he frames his charge does nothing to authenticate his claim that he disapproves of "smear tactics."

Thus, he calls *Social Progress* "a typical left-liberal brainwashing organ"; and says that continuous reading and uncritical acceptance of the material in it could not lead "the average uninformed reader to anything but a propaganda-soaked and liberal-doped mental condition akin to Soviet mental robotry." His own "personal bias and emotions" seem to show through, here, in a way that Bundy, the analyst, could not approve.

Over the years, Bundy's *News and Views* has had a striking range of targets. Thus, in May 1957 the target was foreign aid; in November 1959, Chautauqua Institution; in February 1960, The Foreign Policy Association. The June 1962 issue was headed *Communism on the Campuses*. And the following issue, July 1962—headed *The Wrong-Wing versus the Right-Wing*—disposed of "The New York Times, Time, Look, Life, Reporter Magazine, the mis-named Christian Century, and the Washington Post" as "extremist haters of 'extremists.' "

As our chief exhibit of the Bundy style, we wish to turn, however, to the September 1959 issue of *News and Views*—which is devoted to "The National Parent Teachers Association." In it, Bundy undertakes to prove that "a content analysis of the *National Parent Teacher* for the past twenty-two years, and embracing some 220 issues," shows a "decided preference" for liberal rather than conservative speakers at conventions and an "unquestionable preference for left-wing writers as contributors to the magazine." Further, he portrays the magazine as decidedly leftist in its choice of books to be reviewed.

Under a section heading *Bias to the Left*, Bundy writes, "During the past twelve years the following individuals have appeared either as speakers at national conventions of the National Congress of Parents and Teachers or have contributed one or more articles to the official magazine." Since he was writing in 1959, the "past twelve years" would presumably be 1947–1959. The twenty-one persons whom he names are Ethel Alpenfels, Algernon Black, Margaret Bourke-White, Stuart Chase, Henry Steele Commager, Kermit Eby, Sidonie Gruenberg, Robert Havighurst, Frank Kingdon, Eduard C. Lindeman, Erika Mann, Margaret Mead, Ernest O. Melby, Ashley Montagu, Harry Overstreet, Bonaro Overstreet, G. Bromley Oxnam, Holland Roberts, Ralph Sockman, D. Elton Trueblood, and Harold Taylor.

"None of the above," writes Bundy, "would make any serious claim to being a conservative or a long-established, recognized anti-Communist." Then, getting down to cases, he names as Communists two persons on the list: Erika Mann and Holland Roberts.

In the case of Erika Mann, he offers no evidence to support his charge. He simply calls her "a Communist daughter of the well-known pro-Soviet apologist and Communist fronter, Thomas Mann." We do not know whether she was a Communist or not. But we do know that she did not speak for the Congress or write for the *National Parent-Teacher* during the 12-year period with which Bundy claims to be dealing: 1947–1959. She spoke for the Congress just once: at the national convention in San Antonio, in 1942. Her speech appeared also as an article in the June 1942 issue of the magazine. She was widely known in that wartime year as a refugee from Nazism; and it was in this capacity that she was invited to the convention platform—to speak on Hitler's methods of reaching through to young minds.

Bundy took the initiative in saying that the persons listed had spoken for the Congress or written for the magazine during "the past twelve years." Perhaps he will want to explain, then, why—without indicating the fact to the reader—he went back to 1942, to select from a wartime convention program a refugee from Nazism whom he could call a Communist.

During the 12-year period in question, 433 invited outsiders spoke at Congress conventions: at general assemblies, lunches and dinners, and section meetings. By the most accurate count we have been able to make, 900 different individuals wrote for the magazine during the same time-span. Hence, in making up his list of twenty-one, Bundy had slightly over 1300 persons from whom to choose. If the Congress has a marked *Bias to the Left*, would he have been so hard pressed to discover a Communist who had spoken or written for it that he would have had to go beyond these 1300 names?

Next, Bundy writes, "Holland Roberts has been identified in sworn testimony as a Communist. He was Director of the California Labor School in San Francisco for some years. This Communist academy was officially cited by the U.S. Attorney General as Communist and subversive. Roberts contributed an article 'Straight Thinking vs. Crooked.' The *National Parent-Teacher* with delectable understatement described Communist Roberts as being specially interested in teaching English and in the 'democratizing of education.'"

We are going to ask the reader to go back over this Bundy paragraph, studying how it is put together and what implications are built into it; and then to weigh the following facts. Roberts did not write the article in question during the specified 12-year period; and he did not write it while he was Director of the California Labor School. According to the *Guide to Subversive Organizations and Publications* of the House Committee on Un-American Activities, p. 37, the Subversive Activities Control Board cited Roberts, then Director of the California Labor School, as "a Party member" on May 21, 1957. He wrote the article to which Bundy refers in 1938—when he was Assistant Professor of Education at Stanford University.

Perhaps Bundy will want to explain why, writing in 1959, he went back twenty-one years to select a writer whom he could call Communist—without telling the reader of *News and Views* that he had departed from his 12-year period. Perhaps he will want, also, to explain his motive in saying that the magazine "with delectable understatement described Communist Roberts as being specifically interested in teaching English and in the 'democratizing of education.'" Can he offer any shred of evidence to show that the editors of the magazine could have known in 1938 that Roberts was a Communist? Can he prove, even, that Roberts was then a member of the Party? Not least, he may want to explain why, without directly saying so, he loaded his statement with the implication that Roberts wrote the article while he was Director of the Labor School and after he had been cited as a Communist.

In order to collect four others out of the twenty-one persons named, Bundy departed—without saying so—from the 12-year period which he himself chose to specify. G. Bromley Oxnam wrote an article for the magazine in November 1939; Stuart Chase, in December 1939; Frank Kingdon, in December 1940; and Eduard C. Lindeman, in April 1944. Bundy, in brief, chose six people out of twenty-one who did not belong in the 1947–1959 span of years.

The only two whom he names as Communists are Erika Mann and Roberts. He says that Algernon Black and Frank Kingdon were Socialists—and then pronounces his conclusion: "The names of most of the above list will be all too familiar to those possessing specialized knowledge of Communist fronters and fellow travelers." The names of a goodly number of them, we might note, would also be familiar to Americans at large.

Elsewhere in the issue of *News and Views*, he deals with the "records" of a number of the others named, making them up out of whatever random facts and implications he can assemble. We would recommend to the reader that he get hold of the issue and read it with care—studying each "record" to see what it actually says, and what it implies.

Having made the "all too familiar" pronouncement quoted above, Bundy goes on to dispose of evidence that does not fit his thesis: "Whether they were invited to create some semblance of objectivity to the proceedings or were merely used for fig-leaf purposes, it must be noted that Senator Knowland, Rep. Walter Judd, Carlos Romulo, Helen Hayes, and Dorothy Thompson were also invited to address National Congress of Parents and Teachers Conventions." But why impute dubious motives—with no evidence to support the imputation? Why not assume that these speakers, like others, were invited so that the audience could hear them?

Further on in this *News and Views,* we come to a section headed *Blackout on Books.* It begins with a statement that is demonstrably false: "Each issue of the *National Parent Teacher* carries several pages of reviews of a great many new books deemed to be of interest to parents and teachers." Bundy states, we would recall, that his article is based on a "content analysis" of 220 issues of the magazine—for a 22-year period stretching back from 1950. We do not see, then, how the above statement could have been made in good faith.

Webster's *New World Dictionary* defines "several" as "more than two, but not many." A "content analysis" of the 220 issues yields the following figures. In 41 issues no books are reviewed. In 110, the review space is one page; in 20 issues, a single column; in 5 issues, a page and a half; and in 24, two pages. Thus, the word "several" can be applied to the pages given to book reviews in only 20 issues out of 220; and almost without exception, these instances are accounted for by special booklists for children: books for Christmas or for summer reading, or books preferred by children at different age levels.

What motive, then, did Bundy have in writing that *each issue* of the magazine "carries several pages of reviews of a great many new books . . ."? The answer appears to be that he was building up an argument that would have weight only if he portrayed the magazine as one that regularly carries a sizable and general book-review section. In plain fact, it has never, in any regular way, put major stress upon book reviews; and the number of general-interest books to which it has given space has been small indeed. The overwhelming majority of books reviewed have specifically dealt with child life, schooling, and the home.

What Bundy is out to prove is made plain in three sentences: "The works of Otto Klineberg, Walter Reuther, Kermit Eby, Edgar Dale, Elmer Davis, Robert Havighurst, and Edward R. Murrow are naturally given lavish plugs. Needless to say, anything glorifying the U.N. or any of its subsidiary agencies, particularly UNESCO, is sure to receive considerable favorable space. On the other hand, books critical of this sacred cow of the one-worlders and liberals is sure to receive the silent treatment."

No matter how Bundy may feel on the subject, the UN is more than a "sacred cow of the one-worlders and liberals." It happens to be a world body to which our nation belongs. We have no idea how many books about it have been published; but the number must run high. How accurate is Bundy's statement that any book "glorifying the U.N. . . . is sure to receive considerable favorable space"?

We find that between 1944 and 1959, review space was given to the following items—more of them pamphlets than books. While the UN was still only an idea, James T. Shotwell's *The Great Decision* was reviewed in the October 1944 *National Parent-Teacher.* The May 1947 issue carried a review of a 20-page pamphlet—made up more of line drawings than of words—that was designed to show children of the ten-year level and thereabouts how the UN was put together and how it operated. This was Lois Fisher's *You and the U.N.* In January 1950, a review occupying one-fourth of a page is given to a booklet put out by the UN Information Service: *Building for Peace: The Story of the First Four years of the UN, 1945–1949.* Eleanor Roosevelt's *Partners: The United Nations and You* was reviewed in May 1951. The May 1956 issue told readers about a UNESCO booklet called *Vacations Abroad;* and the June issue of that year divided one column between two books on the UN: a history of its first ten years and an analysis of its structure and functions. Finally, the February 1957 issue gave brief mention to *Favorite Recipes from the United Nations*. So far as we have been able to determine, this covers the reviews of books on the subject which appeared during the years of Bundy's "content analysis."

Finally, we come to our favorite passage: "Incredible as it may seem, Arthur Bestor and Mortimer Smith were given some space to excerpt some of their more important points from their respective books—*Educational Wastelands* and *Quackery in the Public Schools*. However, they were quickly blasted off the stage by some rather heavy return fire. . . . David Hulburd's dishonestly one-sided *It Happened in Pasadena* was naturally given a tremendous send-off of praise and publicity. Elmer Davis's *But We Were Born Free* was enthusiastically plugged by Harry Overstreet. Hoover's *Masters of Deceit* was favorably received thereby achieving the unique distinction of being the only book of that sort to break the literary blackout." The part we have omitted in the middle of this paragraph is a list of books that Bundy thinks should have been reviewed, but that were not.

The first sentence of this passage is simply Bundy's way of saying that the two controversial books on education by Bestor and Smith were discussed pro and con—by their authors, and then by persons who disagreed with their theses. If this is not a good American procedure, what is?

The facts about the "tremendous send-off of praise and publicity" given to Hulburd's *It Happened in Pasadena* are as follows. So far as we can find, the book was not reviewed at all. But in the September 1951 issue, in the section of the magazine called *What's Happening in Education*, William D. Boutwell wrote a one-column answer to a question about charges of subversion directed at teachers and public schools.

He included in this a ten-line paragraph recommending *It Happened in Pasadena* as a "case study" book that was much to the point, ending this paragraph by saying, "Whatever interpretation you put on it, *It Happened in Pasadena* contains a lesson for every PTA in the United States, the lesson that vigilance is the price of a successful school."

Both in the way it is put together and in what it leaves unsaid, the passage about the Elmer Davis and J. Edgar Hoover books is 100 percent Bundy. Bundy names Elmer Davis, we would recall, among those whose books "are naturally given lavish plugs." In simple fact, *But We Were Born Free* is the only Davis book that we find reviewed in the *National Parent-Teacher*.

It is one book; and *Masters of Deceit* is one book. Hence, Bundy could have said with exactly the same amount of truth that books by J. Edgar Hoover "are naturally given lavish plugs." But any such statement would have been a total misfit in his argument. Perhaps it would likewise have damaged his thesis to say—which would have been true—that Harry Overstreet reviewed *Masters of Deceit*, in the June 1958 issue; and that his review was not only quite as enthusiastic as that of the Elmer Davis book but also twice as long. For some reason, Bundy does not even mention the fact that an even longer review of Don Whitehead's *The FBI Story*, with a Foreword by Mr. Hoover, appeared in the February 1957 issue.

In conclusion, it must be noted that Bundy's skill with words is not used only to derogate other persons, or groups that he has elected to call leftist. It is used also to build up his own image: a fact to which the biography in the Church League's brochure bears eloquent witness.

With respect to his service record, for example, we have reported earlier that he joined the Air Force in 1941; became an intelligence officer in 1942; was honorably discharged with the rank of Captain in 1946; re-entered the service in August 1947, for one year; joined the Air Force Reserve when he returned to civilian life on September 1, 1948; and received his commission as Major in the Reserve on January 1, 1956—fifteen years after his original enlistment.

His own coverage of the subject reads thus: "Entered the Armed Services in February 1941 and rose in rank from Private to Major, seeing six years of active duty in Air Force intelligence in every major theater of war . . ." In a different context, over toward the end of the biography, he enters the fact that his commission as Major is in the Reserve; but he does not give the 1956 date.

Although very different in purpose, being designed to glorify rather than to derogate, this passage is in its structure very much like the one about the Holland Roberts article and that about the Elmer Davis and J. Edgar Hoover books; and since we are asking people to read Bundy's materials, as well as those of the other persons whom we have discussed in this book, it seems worth while to analyze how such passages are put together. Any number of them occur in Bundy's writings—and each calls for a sorting out of facts and implications.

In the section about the Holland Roberts article, Bundy makes a succession of true statements: to the effect that Roberts was identified in sworn testimony as a Communist; that he was for some years Director of the California Labor School; and that he wrote a certain article for the *National Parent-Teacher*. But by what he leaves unsaid about the date of the article and the date of Roberts' being cited as a Communist, he creates a false impression.

"Elmer Davis's *But We Were Born Free*," he writes, "was enthusiastically plugged by Harry Overstreet. Hoover's *Masters of Deceit* was favorably received . . ." Harry Overstreet reviewed both books with warm enthusiasm. It can be said, then, that Bundy was speaking literal truth when he said that the Davis book was "enthusiastically plugged" and that the Hoover book was "favorably received." He simply chooses words that make the reception of the two books seem very different—a choice that comes, we would say, within his right of free speech; just as making note of it comes within our own.

In like vein, he simply chooses not to say who reviewed the Hoover book; or that the review of it was twice as long as that of the Davis book. What we have here, in brief, is a fascinating instance of how truths, selectively used and carefully phrased, can be made to foster loaded implications.

And Bundy employs the same basic pattern, with reverse effect, in dealing with his own service record. It is true that he entered the Armed Services in 1941 and rose in rank from Private to Major. He simply leaves unsaid the fact that this rise took place over a fifteen-year period, and that his commission as Major is in the Reserve. Instead of saying this, he goes on, after a comma, to a second truth: that he saw six years of active duty. If the reader concludes, from the way the two parts of the sentence are put together, that Bundy was a Major at the end of his six years of active service, he has merely accepted an implication. He has not been told a falsehood.

To take another example, Bundy testified, in June 1949, before the Senate Appropriations Committee—or, as he puts it, "before full committee in Washington on entire Far Eastern Situation, including China, Siberia, Japan, Manchuria, Korea, the Philippines, South East Asia, and Alaska.

"Testimony lasted two hours . . ." Here, we must do him more justice than he does to himself. Two hours would average out to only fifteen minutes a country—even if South East Asia were treated as a unit, and no time allowed for comments and questions by Committee members. But one reason why the testimony did not last longer is that Bundy entered with the Committee a detailed written report that was a time-saver.

One part of the testimony is given special mention in his biography: the fact that he "predicted under oath that South Korea would be attacked by the North Korean Communist forces. . . . This prediction was made one year and two days before it occurred."

The phrase "predicted under oath" makes it sound as though Bundy had staked his career on the accuracy of his forecasting of events. All that it means, of course, is that he made the prediction while he was under oath because he was giving testimony. No one would be charged with perjury because he made a wrong guess about the future—and in Bundy's case, this is just as well.

The prediction appears as part of a question-and-answer exchange with Senator McCarran—about what would happen to other Far East countries if the Communists took all of China. The relevant portion of the exchange is as follows:

Senator McCarran. If all of China falls, then Japan and the Philippine Islands must fall?

Mr. Bundy. Yes, sir; they must fall.

Senator McCarran. Then what will become of the little part of Korea that is left?

Mr. Bundy. Korea will be invaded by the People's Army of northern Korea, which has been trained and equipped by the Soviet. Not only will Japan and the Philippine Islands fall, but India, Burma, the Malay States and the Dutch East Indies. (1)

We named one chapter in Part I *A Reading Lesson*: and the name would fit, actually, any chapter in this book. Certainly it would fit this one on Bundy. The problem of coping with Radical Rightist materials is, in major degree, a problem of learning how each leader characteristically makes words and phrases do his bidding: how he makes them conduct the reader's mind to the conclusion that he wants it to reach.

The basic weakness of the Radical Rightist cause is shown by the fact that its spokesmen cannot trust simple, forthright statements to do the job they want done. They cannot rely on proof "similar to what would be admissible as evidence in court"; for they do not have that kind of proof at their command. Hence, they have to use adroit phrasings as substitutes for plain statements of fact. The key to whatever success they have is not to be found in the validity or cumulative weight of the objective evidence they present. It is to be found in their way of so utilizing every scrap of evidence or of pseudo-evidence at their command that it implies more than it says.

We have found no short-cut to an understanding of how they build up a case against a target person or group. If we want to defend our minds and our institutions against their peculiar type of assault by words, we have to read enough to learn the verbal mannerisms of those who do the writing. These are what warn us, now at one point and now at another, that the words on the printed page are not telling all: that something is being withheld; or that the reason why a generalization is left empty of facts is that there are no facts with which to fill it; or that a quote had best be checked against the original source.

The "glory" writing that Bundy does in his own biography is harmless enough—except to the extent, perhaps, that it makes his other writings seem more authoritative than they are. But an analysis of it helps to clarify his style. Also, it is highly unbecoming in a man who has, with other people's reputations as his target, so ruthlessly employed words as weapons. Moreover, it does not enhance the credibility of his pronouncements about either these other people or the vast, fateful struggle of our time.

THIRTEEN

BILLY JAMES HARGIS
AND HIS CHRISTIAN CRUSADE

BORN in Texarkana, Texas, in 1925, Billy James Hargis is the youngest leader of a major Radical Rightist organization. Yet in terms of experience, he is a veteran. He started his Christian Echoes National Ministry, commonly known as Christian Crusade, in 1947—eleven years before the founding of the John Birch Society.

After finishing high school, Hargis took a quick course at Ozark Bible College, Bentonville, Arkansas, and was ordained, at the age of eighteen, as a minister in the Disciples of Christ. His first pastorate was in Salisaw, Oklahoma; his second in Granby, Missouri; his third, in Sapulpa, Oklahoma. It was while he was minister of the Sapulpa church that he brought Christian Crusade into being.

Three years later, in 1950, he resigned his pastorate to give full time to his new enterprise—which he describes as "A Force for God and Against Communism." With the organization's headquarters moved to Tulsa, Oklahoma, he settled down to the task of making its work national in scope as well as name.

Christian Crusade did not attract immediate attention. Years later, in 1961, Hargis told John Wicklein, of the New York *Times*, "My biggest break, so far as promotion is concerned, came in 1953. I got the idea of ballooning Bibles into the Iron Curtain countries." (1) This project, sponsored by McIntire's International Council of Christian Churches, gave Hargis his first taste of fame.

But a "break" with bigger consequences came in 1954—when Hargis put the promotional aspect of his Crusade into the hands of L. E. (Pete) White, a Tulsa advertising man who had been responsible for the build-up of radio faith-healer Oral Roberts from a person with $25 to a multimillion-aire. "We set up Hargis along the same pattern as Roberts," White told Donald Quinn of the Oklahoma *Courier*, in 1962; and the results must have been of the same spectacular order.

Eight years after White took on the promotional job, collecting a standard 15 percent commission on intake, Hargis opened a new "international headquarters" in downtown Tulsa; and also purchased, at Manitou Springs, Colorado, an old resort hotel to be refurbished and used as an "anti-communist summer school." Today, the Crusade's program includes radio and TV broadcasts; the monthly *Christian Crusade*; the *Weekly Crusader*; rallies and conferences; an annual anti-Communist leadership school; a Summer Youth University, at Manitou Springs; youth chapters called Torch-bearers; home Bible chapters; and the publication and distribution of a pamphlet series and of Hargis' books.

Also, the Crusade provides a platform for speakers from other far-right groups and an outlet for their publications. Hargis has probably done more, in fact, than any other one person to try to make an effective whole out of the multiple organizations that exist on the Right extreme.

In his 1961 interview with John Wicklein, of the New York *Times*, Hargis explained the logic of his change-over from the regular ministry to the work of the Crusade: "I enjoyed revivals and evangelism is that kind of work, and I decided to become an anti-Communist evangelist." This fusion of anti-Communism with emotion-packed revivalism is the trademark of the Hargis performance; and its results, by objective standards, have not been altogether happy ones.

For one thing, his decision plunged him into the preaching of anti-Communism with no prior disciplined study of what Communism is or how it works. Like Welch, Smoot, McIntire, and Lowman, he treats the term *Communism* as a spacious container that can be made to hold all the religious, social, political, and economic attitudes and policies of which he disapproves.

Not his broad definition of Communism, however, so much as his lack of any definition of it has given him his license to issue a pamphlet called, "The National Council of Churches Indicts Itself on 50 Counts of Treason to God and Country"; to say that "the majority of American newspapers are actively promoting the Communist line"; (2) and to tell a Seattle audience that he regards liberals, not Communists, as "the greatest threat to our nation," because there are more of them and they have more money, and "their socialistic objectives are much the same." (3)

Yet on the basis of this type of sleazy thinking, he goes on, week after week, month after month, asking his followers to dig down into their pockets to support his war against Communism.

A second unfortunate consequence of his commitment to a revivalist method is that he goes on, week after week, month after month, asking these same followers to do a maximum amount of *feeling* about the menace of Communism and a minimum amount of clear, quiet *thinking* about it.

And a third unfortunate consequence is that every subject with which he elects to deal has to be oversimplified to the point where it can be shouted to a mass audience. It has, in brief, to be made as over-simple as the Christian doctrine is made at a revivalist meeting.

This doctrine is not simple: not simple to comprehend in its fullness, and not simple to apply to the daily enterprise of being human. We would not say that there is no place for revival meetings. But they cannot very well constitute the sole approach to the Christian message.

And they certainly cannot do so with reference to all the subjects to which Hargis makes a revivalist approach. Our American form of government is not simple. In its pattern of balanced powers, of freedoms and restraints, it is probably the most demanding of all governmental forms. Our economic system, which has—contrary to Marx's predictions—evolved its own pattern of checks and balances, is far from simple. Again, there is nothing simple about a world wrenched out of shape by colossal forces of change. And international Communism, with its permanent and oft-revised ideology, its conspiratorial tactics, its singular language, its internal tensions, its matching of propaganda to target audience, and its zigs and zags of Party line, is no simple phenomenon.

Yet Hargis imposes upon all these a terrible simplicity. Having begun, as a minister, by asking his congregations to have faith in God's word, he now asks the approximately 100,000 Americans who comprise the Crusade's membership to have faith in whatever word he himself may choose to speak about school textbooks, right-to-work laws, or American foreign policy.

Hargis's basic oversimplification is the same as Robert Welch's: "We conservatives all agree on one thing—that our problem is almost entirely from internal subversion." (4) But this is not a conservative thesis. It is an extremist one. The vast majority of American conservatives would reject it; for they know that the problem of internal subversion in whatever measure it exists, is not self-generated. It is an integral part of a Communist threat that is planetary in scope.

Hargis, however, is satisfied to say that "the Communists are winning World War III without firing a shot," by placing "key men in the American Army, Navy, diplomatic corps, treasury, Congress and other control points of government." (5) He offers no evidence to this effect; and, prudently, he names no names.

We might say that Hargis specializes in generalizations of this type. Thus, on p. 71 of *Communist America—Must It Be?*, he writes, "The American people need desperately to become aware that not only have Communists infiltrated their schools, but they have revised and rewritten school textbooks, and are about the labor of completely rewriting American history . . ."

Boards of education, across America, have approved hundreds—probably thousands—of textbooks. Just as Monsignor Lally asked Welch to name fifty Comsymp priests, and to provide evidence of their being Comsymps, so American educators, with maximum publicity, in the open market place of the mind, should ask Hargis to name, say, one hundred textbooks that have been "revised and rewritten" by the Communists; and to name, say, ten persons who are now engaged in "completely rewriting American history." It would certainly take many more than ten to do the job on the scale on which he asserts that it is being done.

If he knows which textbooks have been "revised and rewritten" under Communist orders, and who is doing the job on the history books, it would be morally irresponsible, and no act of patriotism, for him to refuse to provide names and evidence. If he is merely retailing generalizations that fit his line, thus undercutting public confidence in our schools, and doing so on the basis of no evidence that he is willing to make specific, he is acting in a manner that is both morally irresponsible and unpatriotic.

But Hargis's need to trim down every subject to a "doom-shaped" message that can be shouted makes it almost impossible for him not to talk exaggerated nonsense. On p. 111, for example, of the book from which we have quoted above, he says that, by reason of decisions handed down by the Supreme Court, "America—the American people—today are practically powerless against the enemy"; and on p. 146, "Not only has foreign aid failed, but it is destroying America." Like Welch's "Nobody will ever know" formula, this Hargis formula of over-simple generalizations is good demagoguery, but not good thinking.

How far Hargis is willing to depart from clear and responsible thinking is made plain in an undated letter sent out in the late spring of 1964, under the heading "The National Council of Churches and the 'Bloody Race War' Planned for this Summer!" This document asserts that the pending Civil Rights Bill was being pushed by "liberal preachers" who have gone "crazy with their socialistic and revolutionary schemes . . ." They will, he says, "divide our people and throw us at the mercy of a United Nations' occupation force which undoubtedly will be demanded by the liberals to maintain peace within the U.S. in event of a new civil war between now and the elections in November."

Why *undoubtedly*? Can he name a single "liberal preacher" who has ever even remotely suggested the use of a United Nations force to keep order in our country? Or is he simply scaring his readers in preparation for the latter part of this same letter, in which he urges his Crusaders, "Dig deep into your pocket for a contribution to Christian Crusade this month"?

That the latter may be the case is suggested by his following, in newsletter after newsletter, the formula of first the big fright, and then the urgent appeal. In his newsletter of March 15, 1964, for example, he states as though it were an established fact that "Oswald was an active Castro agent merely obeying orders"; and that the assassination of President Kennedy was part of a complex Communist scheme to discredit American conservatism. Then he declares, "And, I guarantee you we will never know the facts unless there is an AWAKENING this year. It is 'do or die' in 1964. If we don't break this liberal yoke in '64, forget about freedom and liberty. It will become but a memory in the hearts of an enslaved people."

That statement would shout well. But, here, it merely shouts in print—as preface to an appeal: "Dear friends, don't wait an extra day. Rush your gift to Christian Crusade . . ."

Whether on his own initiative, or on the recommendation of "Pete" White, Hargis seems to have undertaken, in recent years, a fairly difficult balancing act. While granting himself the uninhibited privilege of making assertions like those we have quoted, he has begun to demand that he be viewed as a moderate, as an authentic conservative.

The resentment he feels at being classed as an extremist is made plain in the *Weekly Crusader* of February 21, 1964. This issue, headed "The Smear to End All Smears!" is devoted to denouncing an article, "The Fearmongers," in the February 7 issue of *Life*. Wholly oblivious, it would seem, to how funny the statement sounds coming from him, Hargis charges the Editors of *Life* with having made "a broad, sweeping, generalized" attack upon him. They have, he says, called him a segregationist and classed him with those ultra-extremists who, for example, denounce the fluoridation of water.

"This," he writes, "is a dirty, filthy lie . . .I have never written or said anything concerning water fluoridation and you can't produce any writing of mine against the Negroes or any minority race because I haven't written any."

The trouble with this "dirty, filthy lie" reaction is that it all too patently seems to be an extremist overreaction. The extremist of Left or Right gives himself a kind of absolute license to derogate those with whom he disagrees; but he turns into a martyr as soon as he is himself criticized.

Moreover, Hargis, in true extremist fashion, takes on the role of the avenger. He prints in the *Weekly Crusader* the names and addresses of companies that advertised in the offending issue of *Life* and asks his followers to send letters to them protesting their advertising in such a "smear" sheet. Further, he asks them to phone the local distributors of the products of these companies and make similar protests.

"There is one thing for sure. We cannot let this dirty smear go unnoticed. Life magazine must answer for using their columns in such an un-Christian and un-American manner."

Is this just expedient hokum? Or has Hargis managed so to put his ruthless attacks upon others into one compartment of his mind and all criticism of himself into another that he can seriously summon up such hurt self-righteousness? We have no way of knowing. But the objective fact is that Hargis' record is full of items, put there by his own choice, that would invite precisely the interpretation that he accuses *Life* of having unjustly made.

Thus, one Christian Crusade pamphlet is called *The Truth About Segregation.* In this, we read, "The entire problem that confronts America today was bred in the pits of Communist debauchery and conspiracy. . . . Segregation is one of nature's universal laws. . . . It is my conviction that God ordained segregation."

Hargis says that he has never written anything against Negroes. Would he say that he has never written anything against the efforts of Negroes to secure equal rights? In *Communist America—Must It Be?*, p. 97, he says that the entire crisis that has developed in America around "segregation and racism" is an "artificial" one, "instigated by the Communists . . ."

And in the undated letter about the "Bloody Race War" from which we have quoted above, he describes a packet of materials that will be sent to readers upon "receipt of the biggest gift you can rush to Christian Crusade . . ." The description reads as follows:

"(Christian Crusade has received 10,000 informative, legal reports on this Civil Rights Bill the National Council is determined to ram down the throats of our citizenry which details: (1) the cruel and naked facts concerning this proposal; (2) the similarity of this Bill to the Communist Party Platform of 1928; (3) how the Bill fulfills many of the demands of Karl Marx's 'Communist Manifesto'; (4) the pro-Communist records of some of the authors and supporters of this Bill, etc. etc. . . .)"

During the school desegregation crisis in Little Rock, Arkansas, moreover, Hargis distributed a pamphlet called "The Lowdown on Little Rock," by ultra-extremist Joseph P. Kamp—and indicated in a leaflet that he was "proud" to send it out.

The Communists have always been ready to betray the American Negro; and there is no doubt about their being currently on the job. But this seems all the more reason for anti-Communists to support the efforts of responsible Negro groups "to work through traditional American processes to achieve equality." (6) Hargis, by making Communism the author of the "entire problem that confronts America today," betrays the Negro into the hands of the racists and the Communists, the two competing: the racists trying to keep the Negro "in his place"; the Communists trying to make him a tool of their purposes.

Hargis protests that the Editors of *Life* have used the "communist technique of guilt-by-association," classing him with "Ku Klux Klanners, anti-Semites, etc., none of which I support and all of which I hold in utter contempt." But is it really a Communist-type "smear" to assume that Hargis "associates" with those upon whom he calls for advice, whose materials he distributes, whom he invites to work with the Crusade, and whom he invites to speak on Crusade platforms? Do not these free choices constitute a report on the type of person he holds in esteem; not in "utter contempt"?

In the October 1959 *Christian Crusade*, for example, he states that when he was beginning his radio programs, he called for advice on Gerald Winrod—who, although Hargis does not say so, published the "hate" magazine, *The Defender*, and was obtrusively anti-Semitic. "Dr. Winrod explained the operations of an office and the use of letters to underwrite the cost of such an expensive operation."

Also, in the December 1956 issue of *Christian Crusade* he tells of a meeting he had with the publisher of *American Mercury*, and of how the two of them agreed to exchange articles and to offer special subscription rates. Later, he published at least four articles in the *Mercury* in a period when it was blatantly anti-Semitic: in February, October, and December 1957, and in December 1958.

In 1961, he bought the library and files of Allen A. Zoll and appealed to members of Christian Crusade for donations to transport these from New York to Tulsa: a cost set at around $2400. Moreover, the November 1961 *Christian Crusade* pictures Zoll as part of a "Crusade team" that had carried on a money-raising project in Amarillo, Texas, in September of that year—and all this in spite of Zoll's having been a working associate of Gerald L. K. Smith, and of the fact that one of the several organizations he has founded, American Patriots, Inc., was cited as fascist and is on the Attorney General's list.

One final example will serve to show why Hargis' "dirty, filthy lie" protest rings hollow. Among the speakers whom he invited to appear at his 1962 Anti-Communist Leadership School, in Tulsa, was R. Carter Pittman, of Dalton, Georgia—a man who denies that he is a racist but who distinguished himself on the Crusade platform by saying that the chief difference between Negroes in America and in the Congo is that "in the Congo they eat more white people."

Donald Quinn, covering the School for the Oklahoma *Courier*, reports that Hargis stayed out of the room while Pittman spoke, although he had attended all other sessions. Further, his public relations people later expressed regret to the press about some of Pittman's more extravagant statements.

"Yet Hargis himself had whetted the appetite of the participants by telling them that the subject of the coming session would be on the 'race question.' Advance texts were available.

"Newsmen covering the sessions were unanimous in concluding that Hargis was trying to have it both ways." (7)

Had Hargis invited Pittman on some hearsay report, without knowing anything about his racist views? We would find this hard to believe; for an undated leaflet put out by Liberty Lobby, Washington, D.C., in the winter of 1960–1961, indicates that both Hargis and Pittman were members of the Board of Policy of that organization.

"Newsmen . . . were unanimous in concluding that Hargis was trying to have it both ways." On more counts that one, this sentence appears to sum up the reason why Hargis so often finds it necessary to protest the unfairness of judgments that are passed upon him because of what he freely does.

Thus, in his April 1964 newsletter to the Crusaders, he includes the following underlined sentence: *"I think the criticism of me that is most unjust and most unfair, instigated by our pro-red enemies, is that I am engaged in political not Christian activities."*

Then he asks, "If I consider it my Christian responsibility to fight godless, atheistic communism because I want to save this nation and this world in freedom for God, is that a political matter?"

This martyr-response to criticism suggests, however, not the strength of his position, but the weakness of it. As Donald Quinn observes, "Steering through the narrow course of a political ideology by using a religious presentation is almost as tough for Hargis and the crusade as is the problem of avoiding a racist and anti-Semitic tag."

Sometimes he simply does not manage to do this steering with the adroitness it demands. Thus, the United States Senate Subcommittee on Privileges and Elections states in its Report on the 1956 General Election Campaigns that the Presidential campaign of that year was marred by only two instances of "scurrilous and defamatory literature" being distributed; and Hargis was responsible for one of the two. On p. 19 of this official Report, we read, "Rev. Billy James Hargis of the Christian Echoes National Ministry, Inc., of Tulsa, Oklahoma, distributed a mimeographed appeal for funds entitled 'Our 1956 Political Crisis' and a printed leaflet entitled 'Stevenson and Kefauver.' Both of these items were marked by extreme language and by attempts to link Steven-son and Kefauver to communism." (8)

Hargis partially solves, by means of his membership in such other groups as Liberty Lobby and We, The People, his problem of how to talk politics without endangering the Crusade's tax-exempt status. But even with such outlets as these, he cannot wholly forgo the chance to convert members of the Crusade to his political views. Hence, he gives these views a religious coloration, and proclaims it to be most unjust for anyone to call them political.

In many cases, it would take a psychological microscope to discover the religious element in his statements. Thus, in a pamphlet called *The Communist Program for the American Farmer*, he states, with reference to President Kennedy's farm program, "The Communists called for a food stamp program back in 1947 and now that is being put into effect." And in *Communism and American Labor*—another pamphlet —he addresses to "Christian Friends" the following advice: "When in doubt how to vote in an election, you will probably be right 99 out of 100 times if you vote the opposite of the way advised by union bosses." And in his lexicon, anyone who achieves a position of leadership in a union is transmuted into a "union boss."

At his touch, even subjects that we normally think of as profoundly religious suffer a sea-change—or Hargis-change. One of his pamphlets, named *Brotherhood of Man . . . A Smoke Screen*, develops the thesis, for example, that many persons "promoting the brotherhood concept of today will be found among those who follow in varying degrees the marxist class struggle theory. They will be found among those . . . promoting welfare state socialism." By the time he is through with the subject, the whole concept of the brotherhood of man has been made to seem *nothing more* than a smoke screen.

In conclusion, a word must be said about Hargis' continuous and versatile appeals for money. Not even Carl McIntire, whose every radio program is punctuated by such appeals, can match his record. Like McIntire, however, he injects into his appeals a plaintive note; and he permeates them with a sense of urgency.

His January 1964 newsletter begins, *"Frankly, I am more upset and disturbed over the future of our beloved America than I have ever been."* A detailing of his reasons for being thus disturbed leads, on p. 3, to a reminder about his new book, *The Far Left,* and to a statement that the Crusade needs "around $47,000 to get this book published and distributed." Crusaders are invited to send in advance orders to the amount of $100, or to make outright donations.

The March newsletter, addressed to "my dearest friends on earth," declares that the facts about President Kennedy's assassination are being withheld from the public because the truth would implicate "men in high places in Washington, D.C." This theme is prelude to an announcement that "we must have $10,000 in ten days or the Crusade is in big trouble with some creditors who have shown they have no sympathy for our cause."

The April letter, with which we will conclude this chapter, begins with a report on how hard he is working and how tired he is. "I am told that as I stand behind the pulpit desk or speaker's platform, I radiate a most confident manner, and a militant, courageous, fighting attitude. But, many times, if you could just 'scratch the surface' and see beneath the veneer, which is our common possession, my heart is heavy and bleeding, my body is agonizing in physical pain because of the terrific load I constantly carry."

The appeal for funds comes later: *"Everyone writing during the next few weeks with a contribution to Christian Crusade will receive one of the most important packets of material ever assembled and published by Christian Crusade, called 'The Communists' Secret Plans for 1964.' "* And further along, "We must have your help right now . . ."

Thus, the denunciations and charges of pro-Communist leanings go on and on. The portrayals of America as caught in a final stage of crisis go on and on. And no less interminable are the declarations of being misunderstood and unjustly treated, and the appeals for funds. "Dear friends, don't wait an extra day. Rush that gift to Christian Crusade . . ."

PART III

The Radical Rightist Movement

FOURTEEN

HOW UNITED IS THE RADICAL RIGHT?

U NLIKE the Communist Left, the Right extreme is not subject to any over-all discipline. It is an area in which groups and projects multiply with anarchic abandon. No one can say how many of them exist. If their birth rate is high, so is their mortality rate; and confusion is further compounded by the fact that an organizational name may be little more than a façade behind which someone with a mailing list and a home printing press hopefully produces and sends out a statement of purpose, an appeal for funds, and perhaps even a newsletter.

Nonetheless, certain factors that make for united thought and action are indubitably at work on the far Right, binding separate groups together into something that can be called a movement. Our purpose in this chapter will be to take stock of what these factors are and of how they operate.

One of them is the Radical Rightist line. Not laid down by any single authority, this varies in minor detail from group to group. Yet on most major counts it is predictably the same whether it is pronounced by Welch or Smoot or Bundy or by any one of a number of leaders whom we will meet in the chapters ahead. If we were to compress this line into three axioms, these might be stated as follows:

Those who are now on top—in government, education, church Council, labor union, foundation, or whatever—must be pulled down: they are Communists, pro-Communists, or dupes.

Those who are on the outside of the citadels of advantage and exclusiveness must be kept outside: their efforts to become equals and insiders are Communist-inspired;

Wherever America as a nation has become entangled with outsiders—as in the United Nations and the Alliance for Progress—it must disentangle itself: international bodies are Communist-controlled.

If this reduction of the Radical Rightist line to a set of axioms seems to be a *reductio ad absurdum*, it is nonetheless disturbingly accurate in its essentials.

On the political front, now, various voices proclaim that there is a grassroots demand for conservatism, and that extremism is nothing more than an extra measure of zeal in the good conservative cause. We have studied enough far-right materials and action-programs to say that the second part of this compound assertion is nonsense.

We know that there is at the grassroots a widespread sense of anxious frustration; and we suspect that there is a growing conservatism—in the sense that there is a wish to take time out from the pressures of change, to consolidate and evaluate; and a wish to halt certain trends that seem to have developed a steam-roller initiative of their own. But there is nothing in this grassroots conservatism to dictate the Radical Rightist line.

There is nothing that calls for the turning of citizens against their government; of laymen against their ministers and church councils; and of parents against educators. There is nothing that calls for the outlawing of all discussion of controversial issues across lines of disagreement, and for the outlawing of the very concept of a loyal opposition. There is nothing that obligates rank-and-file Americans to play an obedient game of follow-the-leader, and to expose their minds only to materials that represent one side of complex issues.

There is nothing in the grassroots movement to dictate that liberals and Communists be spoken of as well-nigh indistinguishable, and that middle-of-the-road conservatives be charged with Communist leanings if they favor foreign aid or see some good in the United Nations. There is nothing to dictate an effort to split our society down the middle into mutually irreconcilable camps. Finally, there is nothing to dictate an overt repudiation of democracy and a veiled repudiation of the concept of man's brotherhood under God's fatherhood.

The Radical Rightist line is no more an expression of grassroots discontent than Bolshevism was an expression of the workers' discontent. It is, rather, a calculated exploitation of this discontent. The line is a leader-made construct quite as truly as is the Marxist-Leninist line.

Lenin stated that, no matter how discontented the workers might be, they would never of their own accord put a Marxist-Leninist interpretation upon events and problems. This interpretation would have to be brought to them from the outside.

In like manner, the leaders whom we have named in this book, and others whom we will be naming, are bringing to grassroots America an interpretation of events and problems that is not dictated by human experience, by objective evidence, or by our religious-political tradition. One proof that they are doing just this is to be found in the assiduous care with which they ward off from the minds of their followers anything that might challenge their tenuously supported interpretation.

Yet, as the history of Bolshevism testifies, an artificial line may exert tremendous influence in the real world. By insistently driving home the "truth" of their artificial line, the Radical Rightist leaders are both building a movement and consolidating their individual positions of power within their separate groups.

A second way in which they are building a movement is by providing for intergroup collaboration—at the leadership level. If Radical Rightist leaders can agree on a general line and on particular issues to be exploited, the membership groups that they control can remain wholly separate and yet be made to constitute a united pressure-force by the simple device of their leaders all handing down to them similar directives.

A pressure-force that is thus put together when expediency recommends poses no threat to each leader's control of his own separate group. Neither does it mean that any leader, in order to effect a useful measure of collaboration, will have to let other leaders invade his valued sources of revenue. In addition, then, to the types of organizations that we have studied thus far, we must take account of a type that is formed for the sole purpose of bringing together leader-representatives of many groups.

The oldest such organization, so far as we know, is the American Coalition of Patriotic Societies, Washington, D. C. —self-described as a coalition "of more than 100 civic, patriotic and fraternal organizations"; and in one sense, it contradicts what we have said above, in that it was not originally formed by *extremist* leaders. Founded in 1929 by the late John B. Trevor, it was, at the outset, conservative—and on some counts, perhaps, ultra-conservative; but it was not extremist.

Even today, moreover, it would be palpably unjust to apply the term *extremist* to all—or, we would guess, most—of the organizations that make up the Coalition. Recognizing that this term is intrinsically hard to define, and perhaps incurably ambiguous, we hold back from applying it to even ultra-conservative groups so long as their internal structure is democratic, and so long as they do not demand conformity to one "correct" view or try to prevent their members from reading what they want to read and thinking what they want to think. Our quarrel is with the intrusion into our American life of totalitarian, leader-dominated groups that tacitly proclaim un-American methods to be necessary to the saving of American traditions.

What we would want to say about the Coalition, then, would be something like this. It seems, with the passage of time, to have been increasingly neglected by the best members of its best constituent groups; and thus to have become, first, a group declining into futility, and second, a sitting-duck target for extremists who saw in it something worth controlling.

We have attended only one meeting of the Coalition; and our opinion is based on this one experience, on the reading of published materials, on a study of relationships between its current leaders and other organizations that are patently extremist, and on interviews with various members of its non-extremist constituent groups.

The verdict rendered by such evidence would be that, as of now, the Coalition's programs are tailored to fit the Radical Rightist line; and that those who attend meetings are, on the whole, ready to be induced to support this line. A secondary part of the verdict, however, would be to the effect that the organization has a declining membership and is currently suffering from an internal division that is likely to mean a further decline.

Another Washington-based organization that has sought to consolidate the efforts of far-right groups by bringing their leaders together is the Liberty Lobby, which is chiefly concerned with the fate of legislative measures that it opposes or supports. An undated flyer issued in the winter of 1960–1961 listed its policies and invited readers to check their own attitudes against these, to determine whether or not they should become members of the Lobby. This flyer indicates that the group is for States Rights, and for getting America out of the United Nations; and that it is opposed, among other things, to all tax-supported housing projects, aid to education, and plans for medical care for the aged.

At the risk of being repetitious, we would stress again that not everyone who sees danger in the growth of centralized government or who opposes federal housing and aid to education is thereby proved to be an extremist. What counts is the manner in which these issues are interpreted; and our best key to how the Liberty Lobby would interpret them is to be found in the make-up of its Board of Policy—the members of which are listed on the flyer.

The name of Billy James Hargis is present. So is that of R. Carter Pittman, the Georgia racist who spoke at Hargis's 1962 Anti-Communist Leadership School. So is that of Verne Kaub, of the American Council of Christian Laymen: the distributor not only of the leaflet that proclaims the concept of human brotherhood and God's embracing fatherhood to be anti-Biblical, but also of a leaflet called *How Red Is the National Council of Churches?* which flagrantly misrepresents the records of various Council leaders. He is also, we might note, a vice-president of the National Council for American Education—founded by Allen A. Zoll, whose American Patriots, Inc. is on the Attorney General's list of subversive organizations. This Council, to judge by its publications, is out to undercut our basic structure of public schools. We shall have more to say about it in a later chapter.

The names of various other members of the Lobby's Board of Policy may not mean much to the reader at this point. We will be dealing with their organizations in later contexts. But here we will at least introduce them. Harry T. Everingham, for example, is among those present—he being the founder and current President of We, The People. General P. A. del Valle, founder and President of the Defenders of the American Constitution, is on the Board. So is A. G. Heinsohn, Jr., a member of the Council of the John Birch Society. And so is Mary D. Cain, publisher of the Summit, Mississippi, *Sun*, who is a Director-at-large of We, The People, a member of Christian Crusade's National Advisory Committee, and a key figure in an Omaha organization that we shall discuss later: the Congress of Freedom.

Mary D. Cain's name crops up, indeed, in connection with enough "collaboration-making" groups to justify our taking time here to define her viewpoint in her own words. One speech that she gave for the Congress of Freedom is called "From A to Z . . . I'm Indignant"; and it is being offered for sale by the Congress in reprint form for $10 per hundred copies. In this she summarizes, in one sentence or in a few sentences, her outlook on almost fifty different subjects. We will give a sampling:

"Communism—with which we are completely encircled because of (unconstitutional) foreign aid . . .

"Flouridation [sic]—not content with forcing us into a dole system, the PHEW (it smells!) Dept. is urging the nation to put rat poison in its water supply because some people (mostly bureaucrats) think it beneficial to teeth of children under 12—the adult population be hanged! . . .

"Guns—federal attempts being made to force registration of all firearms preliminary steps taken by dictatorships; confiscation the next step . . .

"Kin—the federal government today is trying to govern our kinship with other races, and even tries to tell us who to kiss! . . .

"Races of mankind—about which the federal government apparently knows more than God Himself, although God created them as separate—not mongrel—races."

Further light is thrown on the character of the Liberty Lobby by an all-day convention, or rally, that it held in Washington, D.C., on May 2, 1964. Daytime attendance was small —not more than forty persons being present at either the morning or afternoon session. But in the evening, some three hundred persons crowded into the room to hear Westbrook Pegler.

The master of ceremonies for the occasion was the Reverend Kenneth Goff. Goff was once a member of the Young Communist League, but defected in 1939. By the mid-1940s, if not earlier, he was active in racist and anti-Semitic groups, with his base of operations in Colorado.

Thus, he was associated with Gerald L. K. Smith in the latter's effort, in May 1946, to unite under his own leadership a large number of ultra-nationalistic groups. And in July 1952, he was a speaker at a convention of "nationalists" in Chicago: a convention mobilized in behalf of a campaign which led, later in the summer, to the formation of the Constitution Party. The moderator at this convention was Mrs. Lyrl Clark Van Hyning, head of We, The Mothers, Mobilize for America; and one of Goff's fellow speakers was Conde McGinley, Sr., editor of the newspaper, *Common Sense.*

(When McGinley died, in the summer of 1963, Goff wrote a tribute to him which was published in the memorial issue of *Common Sense*. General P. A. del Valle, named above as a member of Liberty Lobby's Board of Policy, wrote a similar tribute.)

The House Committee on Un-American Activities, in its *Preliminary Report on Neo-Fascist and Hate Groups*, December 17, 1954, devotes a lengthy section (pp. 10 ff.) to Conde McGinley, Sr., who, it says, illustrates a type of "subversion from the extreme right." The Committee takes specific note of the above convention, and of McGinley's "cooperative relationship with two disseminators of anti-Semitic literature from Chicago: Mrs. Elizabeth Dilling and Mrs. Lyrl Clark Van Hyning."

After stating that *Common Sense* "represents itself as 'the Nation's anti-Communist paper,'" the Committee says: "Such patriotic claims provide a poor disguise, however, for some of the most virulent hate propaganda ever to come to the attention of the committee. *Common Sense* defines communism as 'Judaism' and devotes its pages almost exclusively to attacks on the Jewish and to a lesser extent the Negro minorities . . ."

Apart from his anti-Semitic activities, Kenneth Goff, chosen to be master of ceremonies of the Liberty Lobby rally, has several other odd distinctions. He appears to be the original author, for example, of the charge that the fluoridation of water is part of a Communist plot. We have just seen a copy of a sworn affidavit, dated June 22, 1957, and addressed "To Whom it May Concern," in which he tells how, as "a member of the Communist Party," he attended certain "underground training schools" in which there were discussions of the way Soviet Communists were using the fluoridation of water "as a tranquilizer in prison camps."

Also: "The leaders of our school felt that if it could be

induced in the American water supply, it would bring about a spirit of lethargy in the nation; where it would keep the public docile during a steady encroachment of Communism."

While the USSR is still laggard in the field of chemistry and must have been deplorably backward in the 1930s, it is hard to see how it could have relied for long upon a "tranquilizer" that does not have tranquilizing properties. Among three related sets of chemicals—the fluorides, bromides, and iodides—only the bromides could be used as tranquilizers. The fluorides could not be thus used.

For all we know, the Communist schools Goff attended may indeed have discussed what he calls "deadly fluoride" with dead seriousness—though supportive evidence to this effect from other ex-Communists is singularly lacking. But we would note that fluoride begins to be toxic at about 25 parts per million. Where it is added to water supplies, with the aim of reducing tooth decay, in areas where the water does not have it in normal amount from natural sources, the proportion used is 1 part per million.

As we shall note in more detail in a later chapter, Goff appears also, through a singularly unconvincing "document," to be the original author of the now widespread charge that the American mental health movement was Communist-inspired: that it is, indeed, the product of a directive laid down by Beria of the Soviet secret police.

As master of ceremonies, Goff talked ramblingly about Communists in the State Department; his belief, but not certainty, that he once knew Jack Ruby as a Communist; and the fact that Eleanor Roosevelt once entertained at the White House a Communist youth group to which he belonged.

Westbrook Pegler, as chief speaker of the evening, denounced President Johnson for appointing Chief Justice Warren to head up the Commission to investigate President Kennedy's assassination; and said that the reason Johnson had made such haste to be sworn into office and return to Washington was that he was scared to death and wanted to get out of Dallas. He also criticized Johnson for having attended the funeral of former Senator Herbert H. Lehman. He spoke of having known Ruby as an underworld character in Chicago; and stated that Kennedy, during the McCarthy era, had got Mrs. Roosevelt to deliver to him the Communist vote.

Projected against the background of today's world, with all the national and international problems that cry for solution, the whole rally appears tawdry and mean-spirited—and monstrously irrelevant. We do not know what fresh stimulus to collaboration among the member-groups of Liberty Lobby it was supposed to stimulate.

In speaking above of Mary D. Cain, we spoke of the Congress of Freedom, in Omaha—another organ of leader-collaboration. Its general outlook is indicated by a set of Resolutions which it adopted at its 11th Congress, in Houston, Texas, in March 1962; and which it re-adopted, with few changes, at its 1963 Congress in New Orleans.

It is against the United Nations, the International Court of Justice, the Arms Control and Disarmament Agency, foreign aid, Cultural Exchange, the Federal Reserve System, and the current Supreme Court. It is for right-to-work laws and the Liberty Amendment "repealing the personal income tax and forcing the government to sell all business, professional, commercial, financial, or industrial enterprises in which it is unconstitutionally engaged."

Among Board members re-elected in Houston were Milton M. Lory, then President of the American Coalition of Patriotic Societies; R. Carter Pittman; D. B. Lewis, sponsor of the radio-TV *Dan Smoot Report* and President of the Organization to repeal Federal Income Taxes, Inc.; and, again, Verne

Kaub. An undated item which Verne Kaub was mailing out during the 1963–1964 season was a "letter" headed *We Take No Vacations!* In this, he recommended the Birch Society's *Warren Impeachment Packet*; and in it, also, he paid special tribute to Conde McGinley, Sr., whom he described as "a dedicated servant of the Master."

The magazine of the Congress of Freedom, *The Greater Nebraskan* seems to be trying to create an atmosphere in which distrust of our government will approach the 100 per-cent saturation point. In its pages, for example, our Army's counterinsurgency program for training troops to cope with Communism's guerrilla tactics, in Vietnam and similar areas, becomes part of a Kennedy administration plan to suppress every form of opposition—social, economic, and political—here at home.

The February 1962 issue admonishes the reader: "STOP FIGHTING BRUSH FIRES! GET THE REAL FIREBUG!" Then it asks, "Who Is He? or It? or They?"—and lists ten possibilities: "KHRUSHCHEV? United Nations? Income Tax? State Department? Americans for Democratic Action? KENNEDY? Fabian Socialists? Council on Foreign Rela-tions? Federal Reserve? Ambitious Congressmen?"

Again, the October 1963 issue reprints an article from *On Target*, the publication of the super-secret Minutemen: a group, headed by Robert B. De Pugh, which trains itself in the tactics of guerrilla warfare against the time of a Com-munist invasion. This article reports in all seriousness that our government is set to enact a plan, drawn up at an Inter-national Arms Control Symposium, "to confiscate all private firearms by the end of 1965"—this confiscation to be carried out in successive five-state areas, each of which will be blocked off by troops till the job is complete.

It would be easy to dismiss such items without a second thought if the Congress of Freedom were a self-contained "fringe" group and not one that sponsors intergroup collaboration at the leadership level. But among the speakers at its 1960 Congress, in Columbus, Ohio, were, for example, Robert Welch; Willis E. Stone, Chairman of the Liberty Amendment Committee and President of the American Progress Foundation; and Revilo P. Oliver, a member of both the Christian Crusade's National Advisory Council and the Council of the John Birch Society, as well as an Associate Editor of *American Opinion*. Kenneth Goff and Billy James Hargis are listed on the program under the word *Faculty*.

Among those who have served on the Board of the Congress, moreover, are a goodly number of persons who rate in far-right circles as top authorities on Communism: Dan Smoot, for example; and E. Merrill Root. Root is author of *Collectivism on the Campus* and *Brain Washing in the High Schools*. Also, he is on the Textbook Evaluation Committee of America's Future—which, in October 1963, was recommended as a source of information about "suspect" textbooks in both the Birch Society's *Bulletin*, p. 14, and, by the reprint of an approving letter, Gerald L. K. Smith's *The Cross and the Flag*, pp. 25-26.

A final group to consider, here, is the Anti-Communist Liaison—Committee of Correspondence, 1764-1962. This is a Billy James Hargis creation. On March 21, 1962, Hargis called together, in Washington, D.C., a carefully selected number of fellow Rightists. The March 30 issue of the *Weekly Crusader* carried a copy of the invitation he had issued to the members of this chosen company. Addressing them as "Dear Fellow Country-savers," he wrote, "We are coming to Washington to see if we can work out a coordinated effort whereby we can meet monthly or quarterly to be briefed by great conservative statesmen from both political parties on what must be done in the field of education and otherwise to help save our country from internal communism . . ."

No press representatives were allowed at the founding session of the group; but Hargis later gave to the press the names of a five-member committee for the "Co-ordination of Conservative Efforts." Edward Hunter—author of *The Black Book on Red China*, a member of the Advisory Board of Young Americans for Freedom, and a speaker available through the American Opinion Speakers' Bureau of the John Birch Society—was not only made chairman of this committee but is the operating head of the organization. He carries on its business from his own home in Arlington, Virginia, and edits the official publication called *Tactics*. The other four members of the committee were announced to be General Charles Willoughby (retired), Washington representative of Christian Crusade; General Bonner Fellers (retired), now national director of For America; John H. Rousselot, of California—and the John Birch Society; and Benjamin Gitlow.

Hargis is reported to be disappointed with the actual accomplishments of groups that set out to encourage collaboration among leaders—including those of his own Anti-Communist Liaison. He says that the leaders involved are too "individualistic." He might have said that there are too many prima donnas among them; that they all have their own irons in the fire; and that they are not distinguished by any great readiness to operate as equals among equals. Most of them appear to believe in collaboration. But each leader's primary devotion is to his own group, so that he has only a secondary devotion to give to a coordinating committee or coalition.

The groups that we have named in this chapter have all helped, in lesser or greater degree, to weld separate organizations into a Radical Rightist movement—called conservative. They are, moreover, part of what our society is up against in its effort to remain a society of balanced thought and give-and-take practice. They are part of what our schools and churches are up against. Unimpressive, then, as each of them seems to be, they need to be understood as a unifying force on the Right extreme.

FIFTEEN

STRICTLY POLITICAL

ROBERT WELCH declared, in 1958, that the tenth point of his action-program for the Birch Society was the most important: ". . . we would put our weight into the political scales in this country just as fast and far as we could." The argument he put forth was that neither major party could do the organizational work required to reverse, by political means, the trend toward Communism in this country. Nor could this work be done "through the leadership, drive, and loyalty-inspiring qualities of any candidate for the presidency . . .

"We are at a stage, gentlemen, where the only sure political victories are achieved by non-political organization . . . by an organization which has cohesiveness, and strength, and definiteness of direction, which are impossible for the old-line political party organization." (1)

Americans at large would do well to recognize the full import of the attitude that Welch was here expressing. Our two major parties have not been ideologically divided; and because they have both spanned the liberal-conservative opinion-spectrum, three "blessings of liberty" have been insured to us in remarkable measure.

First, we have been able to remain a society in which those who disagree with each other can still talk things over and seek areas of agreement. Both parties have had to support such exchanges of ideas; for they have had to try to keep their liberal and conservative elements on speaking terms with each other.

Second, we have been able to remain a society in which a change of party in power has not had a wrenching effect upon either the daily life-patterns of our people or our relationships to other nations.

And, third, we have been able to remain a society that could swiftly close ranks in a crisis. Our minor parties—our third parties, and fourth—have tended to be all of one piece. They have been built around issues upon which their members have agreed; and some of them have been, in the strict sense of the word, ideological. Our major parties have often been influenced, in an evolutionary way, by minor-party programs; but they have both continued to operate as non-ideological entities. And both of them have taken it for granted that the will to overcome an opponent should always be outweighed by the will to preserve the whole: the basic scheme of things that insures to a losing party the chance to try for victory the next time.

Moreover, the average American—except when he is caught up in campaign fever—makes a moderate reaction to criticism of his party: he has not thought it to be perfect, or to have a corner on the truth. If we compare his reaction with the fierce, vengeful reaction of a Bircher to any criticism of the John Birch Society, we begin to glimpse the nature of the *qualitative* change in our American political system that is implied by Welch's view, broadly accepted by the Radical Right, that

our parties should express the will of non-political organizations that have more singleness of aim than they—the parties
—have.

Perhaps the best way to understand the destructiveness
inherent in the Radical Rightist approach to our two-party
system is to study the Communist imperative that everything
must be "politicalized." Not only those things that we think
of as political, but also those that we think of as apolitical—
friendship, family life, neighborliness, religion, work, and
time off from work—are treated by the Communists as in-
exorably part of the class struggle. And a second part of this
insistent "politicalizing" of life is suggested by Lenin's edict
that the Bolshevik Party "must become infected with intolerance against all who retard its growth." (2)

At several points in earlier chapters, we have spoken of the
effort of the far Right to split our society into mutually
irreconcilable camps. Here, we can put substance into these
statements by a six-item tabulation of what the Rightist
leaders are trying to do in the area of politics.

First, by derogating bipartisanship and what they call "me-
too" attitudes, they are making it seem weak and wrong for
the two major parties of "one nation indivisible" to recognize
that they have large areas of agreement.

Second, they are trying, like the Communists, to "political-
ize" every aspect of life. Whether their followers are reading
a book, talking with a neighbor, going to church, or joining
a PTA, they are supposed to be rendering service to the
Rightist line. The paradox inherent in the position taken by
these Radical Rightist leaders is that they want to reduce the
impact of government upon our daily lives to an absolute
minimum and to increase the impact of politics upon these
same daily lives to an absolute maximum.

Third, they are trying to infect the groups they control with intolerance against all who disagree with them or oppose their aims: not an American-type competitiveness that combines a will to win with a will to live-and-let-live, but a Communist-type intolerance marked by a will to demolish and liquidate.

Fourth, they are trying to make political action, on every front, a constant focus of life. As Welch observed in announcing his plan for letter-writing campaigns, it is important for local members of groups to have "just one more activity, one more thing to do." Or as Verne Kaub stated at the top of his newsletter: "*We Take No Vacations!*"

Fifth, they put high value on secrecy—for much the same reason that the Communists do. The Bircher, for example, who infiltrates a service club or a PTA or a Young Republicans organization cannot very well announce that he and others like him are moving in, under orders, to take over the group.

And sixth—again, like the Communists—they gear their actions to a double standard and permit their followers to do likewise. They have the truth: why should they grant to carriers of falsehood an equal right to influence the minds of men?

In the wake of the U-2 incident, Ulbricht urged upon the people of the Soviet zone of Germany a program of denouncing America. But a number of Germans embarrassingly asked in public whether the Soviet Union did not engage in espionage. Finally, Ulbricht explained that "the collection of military information by 'peace lovers' was not spying, but a humane duty." (3)

In much the same fashion, it is apparently quite all right for Hargis to call the National Education Association a "radical leftist" body that uses "Gestapo" methods; but it is a "dirty, filthy lie" for *Life* magazine to call him a segregationist—even though he has put into print his conviction that God ordained segregation.

Where every aspect of life is something to be "politicalized," it is not easy to distinguish political organizations from those that are labeled religious or educational. The Manion Forum, instituted by Clarence E. Manion, former Dean of the Notre Dame Law College, is a case in point.

The Forum, which calls itself a "non-partisan, non-profit organization," was set up in 1954, under the laws of Indiana, as an "educational trust." Such terms as *forum, non-partisan,* and *educational* incline us to expect that this organization will stimulate a careful weighing of issues and some all-around consideration of public affairs. Yet the Manion Forum —which conducts a weekly radio program, publishes a monthly newsletter, publishes various tracts and pamphlets, and encourages the formation of "Conservative Clubs" throughout the country—is as dedicated to implanting the far-right doctrine as if it frankly declared itself to be engaged in political propaganda.

An issue of the *Wall Street Journal* carried the Forum's statement of purpose: to "wage war" against "(1) the confiscatory, Marxist income tax; (2) wanton foreign aid squandering; (3) Socialistic 'public power'; (4) destruction of states' rights; (5) futile conferences with Kremlin gangsters; (6) ridiculous budgets; (7) federal aid to education, and (8) unrestrained labor bossism." (1)

Obviously, the terminology used here would not be found in an educational brochure. It is the type of terminology that abounds in the writings of both the Left and the Right extreme; and it amounts to an announcement that rage, having parented a "cause," is out to demolish an enemy.

Take the phrase "wanton foreign aid squandering." Supporters of foreign aid do not advocate such squandering. And so far as we can discover, no part of the foreign aid program is approved by Manion. The phrase, in brief, is loaded with the implication that all foreign aid monies are squandered and that the program should be scrapped.

This interpretation seems further validated by the fact that one of the speakers used by the Forum is Walter Harnischfeger, of Milwaukee, Chairman of the Citizens Foreign Aid Committee—which, in spite of its misleading name, is dedicated to a reduction of foreign aid budgets and an eventual ending of the program.

Again, the phrase "Socialistic 'public power'" should be read in the light of Manion's conviction that the TVA should be sold to private interests. This stand on his part was one reason why President Eisenhower, early in 1954, asked him to resign as head of the Commission on Intergovernmental Relations.

Again, the phrase "unrestrained labor bossism" has to be read with the fact in mind that the Manion Forum and the National Right-to-Work Committee, Washington, D.C., are mutually supportive. Edwin S. Dillard, President of the Old Dominion Box Company of Lynchburg, Virginia, was the first Chairman of the Board of the Right-to-Work Committee and has been a Director throughout its history. He has been heard on the Manion Forum; and both he and a fellow Director, Eugene Germany, have been endorsers of the Forum. At least three other members of the Right-to-Work Committee have spoken for the Forum, as have numerous non-Committee supporters of right-to-work laws.

The name of the National Right-to-Work Committee should really be regarded as a euphemism. It reminds us, in fact, of some of the "halo" names adopted by Communist fronts. The Committee plays upon every atom of public impatience with union activities to make it seem that what is needed is the abolishment, by law, of the closed shop: which is to say, of the chief element in labor's bargaining strength. The Committee seems to mean, by the "right to work," the restoration to the worker of the pre-trade-union "right" to stand alone as an isolated individual and bargain as best he can on such matters as wages, hours, and working conditions.

We are not arguing that the union movement is wholly free of corruption and bossism. But if we are going to start abolishing, instead of reforming, all the areas of our life in which corruption and power-seeking can be found, we are going to have to dispose of management as well as organized labor.

All extremists, we must realize, whether of the Left or the Right, would rather demolish than reform. What the National Right-to-Work Committee stands for is, in one basic way, akin to what the National Council for American Education—Allen A. Zoll's brain-child—stands for in relation to the public schools. Both illustrate the extremist tendency to exploit and magnify the shortcomings of a target institution in order to build up, not a public interest in reforming the institution, but a public opinion in favor of abolishing it.

While we have digressed from the subject of the Manion Forum to make these observations on the National Right-to-Work Committee, the digression in itself emphasizes, we think, the type of program the Forum has favored. Among the speakers whom it has featured, for example, are Dan Smoot; T. Coleman Andrews, who ran for President in 1956 on the States Rights Ticket; General Bonner Fellers (retired), National Director of For America and a member of the Coordinating Committee of Hargis's Anti-Communist Liaison; and Willis Stone, Chairman of the Liberty Amendment Committee. Manion himself is a member of both the Editorial Committee of the Birch Society's *American Opinion* and the National Advisory Committee of Christian Crusade.

In naming members of the Board of Policy of Liberty Lobby, we spoke of Harry T. Everingham, founder and currently President of the Chicago-based group called We, The People. Started in 1955, this organization is self-described as a "National Coalition of American Patriots to Save America from Socialism." Hargis is its President Emeritus; and another past president was the late Kit Clardy, Congressman from Michigan—who also, until his death, was on the Board of Liberty Lobby.

The Honorary Chairman—preceded in this post by Ezra Taft Benson—is Thomas J. Anderson, publisher of *Farm and Ranch Magazine*, Nashville, Tennessee; a Council member of the John Birch Society; a member of the National Advisory Committee of Christian Crusade; and a Trustee of For America. One Director-at-large is Mary D. Cain, from whose "A to Z . . . I'm Indignant" we have quoted in the preceding chapter. Another is Milton M. Lory, Board member of the Congress of Freedom, Omaha, and immediate past president of the American Coalition of Patriotic Societies. The official publication of We, The People—edited by Everingham—is a monthly newspaper called *Free Enterprise*, subtitled "Action News for Anti-Communists."

But what chiefly interests us here is the organization's year-round program to support or defeat specific legislation and to build political opinion at the community level. This program is carried on through a Minuteman Network and Strategic Action Councils. We do not know the present number of these; but as far back as December 1961, *Free Enterprise* spoke of there being affiliates in 1700 communities, in all fifty states.

In a recent form-letter addressed to "Dear Friend and Patriot," Everingham, explaining the "Minuteman Network telephone chain," said that whenever a critical issue "that we can do something about" comes up in Congress, a directive with respect to it is flashed from the Chicago office to "every member of We, The People." Each person who gets this "Flash Bulletin" is supposed to phone four others "*who have already agreed to call four others* etc. *etc.* so that all *write to your Congressman* on the same subject at the same time!"

The Strategic Action Councils meet monthly to go over outlines of issues sent to them by the Chicago office; and to plan, on a neighbor-to-neighbor basis, a strategy for building the prescribed public opinion with respect to these issues. The Everingham letter states, "We have in the U.S. today *'Government by rival pressure groups.'* . . . We need *10 million Americans*—working through our conservative groups— *to make ourselves heard and felt!*

"Does your neighbor know the score? Have you ever really told him? If you don't, who will? *America can be lost before he knows it.*"

Here again, in brief, as in the case of the Manion Forum, we find a plan, organized on a national scale, to persuade Americans at the grassroots to write letters and cast votes on the basis of a one-sided, supercharged presentation of key issues.

On the night of Saturday, July 11, 1964—with the Republican National Convention set to open on July 13—525 persons crowded into a meeting room in a San Francisco motel for a rally sponsored by Kent and Phoebe Courtney, of New Orleans, founders of the Conservative Society of America, and publishers of the *Independent American.*

Two speakers were featured: J. Bracken Lee, Mayor of Salt Lake City and a member of both the Liberty Lobby Board and the Advisory Committee of Christian Crusade; and Thomas J. Anderson, whom we have mentioned above as Honorary Chairman of We, The People. Lee elaborated the need to give the people a clear choice. Anderson expressed the hope that the Republican Party would drop dead on the spot if it did not nominate Senator Goldwater. He also said, "I'm for drafting Dwight Eisenhower to do sentry duty at the Berlin Wall."

Our interest here, however, is not in these speakers, but in the Courtneys. Kent Courtney, opening the Rally, told how he had, at the time of the California primary, flooded that state with reprints of an article that described Governor Nelson Rockefeller as an "international Socialist." He claimed considerable credit, also, for Governor William Scranton's "failure to get any more delegates"—on the basis that he had distributed 108,000 anti-Scranton pamphlets. These portrayed Scranton as a leftist and as soft on Communism.

But the vital center of Courtney's message was a statement that a Goldwater victory must be followed by "a purge of liberals from the Republican Party." (5) What makes this statement particularly interesting to us is the fact that it was made, not by a man who has consistently supported the Republican Party, but by a consistent advocate of a third party: a far-right party. Anderson declared that the Republican Party should drop dead if Goldwater was not nominated. But Courtney declared, in effect, that it should drop dead after Goldwater was nominated—and then be reborn, Phoenix-wise, bearing its old name, but shaped in the image of the third party which he, for years, has been sponsoring.

In 1960, Courtney ran for governor of Louisiana on a States Rights Ticket and received, according to the New York *Times* of April 20, 1960, less than 3 percent of the vote. He thereupon turned to national politics and called a "New Party Rally" in Chicago, in April 1961, hoping to sell the third-party idea to nationwide leaders of far-right groups.

The Rally adopted a "declaration of conservative principles," calling for the withdrawal of the United States from the United Nations; liberation of Cuba, by force if need be; repeal of the income tax amendment; adoption of right-to-work laws; and the breaking off of diplomatic relations with all Communist countries. But it took not even one step toward forming a new party.

One reason for this may have been Birch Society opposition: for Welch's preferred method is that of infiltrating and taking over a party that others have created. One speaker at the Chicago Rally was Representative Edgar W. Hiestand, of California, a Birch Society member. It seems probable that he spoke for Welch as well as himself when he said that to build a third party would be "a disaster to the nation." By 1961, the Birch Society was already moving in on the Republican Party at points where a grab for power could later be made. (By the 1964 Republican Party Convention, 100 delegates and alternates were self-identified Birchers.)

After this Rally, the Courtneys devoted themselves to the double task of carrying on the projects of their Conservative Society of America and of getting units of a Conservative Party started in one state after another. Kent Courtney has a weekly radio program; and his wife, Phoebe, edits *The Independent American*. She has also authored several books: one, a tribute to Major General Edwin A. Walker; another, *America's Unelected Rulers*, an assertion that the Council on Foreign Relations is the secret shaper of American foreign policy—and shapes it to satisfy Moscow.

The Courtneys' best attention-getter and money-maker is, however, their pamphlet series, *Tax Fax*—which is bought in bulk by a number of companies to distribute to their workers. Among the titles we find *The Income Tax Can Be Repealed; Beware of World Court!* and *Is Foreign Aid a Fantastic Fraud?* But one of the most revealing pamphlets, authored by Phoebe Courtney, is *Tax Fax* No. 38: *Beware of Phony Anti-Communists!*

The "phony anti-Communists" against whom she warns are Colonel William Kintner, author of *The Front Is Everywhere* and co-author of *The New Frontier of War;* and Robert Strausz-Hupé, Editor and co-author of *Protracted Conflict*. The fact that both men are associated with the Foreign Policy Research Institute of the University of Pennsylvania means to Phoebe Courtney that they are among the secret makers of American foreign policy.

Moreover, Colonel Kintner has criticized the Birch Society. And on May 25, 1962, in Baton Rouge, at an anti-Communist seminar sponsored by the American Bar Association's Committee on Education Against Communism, Kintner said, "We must move toward greater cooperation with our principal allies." Phoebe Courtney interprets: "This is the Atlantic Community, or Atlantic 'partnership' scheme advocated by President Kennedy on July 4, 1962, under which the United States would lose its national sovereignty and become a mere satellite in an eventual World Socialist government."

Hence: "If such self-proclaimed anti-Communists as Col. Kintner and Mr. Strausz-Hupé are scheduled to address an anti-Communist seminar in your city, draw up a list of incisive questions to ask these men during the question and answer period. As these so-called anti-Communists attempt to answer, or dodge pertinent questions, they will reveal to the entire audience the speciousness of their claim to be anti-Communists."

As always, the pattern of collaboration is revealing. A flyer advertising *The Independent American* carries testimonials by Clarence Manion, J. Bracken Lee, and Willis E. Stone, of the Liberty Amendment Committee. Edith Kermit Roosevelt, from whom Dan Smoot took his lead in denouncing Walter Millis, has a regular column in the paper; and articles by and about Senator Strom Thurmond, Thomas J. Anderson, and Governor George Wallace of Alabama are frequently featured. Kent Courtney has spoken for Christian Crusade; and at the national meetings of their Conservative Society, the Courtneys repeatedly feature speakers from the National Right-to-Work Committee. At the 1959 meeting alone, there were four persons from the Committee on the program: the President, William T. Harrison, gave a speech; and he and three others made up a panel, presided over by Kent Courtney. The relationships go round and round.

We do not know when the Courtneys made the decision to support Senator Goldwater and to try to turn the Republican Party into the equivalent of their planned third party. Aside from a brief period when they favored Major General Edwin A. Walker, their preferred candidate has been Senator Strom Thurmond; and Governor Wallace has occasionally seemed to be edging in as an alternate.

The July-August 1963 *Independent American* reports the outcome of a choice-of-candidate poll taken among its readers. Strom Thurmond held top place; but there was a percentage gap of only six points between him and Senator Goldwater. Then, in order, came Edwin A. Walker, Thomas J. Anderson, Clarence Manion, and Dan Smoot.

The November-December 1963 issue, however, reported that Courtney had been, on November 2nd, the keynote speaker at the founding of the Conservative Party of Kansas; and that he had said, "We're going to force the Republicans to run (Arizona Sen. Barry) Goldwater or they'll go out of business."

There is nothing in the Courtneys' record to suggest their being ready to support him as a member of the traditional Republican Party. Rather, it would seem, they were even then thinking of how the Party could be remade into their third party: a party safely purged of all liberals. Goldwater was to them, it would appear, simply the man who could give them a victory to be capitalized in their own way.

In the introductory chapter to this book, we said that most conservatives have not had as much experience with the tactics of extremists as liberals have had—because the Communists got on the job, working to deceive liberals, before today's Radical Rightists got on the job, working to deceive conservatives. But the time has come for the conservatives to do an intensive job of learning—in behalf of our society as a whole: a society that cannot remain itself unless it can preserve the strength of the liberal-conservative center.

SIXTEEN

OF THE RANK AND FILE

THROUGHOUT this book, we have talked chiefly about leaders; not about the led. Here, we wish to talk about the latter and the fact that they can be of many different types. A startling number of persons affiliated with far-right groups obviously welcome the chances given them by their leaders to work off a pent-up store of rage and frustration. Every barrage of letters testifies to this fact by the examples it provides of vituperation and invective. But also the Radical Right, like the Communist Left, has its dupes: persons who have been misled by appeals that have seemed to be in line with their own anxieties and beliefs and who do not understand the full nature of the cause to which they are giving support.

To apply the term *dupes* to all who follow far-right leaders would be as sentimental as to exonerate of pro-Communist intentions all who have become involved in Communist fronts. A great many Rightist followers are, in terms of attitude, small-time replicas of those whom they follow. The response of one audience to one speech given by Dr. Revilo P. Oliver will show what we mean.

Dr. Oliver, a professor of classics at the University of Illinois, is a member of both the National Advisory Council of Christian Crusade and the Council of the John Birch Society. The speech to which we refer was made at Hargis' 1962 Anti-Communist Leadership School in Tulsa. In it, Dr. Oliver described liberal intellectuals as "witch doctors and fakers with a sanctified itch to save the world," and said that they are causing Americans to be taxed to death to "win the favor of every mangy cannibal in Africa." According to the St. Louis *Post-Dispatch*, which covered the school, his speech got "a whistling, cheering, standing ovation." (1) It would be silly to apply the word *dupes* to those who whistled and cheered.

It would be silly, likewise, to apply the term to persons who are receptive to patently extremist published materials. We have before us an item that comes from the Defenders of the American Constitution, Inc., Ormond Beach, Florida. It is called ALERT NO. 14; is dated June 5, 1964; and is signed by the head of the Defenders, General P. A. del Valle (retired).

The text begins: "Mongrelization of this nation will commence with the passage of any of the bills now before Congress designed to break down the immigration barriers set up by the McCarran-Walter Act!"

Then, in a section called FACTS, we read that these bills—the Hart Bill (S. 747), for example—are sponsored by "The International Treason Trust"; and that they are part of a plan "to destroy this country as a 'NATION UNDER GOD' by atheistic destruction of our Christian Faith, and destruction of our White Race by miscegenation." Readers are urged either to reproduce the ALERT or buy it in bulk lots "and mail copies to as many patriots as possible."

On the reverse side of the sheet, H. S. Riecke, Jr., founder and head of "Paul Revere Assoc. Yeomen, Inc.," New Orleans, states that the "PAUL REVERES agree 100% with the ALERT by General P. A. del Valle . . ." Then Riecke makes his own pronouncement: "The 'Establishment' intends to FLOOD the U.S. with some 700,000 TRAINED REVOLU-TIONARIES" as soon as immigration barriers are lowered. These "HORDES" are "already waiting and ready to rush into America over our Northern and Southern borders!"

It is no mark of extremism to be opposed to the Hart Bill or any other immigration bill. There is nothing sacrosanct about such measures. They belong in the area of legitimate controversy and disagreement. But what is a mark of ex-tremism is to *remove* them from this area by branding as traitors those who support them, and "revealing" them to be part of an international plot.

It is too early to know whether this particular ALERT will be given a wide mailing by its readers. But previous ALERTS from the same source have evoked a considerable response. One thing that we have learned, indeed, in the course of this study is that when an item of the above type has once been put into circulation, quotes from it tend to crop up in a host of leaflets and letters. Hence, we must conclude that many followers on the far Right have a mind-set that makes them able and eager to credit charges of treason and conspiracy.

The del Valle sheet can, we realize, be catalogued as a "fringe" product. Does this mean that those who would credit and circulate the ALERT would be a small "fringe" minority, and not representative of the general run of Rightist rank-and-filers?

When we began this study, we were convinced that a line could be and should be drawn between extremists and ultra-extremists. We were prepared, in fact, to draw another line between almost-conservatives and extremists. We are less sure now than we were then that such lines can be drawn; and those who have made us unsure are precisely the leaders whom we have been discussing in this book.

The two among these leaders who have the largest followings are probably Welch and Hargis. What they offer—and give others a chance to offer, on the platform and in print—must be acceptable, then, to more than a "fringe" few; and it is hard to draw a meaningful line between their offerings and those of del Valle and Riecke. What difference *in kind* is there, for example, between del Valle's "revelation" of conspiracy and Welch's declaration that the U-2 incident could not have been anything other than part of a treasonable plot in which President Eisenhower knowingly took orders from Khrushchev?

American Opinion, February 1964, yields an equally striking example of the Birch Society's readiness to sponsor a conspiratorial view of history. Here, Revilo P. Oliver, an Associate Editor of the magazine, has an article entitled MARXMANSHIP: *IN Dallas.* In it, he gives a 16-page elaboration of the Communist "plot" responsible for the assassination of President Kennedy. His sources of information are unnamed "competent observers," unnamed "analysts," and other unnamed "authorities."

The Oliver thesis is that a Communist plot for taking over the United States in 1963 was falling behind schedule because of the efforts of the Birchers and other "conservative" patriots, and because President Kennedy was not delivering the assigned quota of conspiratorial gains.

The assassinated President, says Oliver, was the same "John F. Kennedy who, in close collaboration with Khrushchev, staged the phony 'embargo' that was improvised both to befuddle the suckers on election day in 1962 and to provide for several months a cover for the steady and rapid transfer of Soviet weapons to Cuba . . ." He was the same "John F. Kennedy who, by shameless intimidation, bribery, and blackmail, induced weaklings in Congress to approve treasonable acts designed to disarm us and to make us the helpless prey of the affiliated criminals and savages of the 'United Nations.'"

Nonetheless, according to Oliver, Kennedy was becoming a "political liability" because his power to deceive Americans was on the wane. Hence, the Conspiracy, needing some "drastic means of checking the growth of American patriotism," decided to liquidate him and blame the assassination on the patriots. Thus the plot unfolds through 16 pages; and Oliver prepares his readers for the glaring discrepancy between his thesis and any report likely to come from the Warren Commission and the FBI by warning that the former is made up of traitors and suspect characters and that the same higher-up conspirators who engineered their appointment will prevent the FBI's ever being permitted to tell the truth that it well knows.

Oliver's article appears in a well-printed magazine that is the chief publication of a society reputed to have between 60,000 and 100,000 members. But is it, in its essential character, very different from the cry of treason on del Valle's random sheet? How would a line be drawn between the two, or between the rank-and-filers who read and believe and applaud the one and those who read and believe and applaud the other?

Most of the leaders we have talked of in this book insist that they are true conservatives, and resent being called extremists. Yet if they, individually, ever say to themselves,

"This far I will go, and no farther," we have been unable to discover any evidence of the fact. On the contrary, there is considerable evidence to suggest that they have not faced up to the question of how far they will let expediency lead them. Because they have, in effect, evaded this question, they have tacitly encouraged their followers to do the same.

Every so often, to be sure, one of them says that those who undisguisedly operate on the "fringe" are "nuts." Thus, Hargis told reporters at his 1962 Anti-Communist Leadership School, "The nuts are a burden to me. They are my heartache." He told them further that he had chosen his faculty with great care, to be sure that there were no extremists among them. Yet these statements, taken in the context of surrounding events, do more to render ambiguous than to clarify Hargis's definition of the term *extremist*.

At the opening session of the School, according to Harold H. Martin's report in the *Saturday Evening Post* of April 28, 1962, Hargis "warned the assembly that there must be no intemperate statements either from the platform or the floor. 'We cannot tolerate anti-Semitic statements, anti-Negro statements; we are not here to fight Jews or Protestants, white people or Negroes. We are here to fight Communists.'"

We do not doubt that Hargis really thought that he meant what he said. He meant it, we are certain, just as Robert Welch meant what he said when he announced in *The Blue Book*, "We are fighting the Communists—*nobody else.*" Yet three questions with respect to Hargis's warning call for an answer. Who was responsible for its being necessary? Why was it futile? And why did he let speakers disregard it?

This was the precise School at which Oliver talked about "every mangy cannibal in Africa"; and at which R. Carter Pittman declared the chief difference between Negroes in the Congo and in the United States to be that "in the Congo they eat more white people." If Hargis seriously meant that he could not "tolerate" anti-Negro statements, why did he do nothing more effective than to take refuge in an anti-censorship pronouncement, reduce somewhat the time allotted to Pittman, and absent himself from the hall during his speech—after building up the audience's interest in it?

Our own guess is that he did nothing because he did not know what to do. In 1962, Christian Crusade was fifteen years old. But there is no evidence that Hargis, during those years, had ever defined for himself, or disciplined himself by, a standard that could serve as his unshakable ally in a crisis of this type. For fifteen years, he had himself, on the record, shouted about issues instead of analyzing them; portrayed the civil rights movement as wholly a Communist invention; virtually erased the line between Communists and liberals; and indulged to his heart's content in generalizations unsupported by evidence. The warning he sounded in 1962 was made necessary, in brief, by a veritable host of intellectual and emotional intemperances that antedated 1962; and it was made futile by these same intemperances.

He had selected the speakers, and he can not have done it blindly. Oliver is on his National Advisory Committee, and he knew Pittman before 1962 as a co-member of the Board of Policy of Liberty Lobby. More than this, for a decade and a half he had been drawing to himself as followers persons who like his way of going at subjects and the type of speakers he invited to the Crusade platform. Those who gave Oliver "a whistling, cheering, standing ovation" were not alien gate-crashers. Each of them was a person who had enough confidence in Hargis to pay $100 as a tuition fee to attend the School.

It may seem, in the light of the examples given above—and, indeed, of the multiple examples given in earlier chapters—that only the deaf and blind could become dupes of the

Radical Right. Yet we are convinced that a veritable host of non-extremist Americans have been sold, and are being sold, a bill of goods in a patriotic-religious package. They are being persuaded to lend their support to "good causes" without understanding even a fraction of the implications inherent in the full-scale Radical Rightist program.

How, then, do people become dupes? The process appears to be much the same as that by which other people have become dupes of Communism. Lenin recognized that certain types of individuals make bad risks as Party members and had best be used in fronts or, even more remotely, as spokesmen for a Party line that they accept at face value because the words, *as they understand them,* sound good and true. In much the same way, Radical Rightist groups can use individuals who like what they think they are being offered, and who like what they think they are being asked to do.

Lenin warned that intellectuals, in particular, should not, as a rule, be drawn too close to the hard-core of the Party— because they are too susceptible to "bourgeois" considerations of "abstract morality and justice." Those who become dupes of the Radical Right are not as likely, we think, to be intellectuals as to be just plain decent people who have felt increasingly shut out of vast affairs that seem to threaten their way of life; who want to "do something about Communism"; and who can be captured by an appeal that seems to offer them a chance to get in on the task of defending their country.

Once they have been even partially captured, they are encouraged to study and become well-informed; and they have little chance to check up on the accuracy or fairness of the materials offered them. Progressively, also, they are encouraged to trust someone as *a person who knows;* and to hold certain specified individuals and groups responsible for our nation's troubles. Not least, they are encouraged to send one donation, and then another, and then another. And they are paid in the coin of feeling useful, of feeling informed, and of having companions with whom to talk about important matters without becoming confused in the process.

The Birch Society in its early stages was probably the most successful collector to date of persons who did not really belong in it but who gave it that aura of respectability that drew into it yet others who did not really belong there. Anyone who has ever signed a Communist-sponsored petition because of names he saw already on it should be able to understand the process involved in all this.

The first local units of the Birch Society were set up in January 1959—forty-one years to the month after Lenin's Bolsheviks broke up the duly elected Constituent Assembly in Russia and imposed the dictatorship of the Party. Back of Welch's success in capturing well-intentioned Americans who wanted to "do something about Communism" was the tragic fact that, after forty years, the Communist issue was still lying around unclaimed, for him to pick up and exploit.

Welch did what had not been done by either the genuine liberals or the genuine conservatives. He offered Americans at the local level a chance to study about Communism and to get in on the defense of freedom; and he provided study materials. If these materials and the program in behalf of which they were offered were spurious—even though Welch himself probably thought them genuine—there was nothing spurious about the gratitude with which a host of concerned Americans responded to them.

With the passage of time, the extremist character of Welch's outlook and the Birch Society program have become more apparent. From all that we can learn—which is admittedly far from conclusive—those who are currently being drawn into the Society are less and less often of a type to be called dupes. Most of them are people who can follow Welch with alacrity because his extremism provides, through each month's *Bulletin*, fresh outlets for their own.

For another example of how dupes are made, we can turn to the local Strategic Action Councils of We, The People. As we have noted earlier, these Councils receive monthly from the Chicago headquarters an outline of views on legislation which they are to "sell" to friends and neighbors.

How many of these friends and neighbors who are told—over a cup of coffee, or on the golf links, or at the bridge table—about the terrible danger inherent in some bill of which they have scarcely heard, are likely to have any idea of the standards by which We, The People judges a bill to be dangerous? How many of them, if they write their Congressmen or vote for candidates who, they are told, have taken a firm anti-Communist stand, will know anything about the total Radical Rightist program that is serviced by their small effort?

A different type of example is provided by an effort Hargis is currently making to build up the membership of Christian Crusade by means of Home Bible Chapters. In a set of instructions which he has issued, we read that a Chapter can be formed by any "supporter of Christian Crusade who is willing to hold meetings regularly in a Christian atmosphere and run these chapters according to the program and suggestions from the headquarters of Christian Crusade in Tulsa."

The last part of this statement contains the essence of the matter. All the founder of a Chapter is asked to do is to invite in nine couples to form the group—membership in each Chapter being limited to twenty—and to remind them of each meeting by phone. "The entire program will be on tape recordings sent from the Tulsa headquarters each month . . ." And the phrase *entire program* means what it says. The tapes will provide not only the "Bible Lesson" but also the prayer, the hymns, and an outline of "profitable discussion subjects."

Hargis specifies that no one likely to raise a dissenting voice or to ask questions not indicated by the tape should be invited. The spirit should be one of harmony. "The idea is to make converts"; but this does not mean converts to Christianity in the broad Protestant sense. It means converts who will be "in sympathy with the Christian Conservative cause"; who will, in brief, accept the interpretation which Hargis puts upon social, political, and economic issues—and calls Biblical.

Hargis hopes to have 1,000 such Home Bible Chapters, with twenty members each, "by December 21, 1964"; and each member, he indicates, would have to "join the Christian Crusade and pay the $10.00 annual membership." How many of these individuals, invited into a neighbor's home for Bible study, and held in the group by companionship as well as program, would get any over-all sense of what Hargis stands for—not only as head of Christian Crusade, but as a member of Liberty Lobby, We, The People, and Anti-Communist Liaison? How many would recognize that the ruling against the presence of anyone likely to dissent from the taped "Bible Lesson" is, in effect, a ruling against the exposure of the members' minds to more than one side of highly controversial and complex public issues?

Finally, the Radical Right, like the Communist Party, can use people without having them join anything. The Right extremists, for example—wanting the minds of the young to be shaped to their specifications—try by every means to make parents vaguely distrustful of current classroom procedures, textbooks, and professional educators. To plant such distrust they need not draw the public into group membership. It is enough to encourage people to listen to certain radio programs and to read certain printed materials. If these can make even a few individuals suspect that whatever is wrong with our schools is rooted somewhere in liberal-leftist influence, or in actual subversion, the *somewhere* need not be specified. Doubts, once planted, can be trusted to grow—and to seek expression.

One man, for example, who constantly works to drive home, by way of a radio program, the Radical Rightist line with respect to subversive influences in our public schools is Hurst B. Amyx of Tucson, Arizona—who has recently become, also, one of Hargis' speakers for Christian Crusade. His daily program—described as "Emphasizing the Perils of Communism"—is called *Know Your Enemy*.

Amyx gives plausibility to his programs by building them on two indubitable truths: first, that the Communists want to extend their influence into our school system; and second, that even one Communist teacher, working to subvert the minds of children, is one too many. Also, he creates the impression of being almost pedantically careful about his quotes and his logic. But upon this base of indubitable truth and seeming logic, he erects a structure of innuendo, nonsequitur, and generalization.

Amyx is careful to say that very few classroom teachers are actually subversive. His stressing of this point could well make him sound to uncritical listeners like a scrupulously fair and moderate man. But his fairness is much like that which would be embodied in a statement that Mr. X very rarely beats his wife. In brief, he deliberately plants the idea that *some* classroom teachers are subversives. Then, carefully, he shies away from ever identifying any one of these few. Thus, he plays safe while he creates the feeling that subversive teachers, being somewhere, must be looked for everywhere.

How are they to be identified? He does not say. At least, in the forty-two scripts of his program that we have read we have found not even one clue that would help any parent or any school board to identify a subversive teacher. What Amyx does is to exploit the atmosphere of doubt which he has created in order to get in a requisite number of jabs at such standard targets as John Dewey, UNESCO, progressive education, socialists, and liberals.

The Amyx approach can be made clear, perhaps, by our quoting from Script #488–98A. "The vast number of teachers in Arizona are loyal Americans, and a credit to their country; but, like most professional people, they are clannish, resentful of any derogatory inference against their profession and always willing to come to the aid of their fellow teachers." Further, "most of them are thoroughly brainwashed by the leftwing influences of the various educational groups and associations"; and they are naive. Hence, they are "easy targets for the small clique of organized, dedicated leftwing educators."

Here, again, is a statement that calls for a program of checking up. There is no possible way in which Amyx can know that "most" Arizona teachers are resentful, self-defensive, brainwashed, naive, "easy targets" unless he knows it to be true of enough *individuals* to add up to a majority. It would seem in order for every teacher in Arizona to direct to him an individual inquiry: "Am I among those whom you are thus characterizing?"

If he is willing to commit himself to an extent that would validate the charge he has made—which is to say, in more than 50 percent of the instances—he should be asked to produce his evidence. If he is not willing to commit himself with respect to *individuals,* then his claim that he possesses knowledge of the above type with respect to "most" teachers is plain nonsense—and should be publicized as such. It is

time, in brief, for Americans to stop being passive dupes of
Radical Rightist generalizations.

There are, in fact, any number of ways in which people
can be drawn into the service of a movement which they in
nowise understand. It is as unfair to label as a right-wing
extremist every person who has joined a Radical Rightist
group or who has been confused by Radical Rightist propaganda as it is to label as pro-Communist every person who
has signed an appeal sponsored by the Communists, or who
has joined a Communist front, or who has been confused by
Communist propaganda.

In terms of their make-up as individuals, many persons
who have strayed to one extreme or the other belong to the
liberal-conservative center. If we want them to come home
to this center—to defect from the Left or from the Right,
as the case may be—we do ill to put them on the defensive
by careless, or ruthless, name-calling. But we have every
right to put on the defensive those who propagate the Communist and Radical Rightist lines: not by calling them names,
but by asking them to substantiate every charge they make;
and by giving the fullest possible publicity, then, to their
responses.

SEVENTEEN

FOUR TARGETS

W E will be dealing, here, with four targets that are given no respite from attack. These are our public schools, together with organizations of educators; local PTAs, together with State and National Congresses of Parents and Teachers; the mental health movement, local and national; and public libraries.

These vital elements of our society all have to do with the individual's right to grow and the mind's right to explore the complexities of life in search of truth. Hence, they are all peculiarly subject to pressures from those who want minds to be arbitrarily directed toward an acceptance of some one special doctrine: political, social, economic, religious.

Taking the schools first, we will begin with attacks on textbooks, particularly in the fields of social science and history. Here, the pattern of denunciation is fairly standard. Textbooks are said to implant a collectivist philosophy, to downgrade patriotism, to be critical of the United States, to praise the Soviet Union, to favor the Welfare State, to favor world government, and to belittle the profit motive.

One remarkable thing about these attacks on textbooks is the range of people who feel qualified to make them. We have noted earlier, for example, Hargis' pronouncement that Communists "have revised and rewritten school textbooks, and are about the labor of completely rewriting American history . . ." And his statement is neither better nor worse than are the statements of a veritable host of individuals and groups that claim to know what is in textbooks they have never read, and to know exactly what should be in textbooks dealing with subjects which they have never studied with professional accuracy.

Thus, the Kansas City *Star* of December 3, 1961, reports an interview which a member of its staff, Steve Underwood, had with Robert De Pugh, founder and National Co-ordinator of the Minutemen. Underwood states that one reason given by De Pugh for the supersecrecy of this private guerrilla-warfare organization was that it was called for by a project on schools and textbooks.

"Minutemen feel," said De Pugh, "if their identities are unknown they will be in a better position to obtain information on the infiltration of school systems by Communists and subversives." And he added that a systematic study of textbooks and how they are selected was already under way.

More recently, however, De Pugh is reported to have said that the Minutemen are willing to leave most of the work in this special area to the Textbook Evaluation Committee of America's Future, New Rochelle, New York. This would be a logical decision; for De Pugh is a member of the John Birch Society, and the work of the Committee is highly recommended by Robert Welch.

This recommendation is logical, also. Two members of the

Board of Trustees of America's Future—Thomas J. Anderson and F. Gano Chance—are members of the Council of the John Birch Society; and on the sixteen-member Text Book Evaluation Committee we find three other persons associated with the Society's magazine, *American Opinion*. Two of them, Charles Callan Tansill and Hans F. Sennholz, are Contributing Editors; the third, E. Merrill Root, is an Advisory Editor. Two previous members of the Text Book Committee have had like connections with *American Opinion*: J. B. Matthews as an Associate Editor, and Medford Evans as a Contributing Editor.

E. Merrill Root, a former English Professor at Earlham College, deserves particular mention. He is the author of *Collectivism on the Campus* and *Brainwashing in the High Schools*. The latter, which reports his estimate of eleven high school social science and history textbooks, has an introductory note by Edgar C. Bundy. Root is the author, also, of *Tax Fax* No. 37, *Subversion in the Schools*, published by Kent and Phoebe Courtney's Conservative Society of America. And he was listed as a member of the Board of Directors of Allen Zoll's National Council of American Education in a leaflet issued by this group on February 1, 1953: "Must American Youth Be Taught that Communism and Socialism Are Superior to Americanism?"

We cannot make a complete analysis, here, of *Brainwashing in the High Schools*—which has become a kind of "bible" on the subject all across the far Right. But in many respects—including the inexact use of the term *brainwashing*—it represents a peculiar travesty upon scholarly documentation. For those who want to know what brainwashing really is, and how different it is from what Root is talking about, we recommend three books: Robert Lifton's *Thought Reform and the Psychology of Totalism;* Joost A. M. Meerloo's *The Rape of the Mind;* and William Sargant's *Battle for the Mind.*

In his Chapter I, "Why We are Losing the Cold War," Root gives considerable space to the report of Major William E. Mayer on the educational unpreparedness of American prisoners of war to withstand Communist propaganda. Hence, the reader expects that he is going to establish the relevance of this report to his own analysis of the eleven high school textbooks. But he does not do so. Obviously, American soldiers in Korea in 1950 could not have studied any one of these textbooks; for they were all published between 1950 and 1954. To give the Mayer report the relevance, then, which this chapter seems to attribute to it, Root would have to show at least a few points of resemblance between these eleven texts and those studied in high school by prisoners of war who later proved to be undereducated with respect to American history and institutions.

Oddly enough, however, he does not identify a single book that was actually studied by any vulnerable soldier; so the reader of his book has no chance to determine whether or not any one of the eleven books which he is derogating could be expected to exert a similar influence. Moreover, he does not tell the reader that eighteen out of the twenty-one American prisoners who became "turncoats" were not high school graduates at all: and the same holds true for a startling number of the other men who were prone to credit, or unable to answer, Communist propaganda. If these soldiers were inadequately informed about the American past and present, the blame can scarcely be placed upon high schools which they did not attend—and then transferred to textbooks that had not been published yet when they went to Korea.

One of the eleven books which Root portrays as an instrument for brainwashing students is *A History of Our Country*, by David Saville Muzzey—published by Ginn and Company in 1950. He accuses Dr. Muzzey, and the other historians of whom he speaks, of preaching "class war"; of not making it clear that America is a republic, not a democracy; and of playing down the success of the American venture.

So far as we can discover, Dr. Muzzey does not even use the term "class war." Root himself seems to have imported it into the discussion. No responsible historian would present any country's record as wholly a success story; but what is basic to Dr. Muzzey's view of America is fairly represented, we think, by the following passages from pages 635 and 639:

"The founding fathers set up an ideal of liberty within the wholesome restraint of law. They conceived of a republic in which the opportunity to make the most of one's talent and industry should be open to all, irrespective of birth, creed, or condition"; and: "The torch of our history was kindled at the sacred altar of liberty. Let it be your pledge and mine to bear it high like a beacon."

Some of Root's odd conclusions result from his use of odd methods. On pp. 182–183 of *Brainwashing in the High Schools*, he instructs the reader, "Turn to the indices of these volumes [the eleven textbooks]: look up the number of lines of reference devoted to Presidents Coolidge and Hoover, on the one hand, and to Presidents Wilson and Franklin D. Roosevelt on the other." From the fact that there are more index references to the latter two presidents than to the former two, Root concludes that the authors of the books were prejudiced in favor of Democratic Presidents, and against Republican. And to fortify this view, he counts the references to Lincoln. "(And let us remember that Abraham Lincoln was a *Republican*) . . .

"Here is a curious lack of perspective! Abraham Lincoln, tested by time and universally accepted as one of our two greatest presidents, rates only 107 lines in the indices of these texts. He is surpassed by Wilson, who rates 110 lines. He is surpassed almost 50 percent by Franklin D. Roosevelt.

And the steady, patient, deeply rooted Herbert Hoover . . . is given only 67 lines . . . Coolidge received 35."

Root credits Muzzey with 11 references to Coolidge; 13 to Hoover; 21 to Wilson; 16 to Roosevelt; and 12 to Lincoln. But why take the number of *index references* instead of *the amount of page-space* as a guide to the attention given by an author to this or that individual? Did Root read the eleven books that he analyzes? If he did, why does he ignore the fact that Lincoln is actually given much more space in the Muzzey text than 12 index references would suggest? And why does he conclude that it was because Wilson and Roosevelt were Democrats that they have more index references than the Republican Coolidge and Hoover? What about the fact that they both, unlike Coolidge and Hoover, served more than one term, and that they were our presidents during the First and Second World Wars?

Other criticisms made by Root seem to say less about the textbooks in question than about his own ignorance of established procedures in the teaching of American history. He complains that the books devote more space to the period since 1870 than to the history that preceded this date. The discrepancy is not, in actual fact, as great as he makes it seem to be. But in any event, our public-school plan for the teaching of American history is an over-all plan. It provides for the stressing in elementary and junior high schools, where the highest percentage of our population is reached, of the period that covers the founding of our country, the forming of its basic institutions, and its westward growth. The post-Reconstruction period receives its heaviest stress in the senior high school—for which the eleven texts were prepared.

When it announced the forming of the Textbook Evaluation Committee, in the fall of 1958, America's Future said, "Through the textbooks used in the public schools in 'social sciences,' the progressive revolutionaries have done their most damaging work . . ." Root's book seems designed to support this presupposition rather than to make an objective appraisal of the eleven social science and history texts.

It is hard for the average teacher or average citizen to estimate the fairness and accuracy of a book that claims to expose the latent anti-Americanism in eleven other books. We do not think, however, that it would be an impossible task for small local committees of history teachers and lay citizens to make a detailed comparison of one of these eleven books—say, the Muzzey text—with what Root says about it in *Brainwashing in the High Schools*. Such a study would, we believe, yield some very useful insights into what passes as documentation when extremists of the Right undertake to derogate high school textbooks.

We will have to summarize very briefly certain other forms of attack to which our schools are now being widely subjected; and we can indicate the nature of one of these by recalling from the previous chapter the theme of the Amyx broadcast.

Assurances that most classroom teachers are loyal are combined with non-specific charges that a few subversives are at work among them: enough of these subversives, in fact, to "brainwash" the majority. Thus, a general impression is created that Communist *influence* in our public schools has reached dangerous proportions.

Closely related to this form of attack is another: the effort to turn parents against professional educators. Parents are told that their children are being "collectivized" and robbed of their individual initiative by being herded into group activities; that they are wasting time on "frills" that should be spent on basic subjects; that they are given an obscene account of sex; that they are "brainwashed" by counselors;

and that they are being subtly turned against parents, God, and country. Further, parents are encouraged to feel that educators—acting on directives from the National Education Association—have usurped a role that properly belongs to parents and that did belong to them in "the good old days": namely, that of deciding what their children should study and how they should be taught.

Finally, to an extent that few citizens seem yet to realize, our whole public school system is being put under attack, and the idea is being planted that only a return to a system that is basically private can solve our educational problems and safeguard our republic against mob rule.

In 1958, John Kasper—between jail sentences imposed for his having incited to racial violence—issued a pamphlet called, "Abolish the Public Schools! Now!" This and other publications carrying a like message have been widely distributed by White Citizens' Councils and other segregationist groups.

Allen Zoll's National Council for American Education—with which, as we have noted, E. Merrill Root was apparently associated in the 1953 period—espouses a similar anti-public-school doctrine. One of its pamphlets—"Private Schools: The Solution to America's Educational Problem"—is authored by Frank Chodorov, who was Associate Editor of *Human Events*, Washington, D.C., from 1951 to 1954. This does not call outright for the abolishing of public schools. But it proposes that citizens be given a choice between paying taxes to support a public school system and using the money, in small cooperative groups, to build a network of parent-controlled private schools. The cost of these, he suggests, could be held to a minimum by keeping their enrollments down and making each of them a part of the residence community where the students live.

It is time for Americans at large to realize that elitist

attitudes and segregationist attitudes—the two so often combined in the same individual—are fostering among us a dangerous effort to destroy our public school system altogether.

PTAs are targets of attack because of their closeness to the public school system. One part of the Radical Rightist effort, where PTAs are concerned, has to do with prying the local unit loose from its moorings in State and National Congresses of Parents and Teachers. The other part has to do with gaining control of the local unit and turning it into a pressure group—to make school administrators and classroom teachers hew to a prescribed line.

One pamphlet called *Parents Are Puppets of the PTA* will serve to illustrate the extremist effort to drive a wedge between local PTAs and the National Congress of Parents and Teachers. Incidentally, it will serve to illustrate, also, the manner in which an attack on one organization can be extended into an attack on many.

The pamphlet was issued—150,000 copies of it—in 1963, by the Tarrant County Public Affairs Forum, Fort Worth, Texas. Its quarrel with the National Congress is two-fold. First, it says that "the National PTA exists, not to do the will of its members, but as a pressure group which dictates and coerces its members into conforming." And second, it says that the program of the National Congress follows, in general, the Communist Party line.

In the course of its 23-page attack upon the National Congress, this pamphlet equates federal aid to education with federal control of education, and declares such aid to be "another extension of the Welfare State." It says that the United Nations and the League of Nations before it were "lifted directly from the Communist Manifesto"; and it denounces UNICEF, UNESCO, and WHO as Communist-controlled.

It charges, further, that the mental health movement "seeks to compel conformity in an individual's political beliefs, social attitudes and personal tastes"; and that the fluoridation of water is "politically inspired." It takes issue with a by-law of the National Congress which states that local PTAs "shall not seek to direct administrative activities of the schools or to control their policies." Finally, it asserts that the members of local units have no choice except to cooperate with and support "school policies shaped and laid down by the National Education Association in Washington . . ."

The extremist effort to win control of local PTAs—in order to pry them loose from the National body, and then use them as instruments of Rightist policy—is based on the practice of infiltration. In the September 1960 *Bulletin* of the John Birch Society, Welch issued the following instruction: "Join your local PTA at the beginning of the school year, get your conservative friends to do likewise, and go to work to take it over. . . . When you and your friends get the local PTA groups straightened out, move up the ladder as soon as you can to assert a wider influence." His concluding piece of advice seems rather remarkable in view of the above: "And don't let the dirty tactics of the opposition get you down."

One speaker at the annual convention of the National Education Association, in Seattle, on July 2, 1964, was Professor W. R. Fulton of the University of Oklahoma—a vice-president of the National Congress of Parents and Teachers. He told the audience that thirty-five state congresses have reported infiltration by extreme rightists. "In twenty states extremists are getting members elected to office—and in one state in as many as 200 units." (1)

Within each local, now, PTA members have to recognize

that those who join as infiltrators, rather than just as parents, will be bringing into the group viewpoints and practices alien to the PTA tradition. They will try to capture key positions—in particular, the office of program chairman. They will come to meetings prepared to ask loaded questions of speakers of whom they disapprove. They will, after the manner of Communist infiltrators, employ disruptive tactics to prevent the passage of motions to which they are opposed; and, again like the Communists, they will outstay other members at meetings in order to push through motions or resolutions that the majority would vote down. Not least, they will try to use PTA meetings as places to distribute materials approved by the outside group which they actually represent.

The aim of the Radical Rightists with respect to the mental health movement is not to gain control of it, but to discredit and demolish it. The natural resource that is theirs to exploit in behalf of this effort is a widespread fear of anything that seems to represent a tampering with the human mind. For many insecure, uninformed persons, the whole psychological and psychiatric enterprise seems like a black-magic invasion of the most private aspects of selfhood.

We still recall, for example, the blend of fear and fascination that we saw on the face of a woman in Dallas several years ago: a woman who planted herself directly in front of us as we came down from a lecture platform. "You're psychologists," she said. "Can you tell what I'm thinking?" We recall, likewise, how a woman in California who had opposed our speaking to a certain group refused to meet us when a mutual acquaintance urged her to do so. We might, she said, revenge ourselves by taking control of her mind.

Such extreme instances represent the nth-degree form of widespread fears that are far too real to those who suffer them for the rest of us to think them funny. They are, moreover, meshed in with the widespread fear that individual lives are being shaped and dominated by forces beyond anyone's power to comprehend or control.

To these resident fears, those who oppose the mental health movement deliberately add others. They plant the idea that the movement is Communist-inspired: that it is part of a vast, made-in-Moscow brainwashing program. They portray it as a device for sending anti-Communists to mental hospitals. They declare child guidance centers to be places where Communists and fellow travelers wean children away from their parents and from our political-religious tradition. They plant the fear that people can, against their will, have their personalities utterly changed by psychosurgery or other forms of treatment. And—inevitably, we might say, in view of the far-right line—they portray mental health services as a useless expense; a "socialistic" measure; and a scheme for promoting world government at the expense of American sovereignty.

One man who includes most of these fear-generating themes in a speech called "The Mental Health Racket" is Tom Sullivan, who is made available as a speaker by the "Free Enterprise Department" of Coast Federal Savings and Loan Association, Los Angeles. It does not seem beside the point to note that Joe Crail, President of this company and founder of its "Free Enterprise Department," is on the Board of Trustees of America's Future—sponsor of the Textbook Evaluation Committee.

The specific target of Sullivan's speech is the mental health act of the State of California: the Short-Doyle Act. Those who would like to compare the provisions of this Act with what Sullivan says about them might profitably write to the San Fernando Valley Mental Health Association, 15231 Sherman Way, Van Nuys, California, and ask for a copy of the pamphlet *The Doctors Speak Up: An Answer to Irresponsible Attacks on the Mental Health Program.*

And this brings us back to a matter to which we gave passing attention in an earlier chapter—where we were discussing Liberty Lobby. We spoke there of the fact that Kenneth Goff, master of ceremonies at the Lobby's meeting in Washington, D.C., on May 2, 1964, had authored a booklet called *Brainwashing* in which he portrays the American mental health movement as Soviet-inspired. Goff's specific thesis is to the effect that in the summer of 1935, Lavrenti P. Beria, later to become head of the NKVD—the Soviet secret police—talked to a group of American students at the Lenin School of Psychopolitical Warfare, and outlined the methods by which the American people should be softened up for a Communist take-over. This speech, Goff asserts, provided the basis for our mental health movement.

Those who authored the pamphlet mentioned above— *The Doctor Speaks Up*—report on p. 15 that they directed to the Senate Internal Security Subcommittee an inquiry about the Beria "document" on which Goff's *Brainwashing* is based. The Research Director of this Committee, in a letter dated November 13, 1961, enclosed a Memorandum about Goff's activities—as a Communist, and as an ex-Communist—and said, with reference to the speech attributed to Beria, "We have no ground to believe that this document is genuine."

Whether or not Beria ever gave the speech in question— of which Goff appears to be the sole reporter—it is hard to believe that anyone except the grossly misinformed and those with an axe to grind would contend that the American mental health movement bears any resemblance to a Communist brainwashing enterprise.

Finally, we come to the fourth target of attack: public libraries. Here again the effort of the Right extremists is a double one. They want to force the removal from the library shelves of books and periodicals that seem to them to express wrong views. And they want to insure the shelves' being stocked with books and periodicals that seem to them to express correct views. The three most frequent charges that they direct against books are that they present a favorable view of Communism; that they do not strongly support the American way of life; or that they are obscene, and tend to undermine sexual morality.

The task of finding out just what is said in every book in a major library is, of course, monumental; and the self-appointed weeders-out-of-the-objectionable resort at times to some odd short-cut methods. Like E. Merrill Root, they let index references be their guide. If certain words—like Communism, class war, revolution, and socialism—appear more times in an index than the censors think they should, the book is regarded as suspect. By this standard, J. Edgar Hoover's *Masters of Deceit* would have to be removed from the shelves. It would not be removed, of course, because the would-be censors know who Mr. Hoover is. But their rule-of-thumb standard could well mean the removal of anti-Communist books by authors with names unfamiliar to them.

Far more serious than this possibility, however, is the wish to turn the public libraries of a free country into places where no ideas will be encountered that are disapproved by this or that special segment of the population: a segment that claims to have so firm a hold on the truth that it knows what other people should and should not read.

Very serious, also, is the assumption made by self-appointed censors that their definitions of Communism, socialism, leftism, and anti-Americanism are correct and authoritative. Charges directed against individuals and groups on the basis of these definitions have often been grossly unjust. Is there any reason to think that charges directed against books would be any less so?

The fact seems to be that the Radical Rightists do not see

our present struggle against Communism as one in which we are supporting the freedom of the mind against a Party-State policy of coercive control over the mind. They see it, rather, as a struggle in which viewpoints known to be absolutely false must be defeated by their absolutely true opposites. Thus, they cannot help but view with alarm, as a threat to our national strength, any all-round presentation of ideas that might, they feel, neutralize people or infect them with doubts.

In the course of the years, many local libraries and the American Library Association have developed tools of self-defense that do not put them on the defensive. They have articulated for themselves standards to which they can firmly hold in time of need. They have established procedures with reference to book-selection. Equipped with these standards and procedures, they can turn to the public and ask for support; for their self-defense is a defense, also, of the public's right to read.

We believe, however, that an ounce of prevention could, in many cases, make unnecessary a pound of cure. It would help enormously to prevent community crises if groups such as PTAs, churches, service clubs, women's clubs, and Legion posts would, when no crisis was impending, secure from the American Library Association, 50 East Huron Street, Chicago 11, Illinois, certain key documents and make them a subject of thorough discussion.

We would suggest, for example, their securing copies of *Library Bill of Rights, Policies and Procedures for Selection of School Library Materials,* and some samples copies of the ALA's newsletter, *On Intellectual Freedom.* If the meaning of such materials could be explored, with the help of local librarians, and with disagreements brought freely into the open, in times of non-crisis—when no one was being put on the spot, when no one was fated to win or lose—there would, we feel certain, be fewer times of crisis.

Not only libraries, but all the target groups we have been discussing, have worked out codes of self-defense: procedures for the handling of attacks. We shall have more to say about these in the Conclusion of this book. Here, we will say only that we have been vastly reassured by the refusal of our schools, PTAs, mental health groups, and public libraries either to yield to extremist pressures or to adopt extremist methods in self-defense.

All these target groups have specified to their members that criticisms must be weighed before they are rejected as unjust. Likewise, they have all taken the stand that where an issue has been joined, all sides should be given a fair hearing in the open market places of the mind.

So long as these vital institutions of our free society refuse to scrap democratic procedures even in their own defense, we feel justified in believing that, under the confusions and angers of our time, there exist a deep strength and a deep faith which constitute our society's best insurance.

EIGHTEEN

SELF-PORTRAIT OF THE RADICAL RIGHTIST

C ERTAIN aspects of Radical Rightism do not become immediately clear even to the person who reads what the leaders of the movement publish. An awareness of them comes slowly, by an accumulation of evidence drawn from the printed page. In this chapter, we shall be trying to summarize a number of these; for some understanding of them is necessary to the building of a sound program for coping with the problems that such Rightism poses.

First, then, today's Right extremism is a phenomenon not covered by any of our ready-made political labels. Persons who are angry about it, but who have not explored it in detail, tend to call it *fascist*. Those who have explored it are more prone to grope for a word and then try out for size, as it were, the term *anarchic*. The paradoxical character of the movement is shown by the fact that it can inspire the application of both these terms.

It is not, properly speaking, fascist. As Webster's *New World Dictionary* points out, fascism calls for "the retention of private ownership of the means of production under centralized governmental control." This concept of the corporate state is far removed from the intense anti-governmentalism of the new Right.

Section Six of Welch's *Blue Book* gives his analysis of the governmental factor in human affairs. We would call it "must" reading; for it illumines not only his outlook but that of other leaders of the Right extreme.

Welch begins by declaring that "all known past human experience" supports his conclusions—and then proceeds to give these conclusions. Anarchy is impractical. Therefore, "some degree of government" must be tolerated. But government is "basically a non-productive expense, an overhead cost . . ." Also, it provides a natural gathering place for men with "criminal tendencies." It is "always and inevitably an enemy of individual freedom." It tends to "squeeze out the middle class." And, "by its size, its momentum, and its authority," it perpetuates evils that would otherwise be corrected.

The quality of government, according to Welch, matters more than the form. No intrinsic merit resides in government of and by the people. This may, indeed, be the type most likely to foster bureaucracy—and, therefore, tyranny. An elite may rule better, while letting the people live their own lives. Finally, what matters most is neither quality nor form, but quantity: the less government the better.

In view of this extreme anti-governmentalism, why is the far-right movement so often called fascist? Two reasons have to do with its methods. It fosters the cult of the Leader, reducing the rank-and-file to a kind of task force, to carry out directives and exert pressures at assigned points. And it openly advocates psychological strong-arm methods, such as the killing of reputations by innuendo, which easily lead on to a tolerance for and a readiness to use physical strong-arm methods.

This is what happened at the national convention of Young Republicans in 1963, in San Francisco. There, the extremists did not stop with smear tactics. They cut telephone wires, rifled filing cabinets, falsified messages, and threatened delegates with reprisals and even violence.

But a third reason why the movement is often called fascist is of a different order. There are certain areas of agreement—with respect to free trade unions, for example, and the civil rights movement—between the new Right extremists and elements in our midst that are actually fascist. In these areas, surreptitious forms of cooperation tend to develop—although any reference to them is denounced as a smear.

It is not really strange, then, that some people call today's Radical Rightism anarchic, while others call it fascist. Neither term fits the complex actuality; and we have found none that does. Our current choice, till we find a better, is *anarchic totalitarianism*—which is self-contradictory enough to cover both the Rightists' fierce objection to being controlled in any way and their readiness to control and coerce others by all expedient means.

In the second place, the Radical Rightist line—the nature of which is made plain by the resolutions adopted at one gathering after another—is not underwritten by any coherent theory. It is a product of anger, not of thought: of anger, and of a will to be on top of *some* heap. It expresses a determination to climb up and to pull down.

During the appalling eleven-minute period at the 1964 Republican National Convention when organized hoodlumism was denying to Governor Nelson Rockefeller a chance to be heard, the editor of a California newspaper studied the contorted faces of those who made up one disruptive claque. Edward P. Morgan of ABC, in his broadcast of July 15, 1964, reported this editor's comment. "It was hard to do," he said, "but they all seemed to wear happy smiles with a snarl." What he was witnessing was the expression of Radical Rightists at a moment when they were *simultaneously* climbing up and pulling down.

What adds an extra dimension of both tawdriness and horror to a performance of this type is that those who make up such a claque pretend to be serving a religion of love and a political heritage based on a Bill of Rights and an affirma tion that "all men are created equal." They have their ways of rationalizing their pretense. They assert that the "social gospel" is anti-Christian; and that the Constitution was designed primarily to safeguard property rights and to prevent the Republic from becoming a democracy. But their arguments add up to a ritual rather than to an ordered system of thought: the proof of this being the fact that their expressed dedication to our American heritage does not inhibit them at any point where expediency recommends a resort to un-American methods.

The more we have studied the published output of the Right extremists, indeed, the more convinced we have become that their thinking is too compartmentalized, and too full of inner contradictions, to support any coherent theory, new or inherited.

Thus, for example, Welch professes to abhor strong centralized government equipped with police powers. Yet he has expressed warm admiration for Franco, Batista, Trujillo, and Salazar. His admiration of these men simply lives in a different compartment of his mind from the one in which he keeps his abhorrence of strong centralized government.

It lives in the compartment inhabited by his contempt for democracy, his advocacy of the *Leader* principle, his feeling that the masses and lesser breeds best exhibit a high sense of responsibility by obeying the dictates of those who know what is best for them, and his conviction that property rights are the highest form of human rights. His admiration of strong-man government is of the same stuff, in short, as his will to construct the John Birch Society as a monolith.

Again, he denounces bureaucracy as an evil machinery for the invasion of private lives. But as head of the John Birch Society, he equips himself with a bureaucracy charged with the task of keeping tab on individuals. On p. 128 of *The Blue Book*, after defining the tasks to be performed by the Society's Coordinators and Major Coordinators, he writes, ". . . and we shall further build the organizational frame-work from the bottom up, as made necessary by sufficient membership, in order to keep strict and careful control of what every chapter is doing, and even every member of every chapter so far as the effective work of the John Birch Society is concerned."

Such compartmentalized thinking seems ubiquitous on the far Right. Thus, all Radical Rightists object with fervor to governmental trespass upon the private sector of the economy. They are quick to denounce, for example, as unconstitutional any law that requires a restaurant owner to serve customers without regard to race. As a private owner, they contend, he has an unalienable right to choose his own customers, to decide whom he will and will not serve. But we are yet to find even one instance of their objecting to any state law that *forbids* restaurants to serve both whites and Negroes. By their standards, a private owner who would like to serve both, who would like to treat people as people, has no unalienable right to choose his own customers, to decide whom he will and will not serve. This privilege of decision uniquely belongs to those who choose not to serve Negroes.

A third point about the Radical Right follows logically from this second one: namely, that its aggressiveness is more than matched by its self-defensiveness—because its strength is more than matched by its weakness. We do not mean its numerical weakness, but something more deep and intrinsic.

Because his thinking is compartmentalized and self-contradictory, the Right extremist cannot afford to let one lobe of his brain, so to speak, know what the other is doing. He cannot afford to have his self-contradictions pulled out into the open, where they would meet one another. Therefore, he cannot afford to engage in a back-and-forth exchange of ideas in the open market places of the mind.

Again, because his thinking is so largely generated out of anger and ambition, the Radical Rightist cannot afford to let objective facts speak for themselves. On the Right extreme, as on the Communist Left, facts must be coerced into proving what is to be proved.

We used to think that the inability of the Radical Rightist to admit error—to say *mea culpa*, and be done with it—was just an individual matter: a normal expression, we might say, of emotional insecurity. But we have had to modify this belief—to take account of the extent to which the pattern of defensiveness is standardized all across the Right extreme.

Each Rightist, certainly, acts as an individual and puts the stamp of his personality upon the standardized pattern of defensiveness. But we have been forced to conclude that the Radical Rightist movement is made up of leaders and followers who have acquired a common vested interest in defending as unquestionable truth a structure of ideas that will not stand critical examination.

It is, we believe, this need to defend a structure of ideas that cannot stand alone, and that cannot stand any rough-and-ready encounter with reality, that accounts for the Radical Rightists' singularly standardized overreaction to criticism: their "dirty, filthy lie" reaction; their quick retreat into martyrdom; their exaggerated determination to demolish the critic.

We believe that it accounts, too, for their hit-and-run tactics: for the way they walk out of a meeting, for example, if a speaker is not bowled over by their surprise attack, rather than stay and engage in an open matching of evidence and ideas.

Further, it seems to account for the way they shift ground and attack from another angle whenever one of their "fully documented" charges is refuted by firm evidence. The importance which the Radical Rightists attach to *never being proved wrong* is quite extraordinary. It is as though they feared that even one admission of error might breach their defenses.

Finally, it seems to account for the odd way in which the Right extremists choose—or, if need be, create—"experts" and "leading authorities." All that they really demand of an "authority," it would appear, is a power and willingness to make facts do what they should: to make them support foregone conclusions. If such an authority happens to have a gimmick—like Lowman's Compilations, or Welch's annual American Opinion Scoreboard—to add weight to his words, so much the better.

Sometimes a person's chief qualification as an expert seems to be the training he does not have. All that is required of him is that he represent some group that the Rightists are setting over against some derogated professional group. In their attacks on the schools, for example, as we noted in the preceding chapter, the Rightists are trying to set parents against educators. At the February 1964 meeting of the American Coalition of Patriotic Societies, in Washington, D.C., one speaker was introduced in a way that precisely supported this effort. Myers Lowman, introducing Mrs. Harry

Alexander, of Mississippi—who was to speak on Communist influences in textbooks—stressed the fact that she was not an educator or, with the word turned into a slur on the National Education Association, an *educationist*; she was "a fine mother and grandmother."

The most highly valued authority on the far Right, however, is the person who makes facts do what they should and who, at some past time, had some unusual access to information: as a member of the Communist Party, as an investigator, or as an informant. In such cases, the individual's past experience is simply carried forward as a permanently valid reason to believe what he says about current situations: even about situations with which he has had no contact.

In mid-December 1963, for example, the John Birch Society published in various leading newspapers a full-page advertisement headed THE TIME HAS COME. In this, it laid down the line, now standard on the far Right, that President Kennedy was assassinated as part of a Communist plot. "It has been pointed out," the advertisement announced, "by Hon. Martin Dies, since the assassination, that 'Lee Harvey Oswald was a Communist,' and that when a Communist commits murder he is acting under orders." There is nothing in this statement to distinguish it from one that might have been made by John Doe. There is nothing to suggest that Mr. Dies had any special access to the facts of the Oswald case. Yet the above quote has been used all across the extreme Right, not only as proof of a Communist plot, but as proof so absolute that all contrary estimates of the assassination—even though based on a most careful weighing of evidence—are ruled out as Communist-inspired.

When we put together all the standardized forms of defense that the Right extremists provide for their structure of proof and logic, we are forced to conclude that this structure must be a very flimsy affair. If these extremists cannot make their type of documentation stick; if they cannot preserve all the separate charges that support their supercharge of conspiracy in high places, they stand to lose everything. Having built a house of cards, they cannot let anyone pull out a card on which other cards rest—lest the whole come tumbling down.

This extreme vulnerability of the Radical Right was made strikingly evident in 1961. In that year, a number of speeches were given, over the country, on the subject of Communism and the churches by William C. Sullivan of the FBI: the same William Sullivan whom the Birch Society's *American Opinion* undertook to demolish because of his expressed wish to eradicate the social injustices that encourage Communism. He is identified in the Bureau's public-information pamphlet, *Know Your FBI,* as Assistant Director in charge of the Domestic Intelligence Division. His public biography indicates that he has been in the Bureau for twenty-four years.

We think that most Americans would, like ourselves, take it for granted that Mr. Sullivan's sources of information would be more accurate than most and that he would not talk in public without being sure of his facts. But so far as the Radical Rightists were concerned, "one William C. Sullivan" committed an unforgivable sin: he declared the Communist infiltration of Protestant churches to be less than the Rightist line requires it to be. His data, therefore, had to be discredited; and he had to be demolished. It was reported to us from Phoenix, Arizona, after he spoke there, that one furious woman declared, "We'll force Mr. Hoover to fire this Sullivan person."

We do not know just when the published reaction began. The earliest item we saw was by Carl McIntire in the *Christian Beacon* of May 25, 1961. Not for a moment did McIntire entertain the possibility that Mr. Sullivan might know what he was talking about. Instead, he reemphasized the Rightist line with respect to infiltration of the churches and National Council of Churches. This, in effect, was what had to be true; so the problem to be dealt with was simply that of explaining away Mr. Sullivan's offering of evidence that seemed to challenge this line.

In the end, declaring it to be "a known fact that the National Council of Churches has had an inside track with the Kennedy Administration," McIntire settled for concluding that the FBI had been put under heavy pressure not to report any findings that would make it difficult for this administration "to get along properly with Nikita Khrushchev."

The August 1961 *Beacon Light Herald,* pp. 5–6, carried an article by "THE TRUMPETER," which was reproduced and sent out by the American National Book News, Wilkes-Barre, Pennsylvania. This quoted Mr. Sullivan as saying that "the Communist party has NOT achieved any substantial success in exerting domination, control or influence over America's clergymen or religious institutions on a National scale." But except for quoting this and another sentence or two, the article did not bother with Mr. Sullivan. "Was Rep. Francis E. Walters' 'Retirement,'" it asked, "direful prelude to J. Edgar Hoover's debut as TURNCOAT?"—and proceeded to conclude that this was the case; and that nothing was left for those who wanted to continue to fight Communism except to go "'UNDERGROUND'—just the way others, in countries outside our borders, were forced 'UNDERGROUND.'"

But the most elaborate effort we have seen to demolish Mr. Sullivan was authored by Edgar C. Bundy and sent out as an 8-page *Special Report to All Church League Members.* And here, as always, Bundy's way of building a case against a person who is to be demolished is worth examining.

First, he accuses Mr. Sullivan of saying that "there has been no Communist infiltration of or influence on American churches"; but he gives no direct quote to this effect, and we very much doubt that he could. Mr. Sullivan, at least, makes no statement that even resembles this, or that could be thus interpreted, in one speech that dates from this 1961 period— and of which we have a copy.

This speech, entitled "Communism and Religion in the United States," was given at the Highland Park Methodist Church, Dallas, Texas, on October 19, 1961; and was later reproduced in quantity by the Church and sold at cost: 4¢ a copy. In it, speaking as a professional, Mr. Sullivan worked his way through one phase of the subject after another. He dealt with the irreconcilability of Communism and religion, as documented in Communist writings from Marx to Khrushchev; the tactics employed by Communists in their efforts to "capture" churches and clergymen; and what they had hoped to gain, through the years, by all this effort. Then he went on to discuss the *extent* of Communist success in infiltrating the clergy; and we would guess that Bundy's perturbation stemmed from what was said at this point.

Communist infiltration and influence with respect to the churches and clergy, Mr. Sullivan said, should be viewed in historical perspective. They were at their height when Communist Party membership and Communist influence throughout our society were likewise at their height, "in the late 1930's and during and just after World War II . . .

"Since the late 1940's, Communist influence within the churches and among the clergy has waned . . ." We might note that this fact is confirmed, however unintentionally, by Myers G. Lowman. When we were working on his compilations, we picked fifteen pages by opening the books at random; took down the dates of "items of public record" on these pages; and plotted the curve of distribution. The resultant graph would support Mr. Sullivan's statement that Communist influence "within the churches and among the clergy has waned" since the late 1940's.

"In view of the great amount of time and money communists have spent propagandizing the American clergy," Mr. Sullivan continued, "it is a remarkable tribute to them that they have resisted so successfully." Ministers who have wittingly or unwittingly served the Communist cause have always been, he asserted, a very small percentage of the "300,000 ordained clergymen in the United States . . ." Moreover, most of those who have been known to be Communists or pro-Communists have been removed from their posts by their churches or denominations.

"To recapitulate, it can be stated factually and without equivocation that any allegation is false which holds that there has been and is, on a national scale, an extensive or substantial infiltration of the American clergy, in particular the Protestant clergy."

This statement could, if widely credited, make Bundy's ongoing enterprise of "exposures" look downright absurd. Hence, since the statement could not be disproved, Mr. Sullivan had to be discredited. Bundy's *Report* can best be understood as a full-scale *argumentum ad hominum.*

First, as we have noted, Bundy attributes to Mr. Sullivan a statement so patently false as to bring into question the competence and good faith of anyone who would make it. Thus, he provides himself with an opponent who is not Mr. Sullivan but a straw man of dubious qualifications and intent.

Next, he asserts that "Christians everywhere" should realize "that Mr. William C. Sullivan is not a Protestant and knows nothing whatever of the conditions existing in Protestantism." This argument deserves a prize for sheer silliness. Must we say that Mr. Sullivan, head of Domestic Intelligence in the FBI, is not a member of the Communist Party and knows nothing whatever of what goes on inside the Party?

In addition to being silly, moreover, the argument is funny; for in the Foreword to *Collectivism in the Churches*, Bundy takes exactly the opposite stand. Defending John T. Flynn, who had "revealed certain collectivist trends in Protestant churches," he roundly condemns as left-wingers those who said that Flynn, being a Catholic, was "incompetent to judge what was going on in the Protestant world." *Bundy vs. Bundy.*

Finally, to deliver the *coup de grace*, Bundy quotes two passages from J. Edgar Hoover. One is from an article, "God or Chaos?" which appeared in *Redbook Magazine*. Except that the italics are Bundy's, although he does not say so, this article begins, "*Many* communist fronts have operated under the guise of some church commission or religious body. It is ghastly to see the monster atheism nourished *in the churches* which it seeks to destroy." But this article appeared in 1949. Mr. Sullivan said, in 1961, "Since the late 1940's, communist influence within the churches and among the clergy has waned . . ."

In January 1962, the *Christian Herald* published an article by Mr. Hoover, entitled, "Let's Fight Communism Sanely!" It begins: "The Communist Party today is waging an aggressive campaign against all sectors of American national life. A foremost objective is the religious life of this Nation—our religious leaders and groups. This campaign, following historic Marxist-Leninist principles, can be expected to continue with unabated zeal."

But Mr. Hoover goes on to say, "Over all, the Party has not had marked success in its attacks against the church. The Communists have found in religion a foe of the greatest tenacity, able to withstand the withering fire-power of Marxist-Leninist chicanery. The overwhelming majority of America's clergy are loyal citizens, devoted to working for the best interests of the Nation . . .

"Americans can be truly thankful for the magnificent contribution which these men have made to our national life."

Now we turn to the second quote Bundy brings in. "The most important testimony of Mr. Hoover, and the most recent," he writes, "was given to the House of Representatives Sub-Committee on Appropriations on March 6, 1961 . . . in which testimony he states on p. 435: 'They (the communists) have infiltrated every conceivable sphere of activity: youth groups, television, radio and motion picture industries, *church* and school, educational and cultural groups, the press, nationality minority groups and civil and political units.' " Bundy does not say so, but it is he who italicizes the word *church*. If we remove from this word the artificial emphasis which he, not Mr. Hoover, has imposed upon it, the church becomes simply one of the multiple groups designated as Communist targets. It does not stand out as having been infiltrated to any exceptional degree.

In conclusion, Bundy writes, "The Church League of America strongly advises its supporters not to go off on tangents or into 'the wild blue yonder' when they hear or read statements by ministers, press agents of the National Council, or even an F.B.I. agent, who may not know what he is talking about."

But again, of course, he may. It does not seem altogether improbable that the Assistant Director of the FBI, in charge of Domestic Intelligence, is as well informed as Edgar C. Bundy. As we have noted in earlier contexts, Bundy's own documentation is not always such as to inspire confidence.

What primarily interests us here, however, is not Bundy's opinion of William C. Sullivan. We have used the responses made to Mr. Sullivan's speeches by McIntire, "THE TRUMPETER," and Bundy only to illustrate the odd fact that, so far as the Radical Right is concerned, nothing can be worse than for things to get better.

One whole section of the extremists' house of cards is built on the interminably reiterated assumption that Communist infiltration of and influence on the Protestant clergy and the National and World Councils of Churches are of massive proportions. Therefore, not Mr. William C. Sullivan, nor even Mr. J. Edgar Hoover, can be permitted to pull out this key card that supports other cards. By the Radical Rightist code, it is better to destroy public confidence in the FBI than to permit the FBI to render more rickety than it already is a "necessary" proof that Communist influence is rampant in high places.

This is one of those points at which Right extremism shows how sharply divergent it is from both conservatism and plain average Americanism. Most Americans can believe that Communism is a threat that must be taken seriously without seeing it as in control of any major sector of our society. Most Americans, again, would welcome trustworthy evidence that church leaders—or educators, or labor leaders, or business men, or government officials—had been learning the score and making it harder than it once was for Communists to infiltrate our institutions. But the Radical Rightists come so far from being able to welcome any such evidence that they feel impelled to demolish the person who presents it.

We said in an earlier chapter that the Radical Rightists' view of the world is "doom-shaped." Here, we would add that they have a vested interest in keeping it so. A sense of impending disaster is their most marketable ware. An understanding of this fact is vital to an understanding of their line and their tactics.

THE TASK AHEAD OF US

We are venturing to inject, here, a personal note. Eleven years have passed since we undertook to make the study of Communism our chief preoccupation. During these years, the overwhelming proportion of the reading we have done has been in this field; and we have, also, given ourselves as many chances as possible to talk with persons who could supplement what we had learned from the printed page with what they had learned by long scholarship, intimate contact with special problems, or experience within the Party or the orbit.

Several years ago, for example, we traveled what might be called the Iron-Bamboo crescent from West Berlin to Hong Kong. As we write, we feel surrounded, as it were, by a cloud of witnesses: Polish, Czech, and Lithuanian refugees with whom we talked in London and Paris; East Germans with whom we talked in West Berlin, Nuremberg, and Munich; Hungarian students in Vienna; Bulgarian sailors in Turkey; Tibetan refugees in India; North Vietnamese in South Vietnam; and refugees from Red China in Hong Kong.

In their remembered presence, we are not inclined to speak lightly of the world's sorrow or of the totalitarian power that authored their homelessness. But neither are we inclined to dismiss as relatively unimportant that extremism of the Right which, at so many points, apes the methods of Communism.

Quite explicitly, in fact, we have been moved to write this book by our study of Communism. This study has convinced us that unless we Americans get down to the task of appraising what extremist methods, of the Left or Right, lead to in the way of human sorrow and an erosion of the moral sense, we stand to lose the best that the centuries have given us.

As matters now stand, what are we called upon to do? If we were to give a covering answer before getting down to specifics, it would be this: we need to release a grassroots ingenuity with respect to certain problems. In matters that range from material production to social institutions, we have been a nation of tinkerers: a nation of people who have liked to fit things together so that they will work. The word *tinkerer* may not sound impressive; but the results of what it stands for are impressive indeed.

Many differences between our system and the Soviet one have been stressed; but one difference has, we think, been too little noticed. We can illustrate it by recalling from Part I that when Stalin wanted to start the Soviet automotive industry, he bought the equipment ready-made, with blueprints and spare parts, from Henry Ford for $30,000,000.

All that he needed to get going, we might say, was delivered to him more than thirty years ago. Yet today Soviet production of cars, trucks, and tractors lags far behind that of the West; and the harvesting of crops is hampered, year after year, by farm machinery's standing idle for lack of repairs and parts. Khrushchev might well ask, in the words of the rich young man in the Bible, "What lack I yet?"

After the war, the Soviet Union carted off and reassembled on its own soil the factories of a conquered East Zone of Germany. By way of plans purloined under cover of war, it exploited the know-how of German scientists to put into orbit the first Sputnik. Today, it is acting to buy, ready-made, entire chemical factories from England.

The Communists tell the underdeveloped countries that they have the formula for a quick advance from backwardness to industrial strength. In plain fact, this formula has been that of the theft or purchase of the ready-made: the ready-made plan, product, and factory. With such a short-cut, they should, it would seem, be well ahead of the game. Instead, all across the board, their rate of economic growth is slowing down. What lack they yet?

We would say that they lack what Henry Ford learned in the process of tinkering the Model T into existence. They lack the experience of starting in the small. They lack the experience of learning by doing. They lack the experience of having their entire country become a kind of material and social workshop in which people face up to problems.

Lenin asked the wrong gift from the genie that emerged from the long corked-up bottle of revolution. He asked for the gigantic: Give me heavy industry, all at once. Give me an all-embracing political structure, ruled from the top down. Worshipers of the mammoth—whether in factory, acreage of wheat, or political organization—Lenin and his successors have planned on a vast scale and have despised the small. Therefore, they have not developed a people whose minds and fingers just naturally take hold of things and set about finding out what can be done with them.

The history of our country has been that of starting in the small and tinkering our way toward the large. Long before our Constitution was drafted, the burghers of Watertown, Connecticut, signed their village charter: "Our intention is to sitt down here close togither." We were a nation of thirteen states before we were a nation of fifty. Back of every major industry are the workshop tinkerers. Back of a myriad established practices are the neighbors who have talked things over, the committees, the voluntary groups in which two or three—or twenty or thirty, or two or three hundred— have been gathered together to wrestle with a problem.

In making this contrast between our own history and that of the Soviet Union, we have not been angling away from the subject of this chapter: the task ahead of us. We have been giving the reason why we believe that the problem of extremism, of the Left and the Right, can be handled in a way that strengthens our country only by turning local ingenuity loose on certain problems and asking it to come up with some answers: partial answers; experimental answers that can invite to further experiment.

Robert Welch spelled out in *The Blue Book*, as we noted in Chapter Seven, what he would do if he were the " 'man on the white horse' on our side in this war" and had enough "accepted authority over one million dedicated supporters" that he could coordinate their activities "with some degree of positiveness and efficiency approaching the coordination by the Communists of their members and fellow travelers."

Our own first act, if we were in the position he describes, would be to get down off the white horse. Then we would want to put four problems to whoever happened to be around; and we would ask them to get busy on these by means of those "debating society methods" that Welch despises.

We would hope that some high-school students might be on hand, and college students. There should be PTAers, librarians, teachers, and women from the AAUW. There should be men from the various service clubs, and from the

Chamber of Commerce and the American Legion. We would want people from the Federated Women's Clubs and the DAR; from nationality groups; from Protestant and Catholic churches and Jewish temples; from the Urban League, the YMCA and YWCA, the Disabled Veterans, mental health groups, press clubs, the NAACP, organizations of "senior citizens," labor unions; and from that blessed *etcetera* that can be stretched to cover all groups that believe in the processes of freedom as well as the pronouncements.

We would say to whoever happened to be on hand as part of this goodly company: We do not know your community as you know it. We do not know its resources, or who there is in it who knows what. But there are four questions to which answers need to be found to make our country's future secure; and we wish you would, in very practical terms, start looking for them.

How can we strengthen the liberal-conservative—or conservative-liberal—center, so that we can not only afford our extremisms but can afford to defend the rights of the extremists as we would defend our own?

How can we begin to build throughout our land the kind of bedrock, accurate knowledge about the aims and tactics of Communism that will make for a strong imperviousness to the Party line?

How can we prevent extremism of the Right from eroding our freedoms and making us afraid of one another, while we also work to draw as many individual extremists as possible back into the liberal-conservative center?

How can we learn to talk about this country, and what we have that is enormously worth preserving and developing: talk about it in quiet ways, factual ways, that will send tingles up the spine?

Is there any reason, we would ask our representatives of community groups, why you cannot, cooperatively, get busy where you are, answering these questions with what you have to work with—and with such help as you want to ask from outside sources?

We have put the first question first—the one about strengthening the center of our society—because we believe that the closer we come to answering this question, the better equipped we are to answer the others. The extent to which the liberal and conservative elements in our national strength have become strangers to each other, in recent decades, and mutually on the defensive, is simply not good for the common welfare.

"Some ages," remarks C. S. Lewis, in *The Screwtape Letters*, "are lukewarm and complacent. . . . Other ages, of which the present is one, are unbalanced and prone to faction." And he goes on to say that in such a period each faction tends to become exclusive; to feed on self-admiration; and to direct hostility outward "without shame because the 'Cause' is its sponsor and it is thought to be impersonal."

We can readily see how this applies to the Left and Right extremes. But a more profound danger to our country lies in the extent to which it applies also to the liberal-conservative center. If the balance-makers have lost their balance, wherewith shall our society be held upright?

We are not thinking, here, of a formal movement for getting liberals and conservatives together. Such a movement would only make them self-conscious and prone to platitude. We are thinking of something as informal as the Caucus Race in *Alice in Wonderland*: that race in which everyone started from where he was, and ran as fast and far as he could; and in which all got prizes.

We would like to see a grassroots effort on the part of responsible liberals and conservatives, and liberal and conservative groups, simply to move toward each other and ask, "What is it, really, that is deeply worrying you about how things are going? What is it in my attitude, as you understand it, that seems to you to be unrealistic and dangerous?"

The issues that we have spoken of in this book—those that we have had repetitively to refer to in connection with the Radical Rightist line—are real issues. The growth of federal power, the processes of foreign aid, the role of the United Nations, the civil rights movement, the shortcomings of our schools: all these are important. The point is that they are too important and too complex to be reduced to stereotypes— with the pronouncement of these stereotypes ritualistically accompanied by the naming of "subversive" villains who are responsible for whatever has gone wrong.

It is time for liberals and conservatives together, at the community level, to start talking out these issues—to discover how much they agree and how much they disagree; and how much they both have still to learn in order to be able to talk accurate, responsible good sense.

No one has yet found an answer to the second question: the question of how Americans, young and old, can be moved to learn enough about the realities of Communist aims and tactics that their informed minds will be freedom's best safe-guard. As a matter of fact, the need for this type of learning seems always to be slipping out of our consciousness: to be crowded out by other matters, or pushed out by our own wish-thinking.

This was brought vividly home to us within the past year at a convention we attended. The convening organization has been harassed by the Radical Right to a point where it has become, almost of necessity, preoccupied with holding its own against irresponsible attacks and against the pressures brought to bear upon its local units. We discussed with vari-ous members the double problem of becoming informed about the tactics of the Radical Right and those of the Communist Left; and we found them to be surprised that we brought up the latter subject.

Three years ago, to our knowledge, this group was more actively concerned with the study of Communism than it is now. We asked several key members why this was so. Their answers seemed to come out of a perplexed vagueness, and were to the general effect that they guessed they had all thought that things were "getting better."

It seems that every time we get even a slight measure of assurance that Party membership has declined or that the infiltration of this or that group has not reached the horrendous proportions announced by the Right extremists, we translate this assurance into permission to relax and forget the problem. It is easy to do so; for the Communists that infiltrate groups obviously do not announce their presence, and people of good will and common sense are embarrassed to keep looking for the invisible.

But if it is irresponsible nonsense for Hurst Amyx to say that most of the teachers in Arizona have been "brainwashed" by subversives among them; or for Hargis to say that the whole civil rights movement has been "instigated by the Communists"; or for Dr. Charles Poling to say that "Practically all our National Council leaders . . . have been following the Communist line," it is also nonsense for the rest of us to forget that even one dedicated Communist, working to promote the Party line within one American institution, is one too many.

It is morally and intellectually shabby for Edgar C. Bundy to give himself a straw man as an opponent by attributing to Assistant Director William C. Sullivan of the FBI the patently inaccurate remark that "there has been no Communist infiltration of or influence on American churches." But it is scarcely less so for any churchman to quote Mr.

Sullivan so selectively as to make it seem that there is no longer any need to worry about Communist infiltration of the churches.

Both Mr. Sullivan and Mr. Hoover have had reassuring things to say about the *extent* of Communist infiltration of the churches. But neither has ever, to our knowledge, voiced this reassurance without also warning that the churches are an everlasting target of Communist effort. If a person prefers a different authority on this subject, he can read the Communist publications, *The Worker* and *Political Affairs.* These contain constant reminders that, while the spirit of religion and that of Marxism are irreconcilable, religion is a "social force"—and that it will, in Communist parlance, be a force of "reaction" if it is not properly directed.

Personally, we believe that the reason why it has been so hard to get a nationwide, fact-centered study of Communism under way is that the people who could best sponsor and plan such a study to fit the resources of given communities have not been clearly asked to do so. To our minds, these people would be representatives of our established local voluntary groups, working together.

The Right extremists have tried to channel into our communities their special dogma to the effect that the danger of Communism comes almost wholly from internal subversion. They have tried to channel into our communities their blurred definition of Communism. But they have actually discouraged their followers from studying the subject in depth—for they have wanted them to believe that all that anyone really needs to know is to be found in books and publications that present the Radical Rightist viewpoint on domestic and foreign policies.

Not only do they fail to teach, in any adequate sense, the history of Communism or the ideology, but they fail to give even the rudiments of the current Party line. We have not found in any of their writings, for example, a fact-giving analysis of the vitally important new Communist Manifesto of 1960, the tactical agreement drawn up by the Parties of the world in their crucial Moscow gathering.

Again, even though the Radical Rightists harp on the subject of internal subversion, they provide their followers with no facts at all about how the Sino-Soviet conflict has been transferred to our soil—so that two branches of the Party are putting into competition, here, their different versions of "useful" trouble-making. They protest Communist speakers' being permitted to appear on college platforms; but they offer no analysis of how these Party planters-of-ideas put a speech together to accomplish what the current Party line calls for. In short, they simultaneously fail to teach about Communism and lull a host of persons into thinking they have learned about it.

Many responsible organizations have encouraged schools to teach about Communism and have provided plans and materials. We will include some of these in a list of sources for materials at the end of this book. But schools exist in communities; and all too often teachers have either been made to feel "subversive" if they tackle the subject at all or have been put under heavy pressure to do a grossly slanted job of dealing with it.

We are convinced that the time has come to take the problem to the grassroots: to ask local groups to get together and come up with a plan with which they can *make a start* toward getting people in their community to study the subject. From this start, they can learn how to proceed.

They can get plenty of help from outside groups—from the American Bar Association's Committee on Education Against Communism, for example. But outsiders cannot— except when they are asked to help out with special projects —move in to do the job. Local resources have to be sized up,

and built up—with as many solid groups as possible cooperatively involved. And incidentally, since one problem is
always that of people's having enough time to read, we
would emphasize the value of using the time and talents of
those who have time: retired people, and the disabled. Another problem is always that of having sound materials to
read. The local librarian is the logical guide, here.

Next comes the highly practical question of how local
groups can best handle attacks from the Radical Right.
Drawing on our own experience, and on that of experienced
church leaders, educators, librarians, PTAers, leaders of the
mental health movement, and others, we will venture the
following suggestions.

Do not wait until an attack has been made on your group
before you begin to let other community groups know the
nature of your program. Where intergroup communication is
soundly established, false charges are not likely to be
credited; and support can be rallied when necessary.

Do not angrily dismiss criticism without weighing it for
whatever merit it may have. Much as we deplore their
methods, the Radical Rightists are not wrong on every
count; and the rest of us are by no means faultless. To
acknowledge error is as important as to refuse to let unjust
criticism pass unchallenged.

Keep the line of communication open between your group
and the press. We voice this as a heartfelt imperative; for we
have had many occasions to learn that the press can be a
tower of strength to the person or group that is unjustly
attacked—*if* the person or group does not sound abused or
dodge questions. The press likes facts. Give them.

If an attack on your group seems serious enough to bother
about, take the discussion of it into the open market places
of the mind—with as many citizens as possible present and

with both sides represented. Again, we speak from experience: the American public, like the American press, can be a tower of strength. But it wants facts—and *should* want them.

If your group is attacked by a virtually autonomous unit of a national organization, do not talk as though the whole organization were back of the attack. Our experience has been that the best thing to do is to refer the problem to the national and get advice on how to handle it. Often, the national will help with the handling—once it is convinced that you have a case.

If you recognize that certain individuals have joined your group as infiltrators, give them work to do that will make them acquainted with the complexities of problems that their own groups have been oversimplifying. After all, we are not trying either to ostracize or to liquidate the Right extremists. The never-to-be-forgotten hope is that most of them will, sooner or later, come home to the liberal-conservative center.

Challenge irresponsible methods openly and firmly. Ask the extremists to fill their generalities with specific content; to say what their statistics and percentages mean; to explain their use of quotes so taken out of context as to misrepresent their meaning; to explain their use of loaded implications. And make this whole process of asking as public as possible at the community level: not to show off, but because the public needs to become familiar with the extremist tactics.

Require that all charges be put into writing and signed. If, for example, as a program chairman, you are subjected to pressures designed to force you to cancel some lecture, require that the charges against the speaker be in writing. And make sure that the speaker is given a chance to answer them before you make your decision. Weakening to avoid controversy invites more chances to weaken to avoid controversy; and that is about all that it accomplishes.

If free speakers are offered to your group, ask for a statement about whom they represent and a brief summary of what they intend to say.

If your organization handles printed materials—as a school or library does—have established procedures for the selection of these materials and for the weighing of criticisms with respect to them; and *hold to these procedures.*

Also, have established procedures in your group for the permitting of announcements and the passing out of materials; for the introduction of resolutions and a vote upon them at a later meeting, not the same meeting; for the closing of meetings; and for any other matters that experience shows to be necessary in order to avoid letting trouble-makers take over; and *hold to these procedures.* The infiltrators cannot object to being treated like everyone else; and there is no reason why they should be treated differently.

These are only suggestions—passed on for what they are worth. Actually, every individual and every group has to learn by experience how to handle unjust attacks. We can only say that we have become very sure of a few things: that there is no need, for example, to become shrill in answering an attack; and that it always pays to trust the American public.

We approach our final question—that of how we can learn to talk about freedom, and about our country—with a certain shyness; for here again we are going to venture to inject a personal note. We have had the happy experience, over the past five years, of talking to various international student groups abroad about freedom and what it means: groups made up largely of young people from Asia and Africa; and made up largely, we might add, of young people with skepticism in their eyes.

We say that the experience has been a happy one; and it has. But also it has been a *testing* experience: one that has called into play all our lifelong caring about the American adventure, and all our ingenuity. We do not offer what we say here as a formula for others to follow. We can only affirm that we have learned, by trial and error, that we best penetrate the skepticism of such young people and reach through to their concern about the future of their homelands when we come up to the subject of freedom, as it were, on the bias.

Also, we feel that we have succeeded best, not when we have told them about the values of our free society, but when they, in the end, have told themselves that the ways of freedom are better than those of dictatorship. Even at the risk, then, of seeming to claim more accomplishment than we mean to claim, we wish to report what we have tried that has, we think, worked reasonably well; for we have tried variations of the same approach with American audiences, young and old, and have enjoyed their thinking along with us, too.

First, then, we have asked the students from Asia and Africa to put a proper value upon the fact that they are members of the first generation of the era of independence in their countries; and we have quoted to them from a tablet that memorializes certain heroes of American independence: "Here the men of Boston proved themselves able and courageous freemen, worthy to raise issues that were to concern the welfare and happiness of millions yet unborn."

Working from this quote, we have asked them to consider with us the importance of a country's making, at the very start, sound decisions about six issues that no country can evade. And to get the discussion under way, we have framed these issues as questions.

How do you intend, in your country, to handle human differences of opinion—since they can be neither wished nor coerced out of existence?

How do you intend to provide for *orderly* change—since change will take place, whether or no?

What concept of law do you intend to incorporate in institution and habit system? Is law to be a tool by means of which the already powerful maintain and increase their power; or is it going to be something by which even the powerful are bound?

How do you propose to release your country's finest resource: the inborn capacities and ingenuities of your people?

What proportion of your people do you intend to have participate in the social process; and by what means?

And, finally, what pattern of centralized and decentralized powers do you want to work out as a safeguard against chaos, on the one hand, and tyranny, on the other?

It has been a heartening and humbling experience, on a number of occasions, to watch skeptical eyes turn thoughtful as young minds have wrestled with these ancient, always-new issues in relation to the future of their own countries. And what has impressed us most, in the end, has been the extent to which these Asian and African students have made it unnecessary for us to put the case for freedom—by putting it themselves.

One by-product of these experiences, one bonus which they have netted us on each separate occasion, has been a deeper gratitude for the kind of sendoff that America's founders gave our country as it entered upon the venture of independence. This gratitude dictates, as it were, five things that we want to say before we bring this book to its close; and, oddly enough, they all begin with the phrase: *Don't be afraid . . .*

Don't be afraid to quote words that have splendor in them. It is a great thing to have back of us, in the line of Western culture, a Socrates who said, with his life at stake, "An unexamined life is not worth the living." It is a great thing to be indebted to Jesus for his saying, "Whatsoever ye would that men should do to you, do ye even so unto them." It is a great thing, when the going gets rough, to have Milton for company: "Though all the winds of doctrine were let loose to play upon the earth, so Truth be in the field, we do ingloriously, by licensing and prohibiting, to misdoubt her strength. Let her and Falsehood grapple: who ever knew Truth put to the worse in a free and open encounter?" It is a great thing to hear Lincoln's reminding voice: "Let us bind up the nation's wounds."

If we were to voice our basic concern about today's schooling—humbly, knowing how tough the problems are that educators have to cope with—it would be to this effect: that young people are not being required to memorize enough of the great words of our tradition so that they will have, all their lives, the supportive companionship of these words when they need them. Our Declaration of Independence; the Gettysburg address: these, and other statements—many of them a single sentence, or a single line of poetry—are what the individual needs most when, in a crowded world, he stands alone with a crisis of the spirit.

Don't be afraid of controversy. It is the stuff of freedom—and it can have many a happy ending. There is no way to believe in freedom of speech and press and religion, and in the two-party system, and, at the same time, avoid issues.

Don't be afraid to say that some types of action are outside the pale. In recent months, for example, the Ku Klux Klans have achieved, in various areas and various minds, a type of quasi-respectability that lawless, secret brutality never deserves. It would be a healthy thing for America if every person who has felt inclined to tolerate terrorist tactics, or to let the terrorists do a type of dirty work that he vaguely wants to have done, were to say to himself, in honest self-confrontation, "I am the kind of person who does not mind having helpless people beaten up, or even killed, by gangs that play safe by hiding their own identity."

Don't be afraid of the American public. It has its share of the world's timid souls; and, we must assume, of the world's misguided and uninformed. But it has far more than its share of those who have learned to come to grips with problems— as individuals, and through the voluntary group process. And, by and large, it has a taste for facts and fairness. Often, it seems to avoid issues as long as it can; but when it has to take hold of them, it does so.

Finally, *don't be afraid* of the concept of democracy. The Communists exploit the word to make their totalitarian system seem to be representative of the people; but we need not relinquish our own use of it on this account. The Radical Rightists downgrade the word, making it seem equivalent to mob rule. One constant theme in their publications is that of setting up a sharp contrast between a republic and a democracy, as if the two were irreconcilable opposites. They urge upon their readers the view that respect for the intent of those who gave us our Constitution bids us repudiate the democratic concept; but in doing so, they appear to be simply bidding for a new elitism.

"It is sometimes asserted," writes Sidney Hook, "that the United States is not a democracy because the word 'democracy' is nowhere to be found in the Constitution. But neither is the word 'republic' although Article IV, Section Four, guarantees to every *state* in the Union 'a republican form of government.' The meaning of this phrase is not further explained, but at the time it was inserted it probably meant no more than opposition to the institution of monarchy." (1)

For our part, we are content to end this book with *The American's Creed*, written by William Tyler Page, a descendant of one of the signers of the Declaration of Independence; and officially accepted by the House of Representatives on April 3, 1918. We find it quoted in J. Edgar Hoover's *A Study of Communism*. We find it quoted in *Flags of American History*, by David Crouthers—a book sent out by the Disabled American Veterans. It is good enough for us—and the italics in it are ours:

I believe in the United States of America as a Government of the people, by the people, for the people; whose just powers are derived from the consent of the governed; *a democracy in a republic;* a sovereign Nation of many sovereign States; a perfect union, one and inseparable; established upon those principles of freedom, equality, justice and humanity for which American patriots sacrificed their lives and fortunes.

I therefore believe it is my duty to my country to love it; to support its Constitution; to obey its laws; to respect its flag, and to defend it against all enemies.

To our minds, the concept of *a democracy in a republic* is a good one to bank on; and we do not believe that anyone who takes seriously the job of serving this concept is likely to find life dull.

NOTES TO THE TEXT

Preliminary to the Whole

(1) Press conference transcript, quoted in the *Twelfth Report* of the Senate Factfinding Subcommittee on Un-American Activities, California Legislature, 1963, pp. 51-52.

(2) "New Campus Speaker Policy: An Act of Confidence"; *California Monthly*, October 1963. University of California, Berkeley.

Chapter One—Monolith on the Right

(1) Helen B. Shaffer, "Secret Societies and Political Action"; *Editorial Research Reports*, May 10, 1961, page 348. Washington, D.C.

(2) *The John Birch Society Bulletin*, August 1963, p. 13.

(3) Robert Welch, *The Blue Book of the John Birch Society*, Seventh Printing, p. 126. Copyright by Robert Welch, 1961.

(4) Ibid., p. 124.

(5) Ibid., p. 126.

(6) Robert Welch, *The Politician*, p. 6. Privately printed. Copyright by Robert Welch, 1963.

(7) *Bulletin*, June 3, 1963, p. 10.

Chapter Two—How Welch Identifies Communists

(1) *The Blue Book*, Seventh Printing, with earlier Forewords and Footnotes included, p. 89.

(2) Ibid., p. 8.

(3) J. Edgar Hoover, "Internal Security," April 17, 1962. Reprint from the *Law Enforcement Bulletin*.

(4) *The Blue Book*, p. 125.

(5) Ibid., p. 73.

(6) *The Politician*, pp. 220-221.

Chapter Three—A Reading Lesson

(1) *The Politician*, pp. xxxii-xxxiii.

(2) *American Opinion*, July-August, and September 1960.

(3) Howard Simons, "Our Fantastic Eye in the Sky"; Washington *Post and Times-Herald*, December 8, 1963.

(4) Ibid.

Chapter Four—Scholarship Limited

(1) *The Blue Book,* p. 22.
(2) Ibid., p. 8.
(3) Ibid., p. 12.
(4) Werner Keller, *East Minus West = Zero,* p. 198. New York: Putnam, 1962.
(5) Ibid., p. 209.
(6) *The Blue Book,* p. 130.
(7) Ibid., p. 125.
(8) V. I. Lenin, *Selected Works,* Vol. IX, p. 400. New York, International Publishers, 1943.
(9) Ibid., Vol. IX, p. 186.

Chapter Five—Spengler According to Welch

(1) *The Blue Book,* p. 35.
(2) Ibid., p. 37.
(3) Oswald Spengler, *The Decline of the West,* Vol. II, p. 94. New York, Knopf, 1928.
(4) Ibid., Vol. II, p. 99.
(5) Ibid., Vol. II, p. 105.
(6) Ibid., Vol. II, p. 470.
(7) Ibid., Vol. II, p. 570.
(8) Ibid., Vol. II, p. 570.

Chapter Six—Of Statistics and Percentages

(1) *American Opinion,* July-August and September 1960, p. 96.

Chapter Seven—Of Men and Methods

(1) *The Blue Book,* p. 60.
(2) Ibid., p. 27.
(3) Ibid., p. 63.
(4) Ibid., pp. 68, 70.
(5) Ibid., p. 73.
(6) Ibid., p. 74.
(7) Ibid., p. 74.
(8) Ibid., p. 82.
(9) Ibid., p. 83.
(10) Senator Thomas H. Kuchel, Speech at Republican Fund-Raising Dinner, New York City, May 6, 1964.

Chapter Eight—Letters Unlimited

(1) *The Blue Book,* p. 66.
(2) Ibid., p. 67.
(3) *Fundamentals of Marxism-Leninism,* pp. 416-417. Moscow, Foreign Languages Publishing House.
(4) Jack Bass, "A Depth Study of the John Birch Society," p. 2. Reprint from the Columbia, S.C., *Record.*

Chapter Nine—The Dan Smoot Report

None

Chapter Ten—Carl McIntire: Maker of Schisms

(1) Carl McIntire, *Servants of Apostasy*, p. 325. Collingswood, New Jersey; Christian Beacon Press, 1955.

(2) V. I. Lenin, *Selected Works*, Vol. II, p. 68. New York: International Publishers, 1943.

(3) *Sowing Dissension in the Churches*, p. 8. The National Council of the Protestant Episcopal Church, Department of Christian Social Relations, 281 Park Avenue South, New York 10, New York.

(4) Obtainable from the *20th Century Reformation Hour*, Collingswood, New Jersey.

(5) Carl McIntire, *UNICEF and the Reds!* A leaflet sent out by the American Council of Christian Laymen, Madison 1, Wisconsin, in a sample packet of its materials, Spring 1904. (The leaflet itself is undated.)

(6) Karl Marx and Friedrich Engels, *Selected Correspondence, 1846–1895*, p. 22. New York: International Publishers, 1934.

(7) V. I. Lenin, *Selected Works*, Vol. IX, p. 475. New York: International Publishers, 1943.

Chapter Eleven—Myers G. Lowman of the Circuit Riders

(1) Atlanta *Journal*, August 3, 1958. See also Atlanta *Constitution*, August 2; and Sunday *Journal-Constitution*, August 10.

Chapter Twelve—Edgar C. Bundy and the Church League of America

(1) Foreign Aid Appropriations Bill, 1950. Hearings Before the Committee on Appropriations, United States Senate, Eighty-First Congress, First Session on H.R. 4830, p. 594. United States Government Printing Office, Washington, D.C., 1949.

Chapter Thirteen—Billy James Hargis and His Christian Crusade

(1) New York *Times*, August 6, 1961.

(2) Billy James Hargis, *Communist America—Must It Be?* p. 29. Butler, Indiana: Higley-Huffman Press, 1960. Distributed by Christian Crusade, Box 977, Tulsa 2, Oklahoma.

(3) Seattle *Times*, August 20, 1962.

(4) New York *Times*, August 6, 1961.

(5) *Communist America—Must It Be?* p. 21.

(6) Roy Wilkins, Interview in the New York *Times*, May 5, 1964.

(7) Donald Quinn, Oklahoma *Courier*, Oklahoma City, March 2, 1962. This quote and the others from Donald Quinn are from a series of three articles which appeared in the *Courier* on February 16 and 23, and March 2—all dealing with Christian Crusade. Also, the entire series was read into the Congressional Record of April 16, 1962, pp. 6576 ff., by Senator Gale McGee.

(8) Section F: *Campaign Literature: 1956 General Election Campaigns:*
Report Together with Minority Views Submitted to the Committee on Rules
and Administration Pursuant to Senate Resolution 176, 84th Congress,
p. 19. Report of Senate Subcommittee on Privileges and Elections, issued
February 1957.

Chapter Fourteen—How United Is the Radical Right?

None.

Chapter Fifteen—Strictly Political

(1) *The Blue Book*, pp. 84-85.
(2) V. I. Lenin, *Selected Works*, Vol. II, p. 64. New York: International
Publishers, 1943.
(3) *Manchester Guardian Weekly*, June 16, 1960, p. 9.
(4) *Wall Street Journal*, March 17, 1958.
(5) Washington *Post and Times-Herald*, signed article by Robert J.
Donovan, July 13, 1964; and news item, July 14, 1964.

Chapter Sixteen—Of the Rank and File

(1) St. Louis *Post-Dispatch*, February 2, 1962.

Chapter Seventeen—Four Targets

(1) Seattle *Times*, July 2, 1964.

Chapter Eighteen—Self-Portrait of the Radical Rightist

None.

Conclusion—The Task Ahead of Us

(1) Sidney Hook, Chapter 2, *Democracy or Republic?; Political Power
and Personal Freedom*, p. 43. New York: Collier Books. 1962. We particularly recommend this ten-page chapter to those who are confused by
efforts to treat democracy and republic as mutually exclusive.

HOW TO GET
FAR-RIGHT PUBLICATIONS DISCUSSED
IN THIS BOOK

Note: Since the key books and periodicals from which we have quoted, and which we would like our readers to explore for themselves, are not readily available at general bookstores or magazine stands, we are giving, here, the home-base addresses of organizations discussed and also certain other sources of these materials.

The address of the John Birch Society is Belmont 78, Massachusetts. *The Blue Book* and *The Politician* can both presumably be secured at this address; and subscriptions to *American Opinion* ($5) can be entered there. Also, American Opinion Bookshops exist in many major cities; *The Blue Book* can be bought at any one of these. We got both of the above books from the Heritage Book Shoppe, 2427 Marconi Avenue, Sacramento, California. They can also be ordered from the American Council of Christian Laymen, Madison 1, Wisconsin. We understand that *The Blue Book*, at least, can be secured through George H. Birdsall, Box 449, Annandale, Va.

The address of *The Dan Smoot Report* is P.O. Box 9538, Lakewood Station, Dallas, Texas. Subscription to this weekly *Report* is $10 per year. Smoot's books can also be ordered from this address. One of these books, *The Invisible Government*, is now available in paperback form for $1. American Opinion Bookshops also carry the Smoot books.

Carl McIntire's newspaper, *The Christian Beacon*, and his book, *Servants of Apostasy*, can be secured from 20th Century Reformation Center, Box 190, Collingswood, New Jersey.

The address of the Circuit Riders, Inc., is 110 Government Place, Cincinnati, Ohio. Myers Lowman's various Compilations can be ordered from this address. They are also available at the American Council of Christian Laymen, Madison 1, Wisconsin.

The Church League of America is located at 422 N. Prospect Street, Wheaton, Illinois. Edgar C. Bundy's *News and Views* (monthly) can be secured through this organization, as can his book, *Collectivism in the Churches*. This is also distributed by Devin-Adair Company, New York 10, New York. Or it can be ordered from the American Council of Christian Laymen, Madison 1, Wisconsin.

The address of Christian Crusade is P.O. Box 977, Tulsa 2, Oklahoma. The monthly *Christian Crusade* and the *Weekly Crusader* are organs of this group. Hargis' books, *Facts about Communism in Our Churches*, *Communist America—Must It Be?*, and *The Far Left*, can be ordered from this address. They are all in paperback.

The Kent and Phoebe Courtney newspaper, *The Independent American* (annual subscription rate, $5) is published at P.O. Box 4223, New Orleans 18, Louisiana. The pamphlet series of their Conservative Society of America, *Tax Fax*, can also be secured from this address.

The address of the Liberty Amendment Committee is 6413 Franklin Avenue, Los Angeles 28, California.

The Congress of Freedom is located at 1330 Turner Boulevard, Omaha, Nebraska; and *The Greater Nebraskan* can be ordered from this address.

The address of the Manion Forum is St. Joseph Bank Building, South Bend, Indiana.

The national headquarters of We, The People! is at 111 North Wabash Avenue, Chicago, Illinois 60602.

America's Future is located at 542 Main Street, New Rochelle, New York.

The American Coalition of Patriotic Societies has its headquarters at 1025 Connecticut Avenue, N.W., Washington, D.C.

E. Merrill Root's *Brainwashing in the High Schools* was originally published by Devin-Adair Co., New York 10, New York; but the paperback edition is published by the Church League of America, the address of which is given above. It can also be ordered from the American Council of Christian Laymen, Madison 1, Wisconsin.

The American Council of Christian Laymen conducts a mail-order business in far-right books and pamphlets; and it is a good place to try for almost any book for which no other specific outlet is known.

The address of Liberty Lobby is 132 3rd Street, S.E., Washington, D.C.

ORGANIZATIONS THAT HAVE
RESOURCE MATERIALS

Note: The organizations listed below have all had considerable experience of being targets of attack; and they have all built up a store of resource materials that can be useful to groups that need advice and lack experience. Also, we would say, they should be given a chance to present their side before any charges against them are taken at face value:

AFL-CIO Publications Relations Dept.
815 16th Street, N.W.
Washington, D.C.

American Book Publishers Council, Inc.
58 West 40th Street
New York 18, New York

American Jewish Committee
165 East 56th Street
New York City, New York

American Library Association
50 East Huron Street
Chicago 11, Illinois

American Textbook Publishers Institute, Inc.
432 Park Avenue S.
New York 16, New York

Anti-Defamation League
Information Service
1640 Rhode Island Avenue, N.W.
Washington, D.C.

NAACP Legal Defense Fund
10 Columbus Circle
New York, New York

National Catholic Welfare Conference
1312 Massachusetts Avenue, N.W.
Washington 5, D.C.

National Congress of Parents and Teachers
700 North Rush Street
Chicago 11, Illinois

National Council of Churches
475 Riverside Drive
New York City, New York

National Education Association
Commission on Professional Rights and Responsibilities
1201 16th Street, N.W.
Washington, D.C.

National Information Bureau
205 E. 42nd Street
New York 17, New York

National Mental Health Association
10 Columbus Circle
New York City, New York

INDEX